Naughty or Nice?

Holiday Card Sketches from 2020-2023

Vol. 4

By Jodi "J3T" Tong

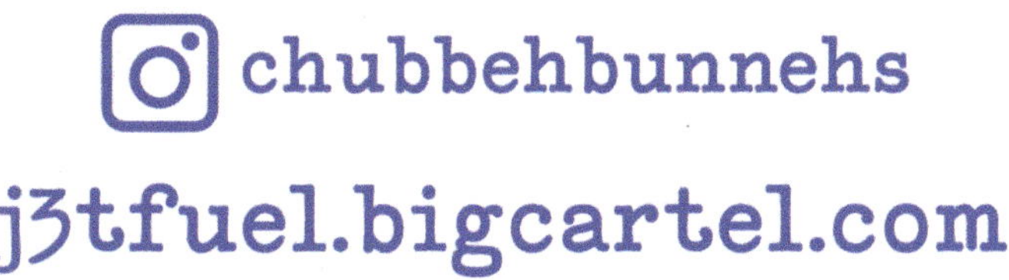

j3tfuel.bigcartel.com

Published by FurPlanet Productions. Printed in 2025

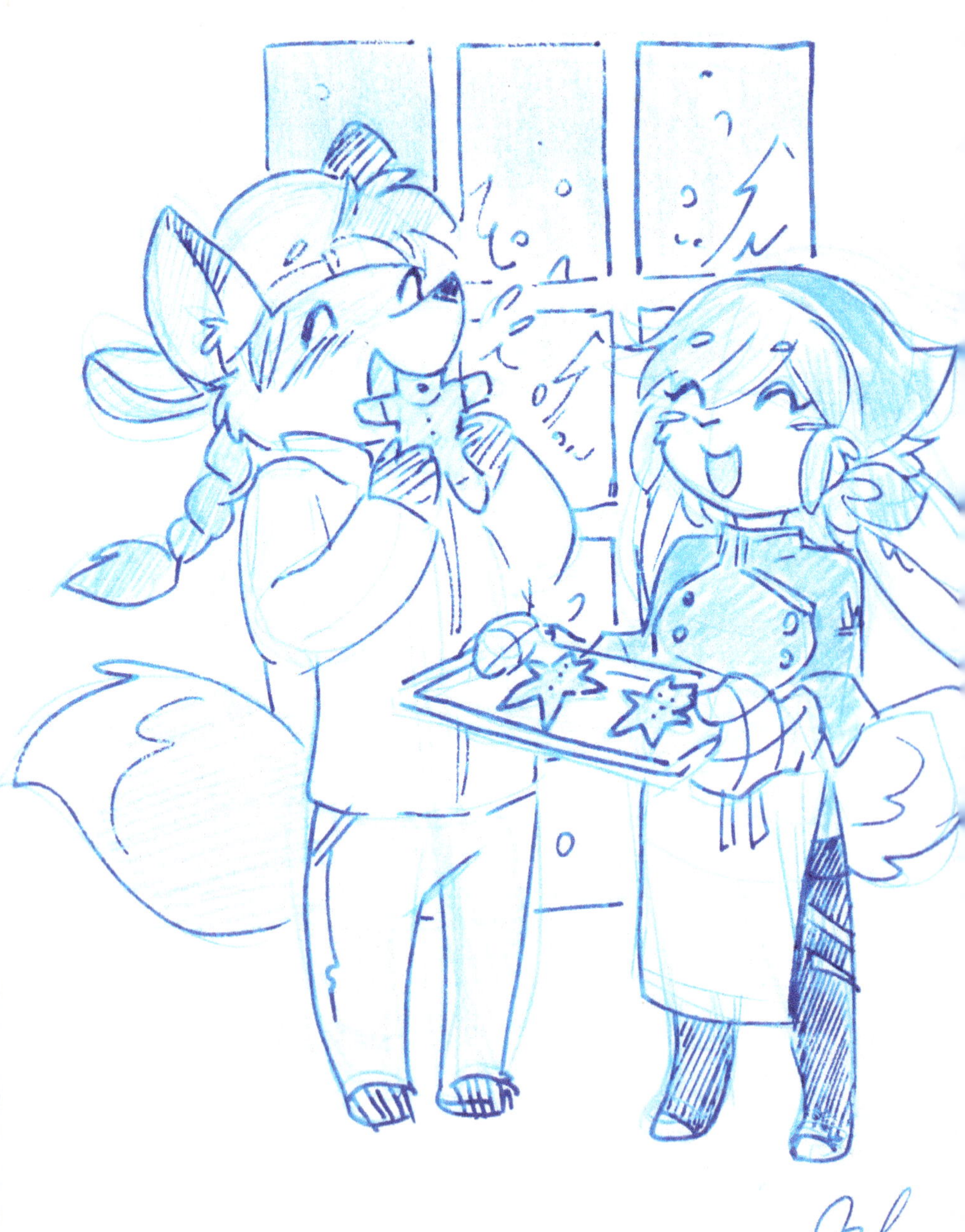

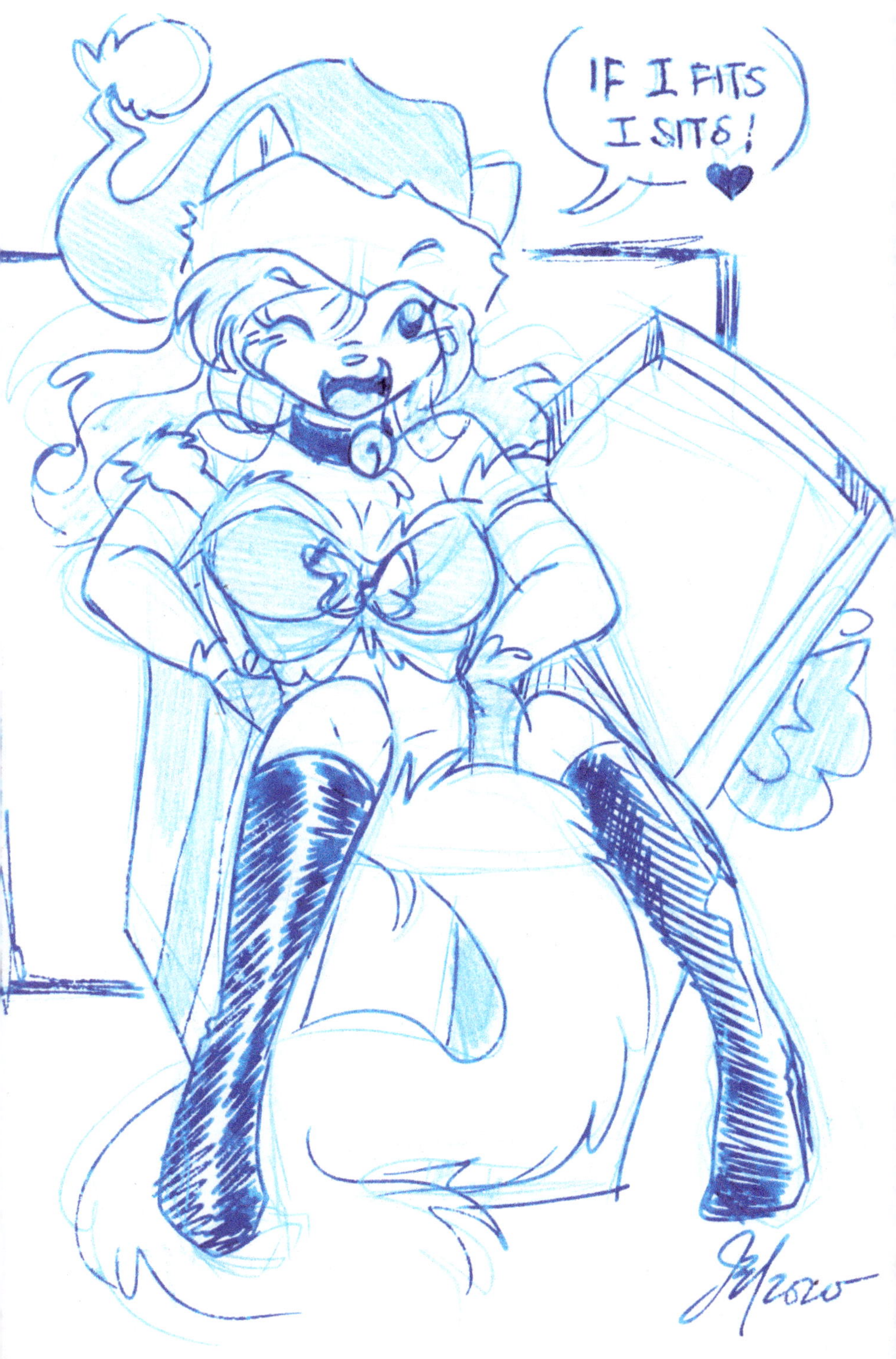
IF I FITS
I SITS!

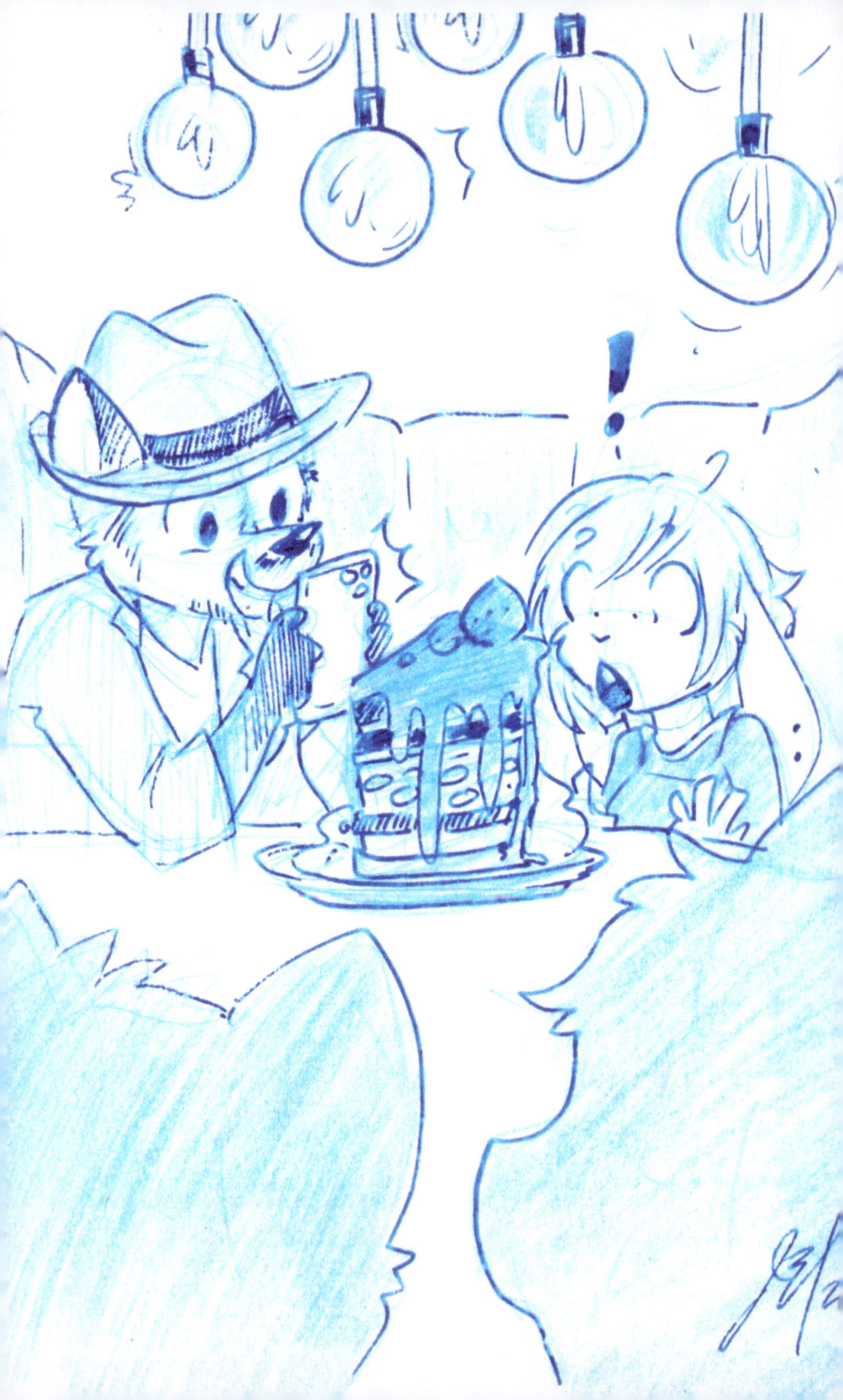

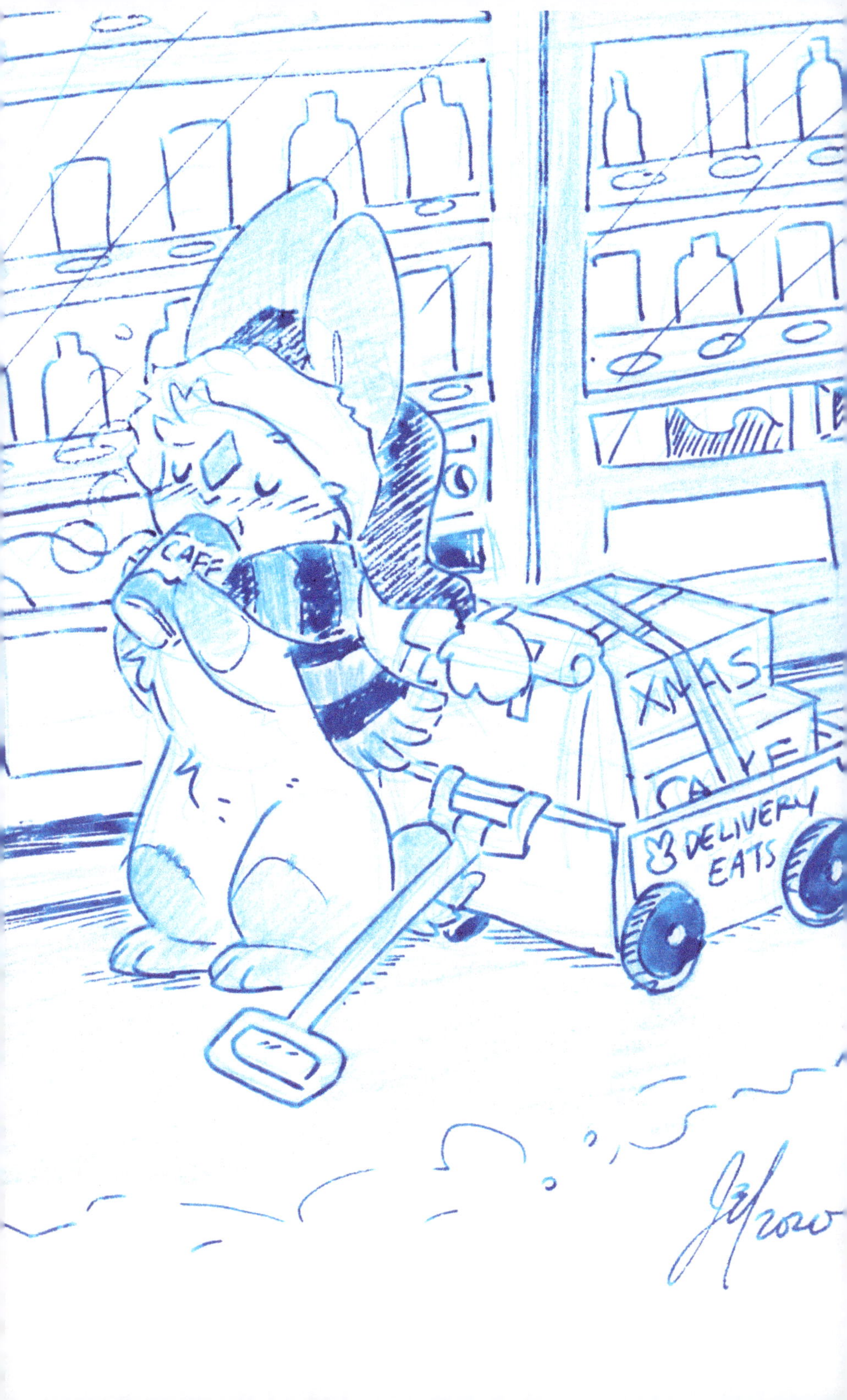

CAFÉ
XMAS
DELIVERY EATS

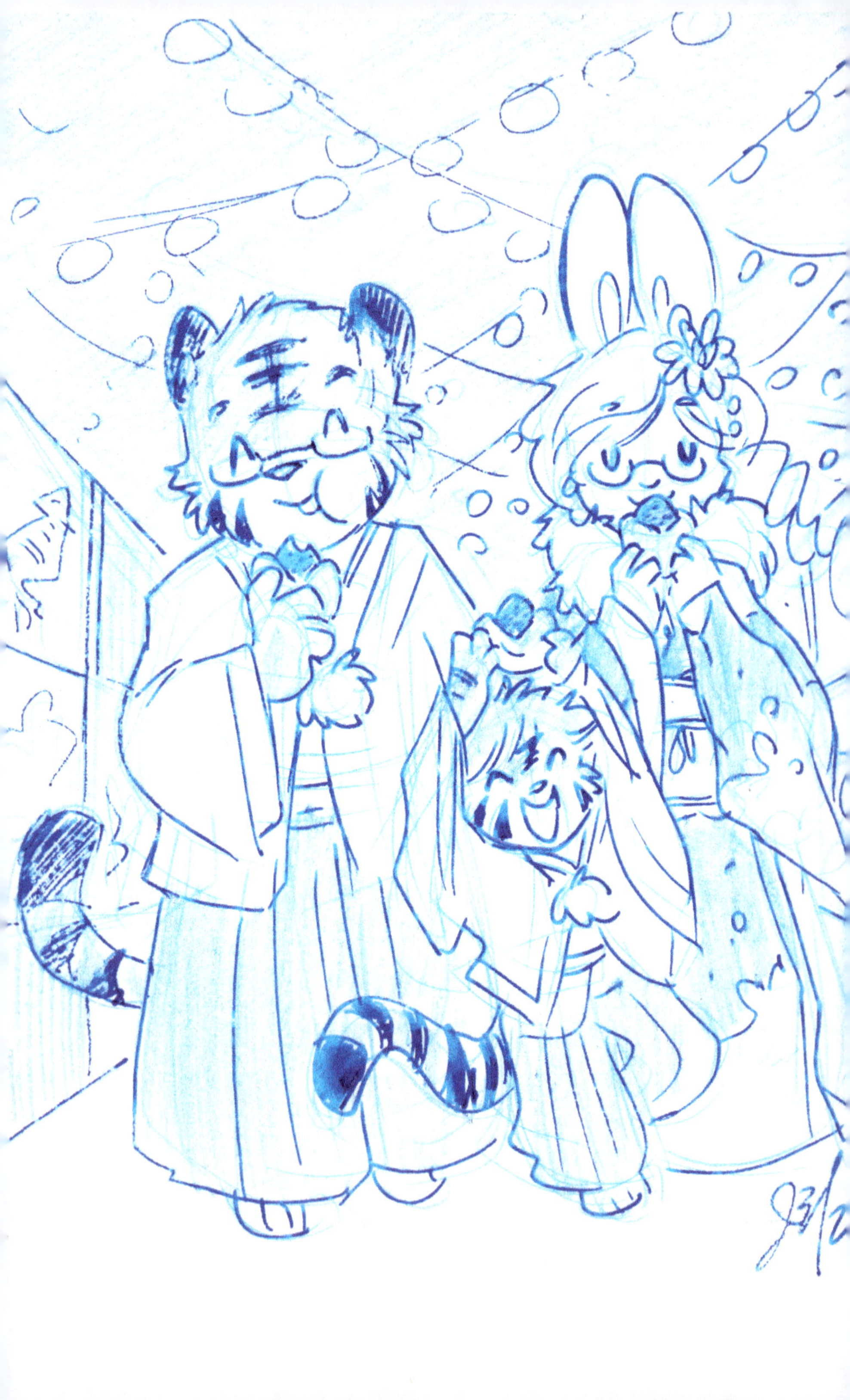

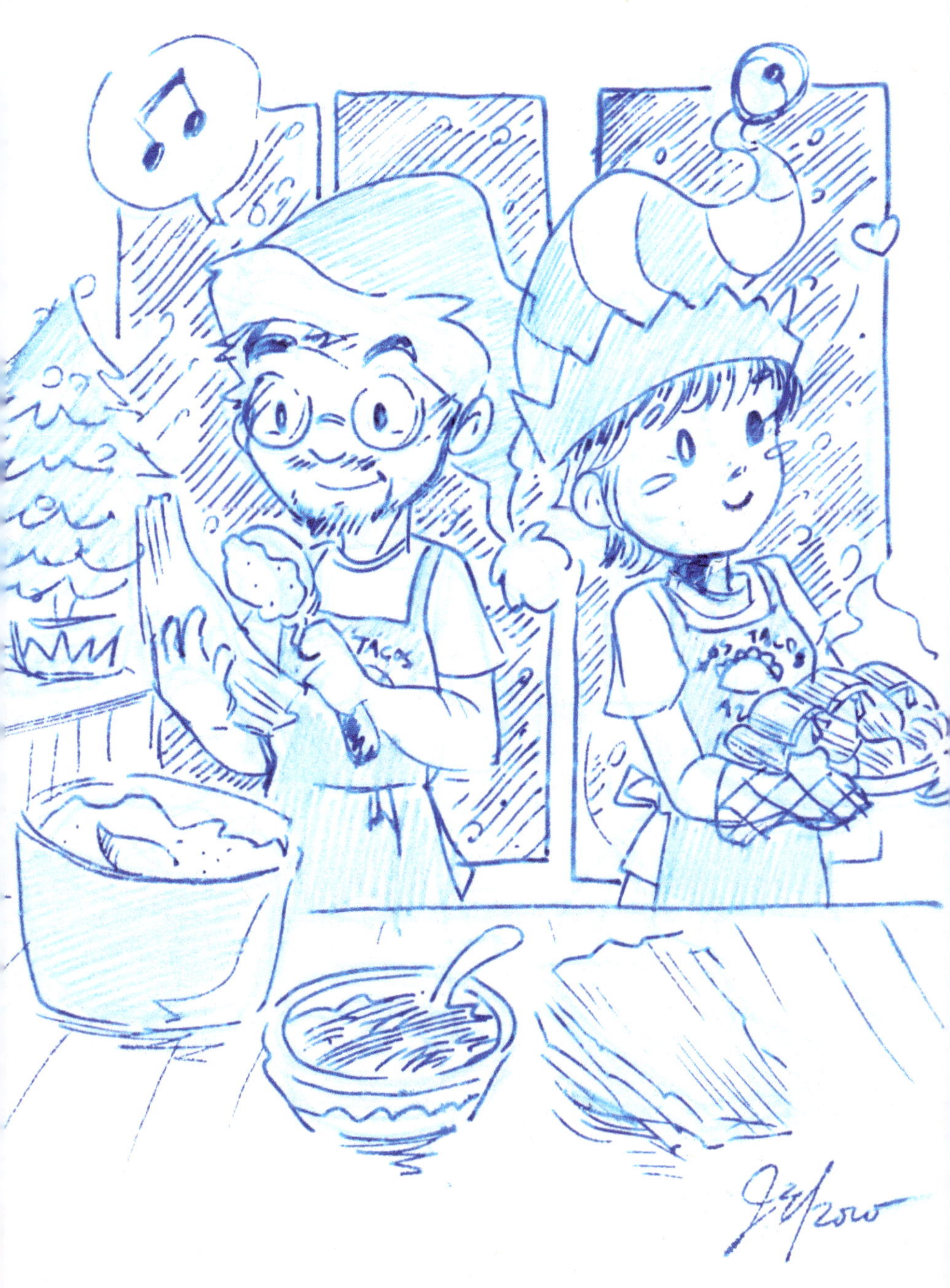

TACOS
AZ TACOS
AZ

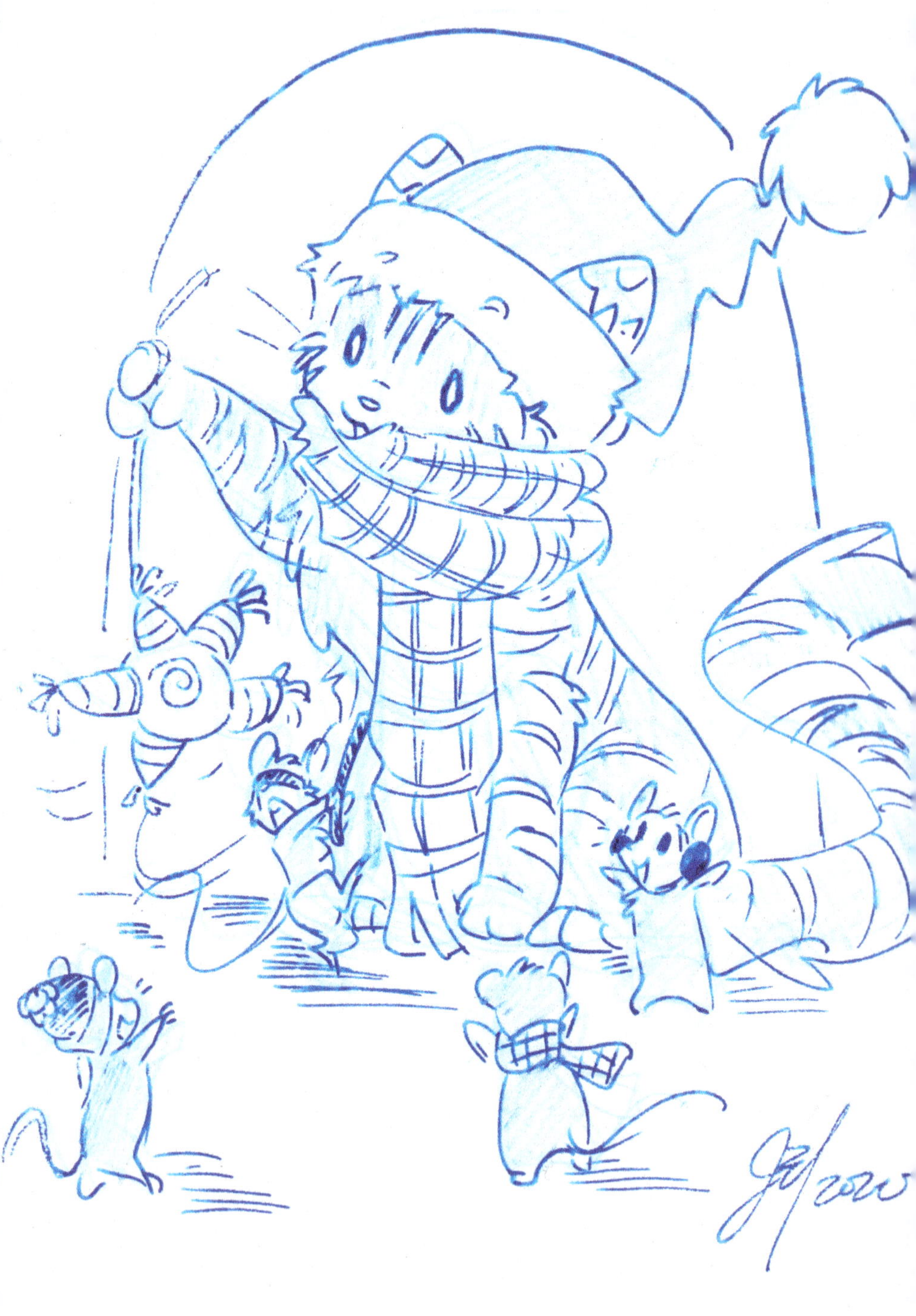

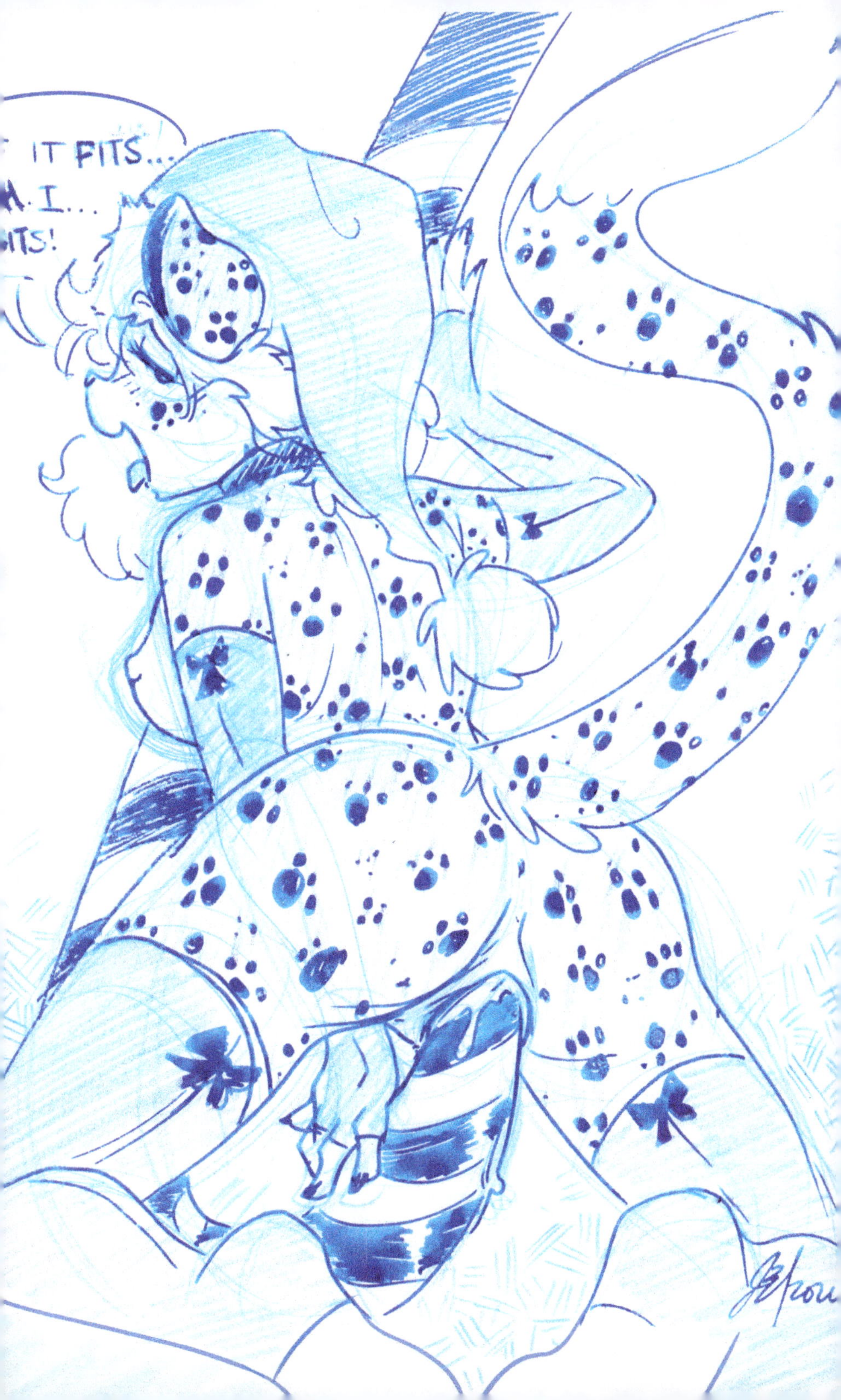

IT FITS...
A. I...
ITS!

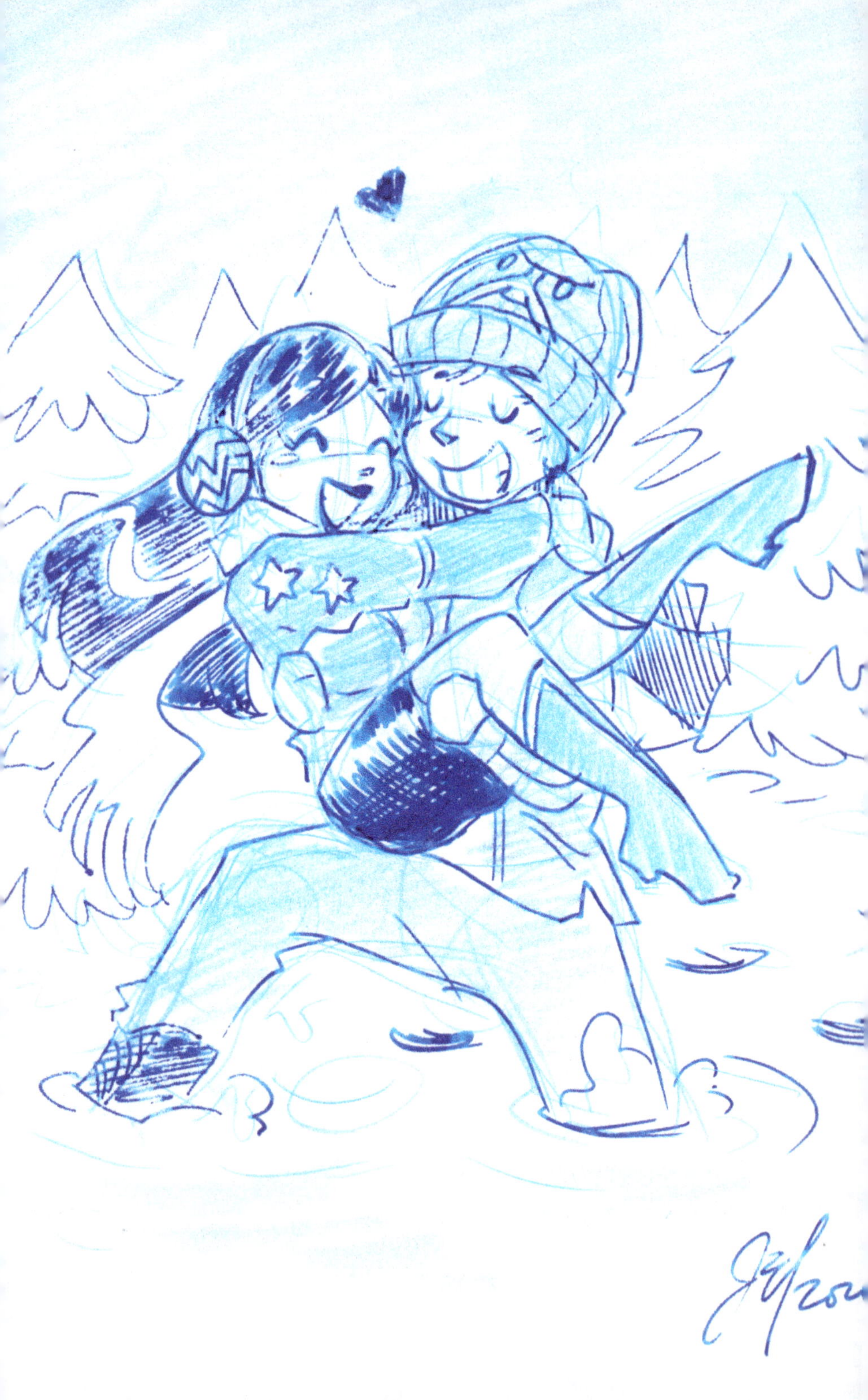

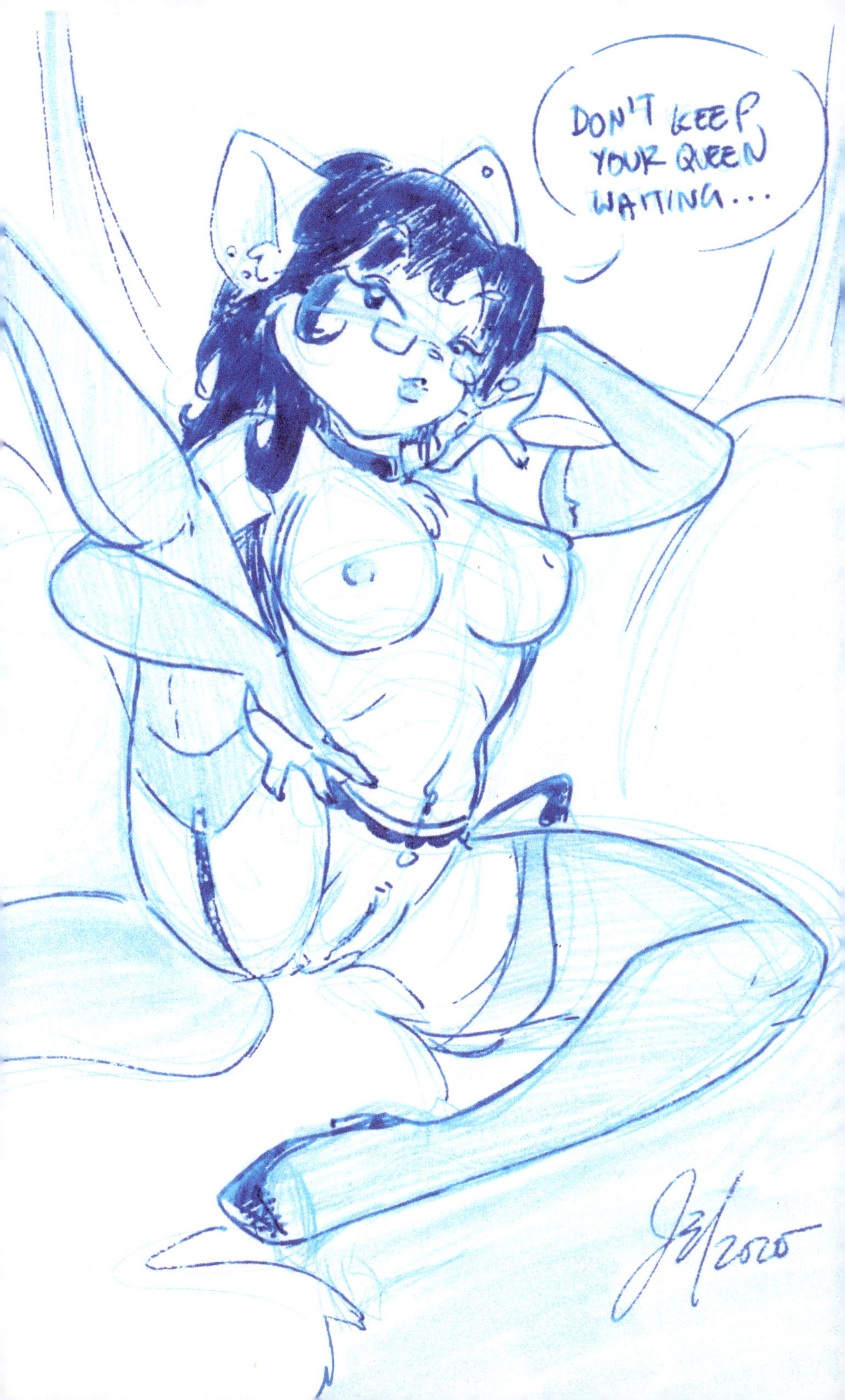

DON'T KEEP
YOUR QUEEN
WAITING....

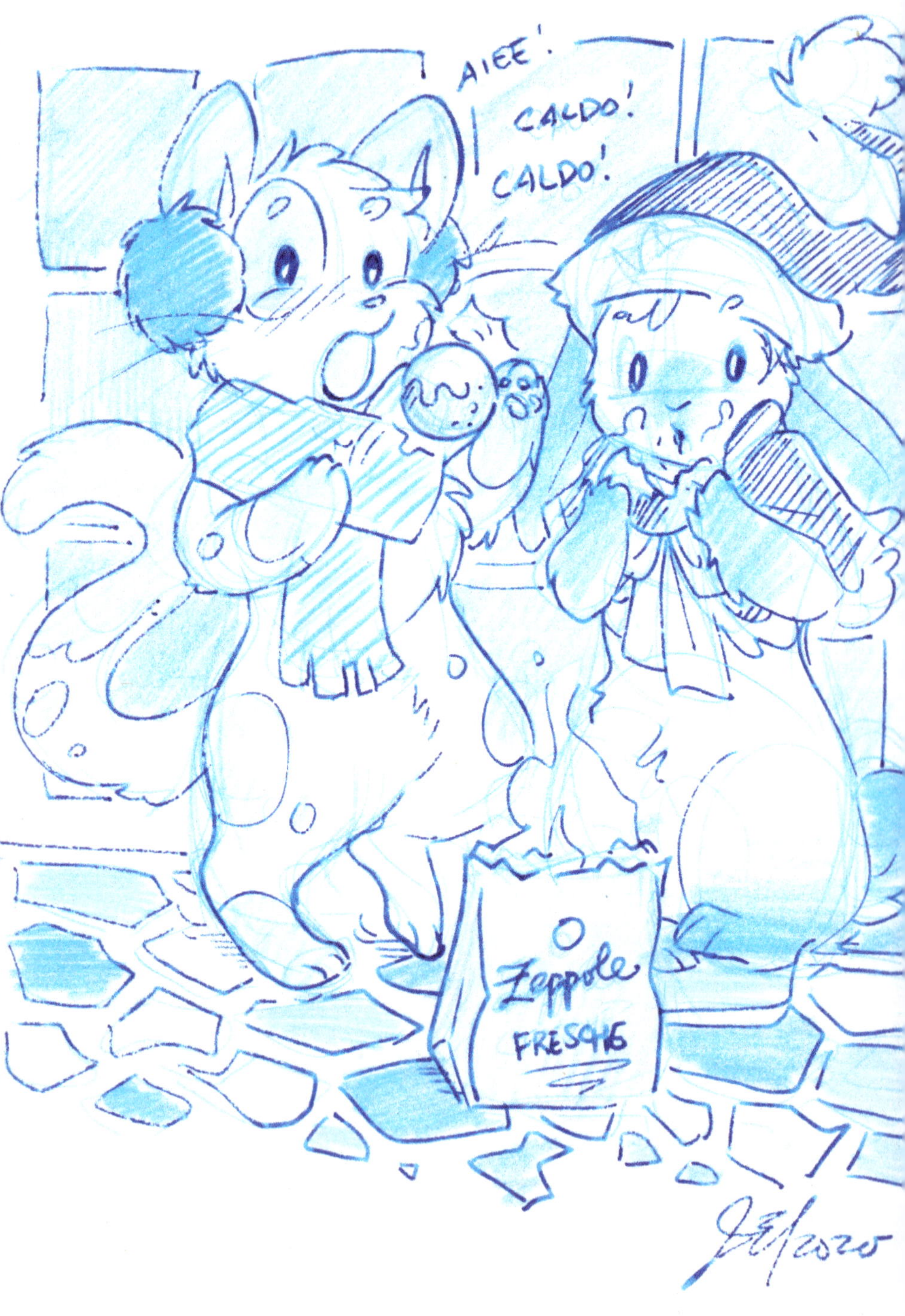

AIEE!
CALDO!
CALDO!
Zeppole
FRESCHE

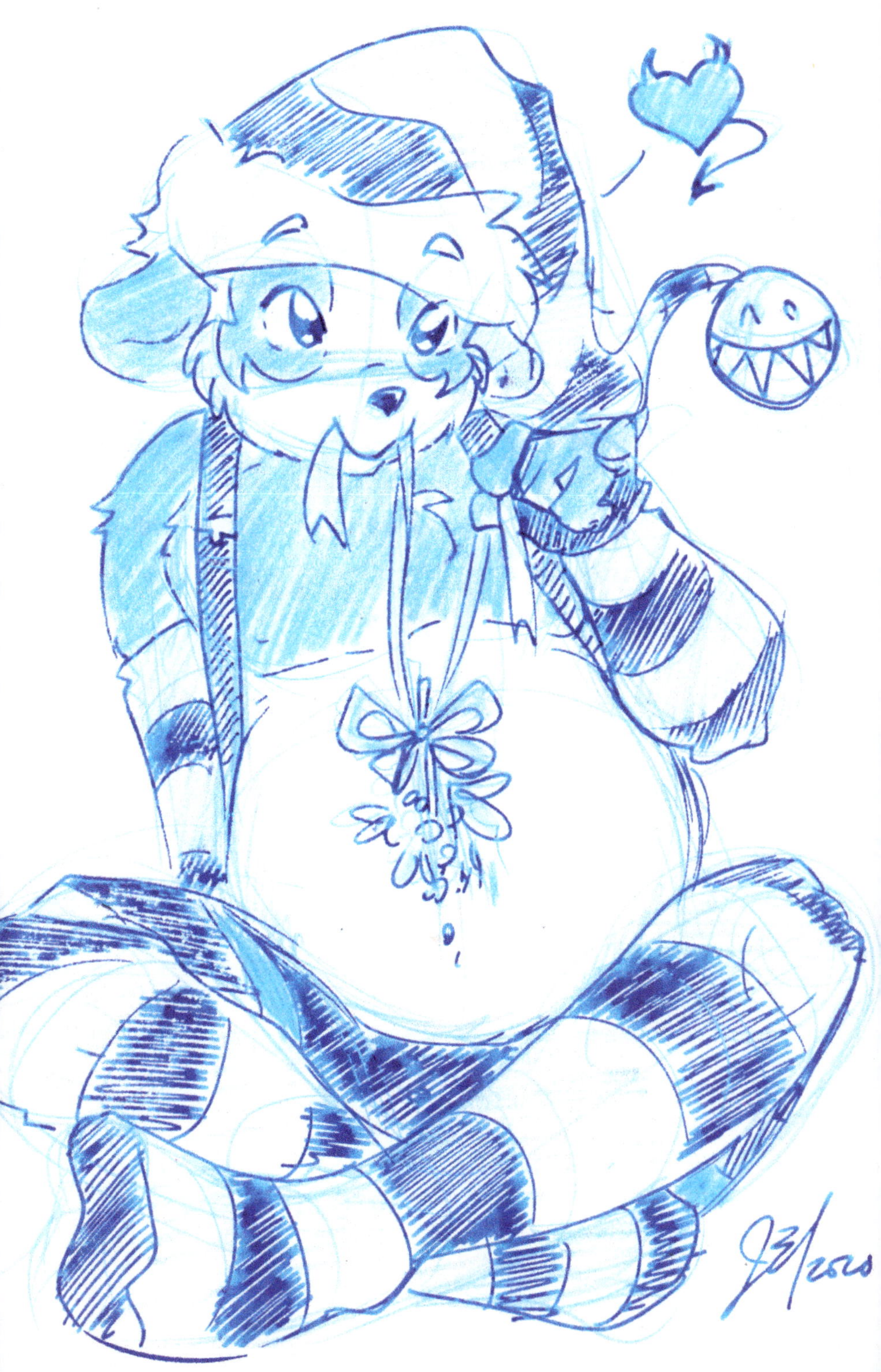

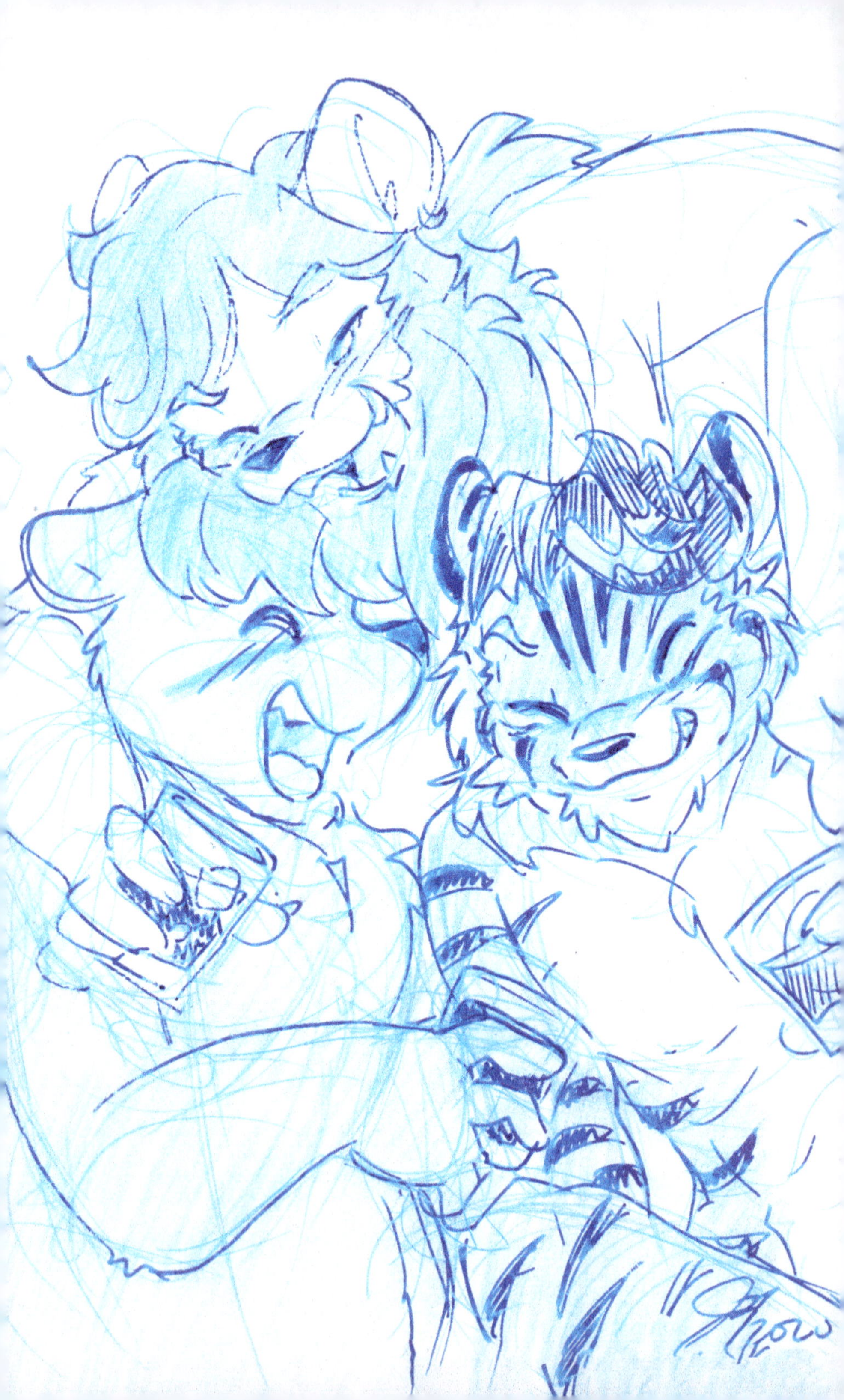

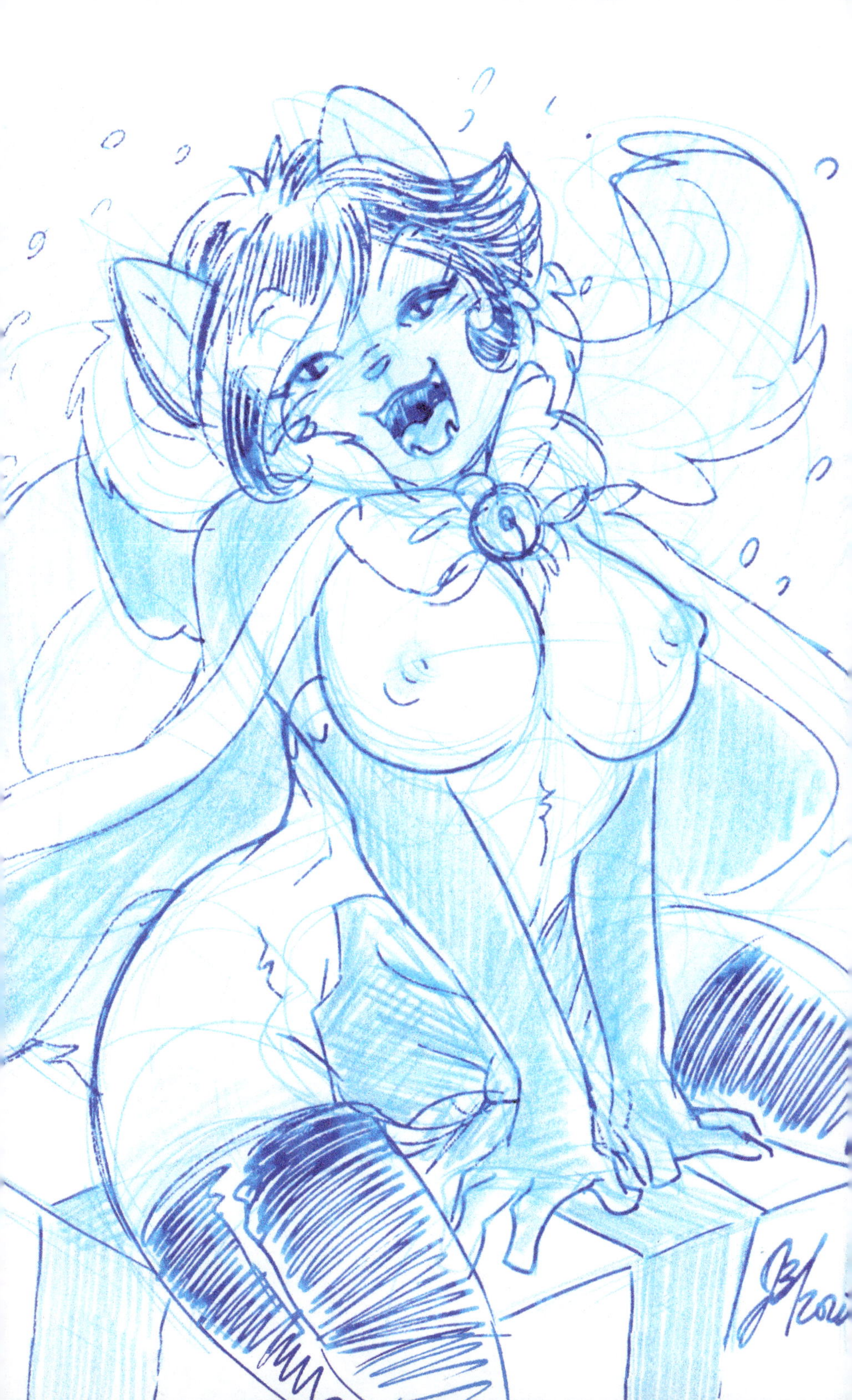

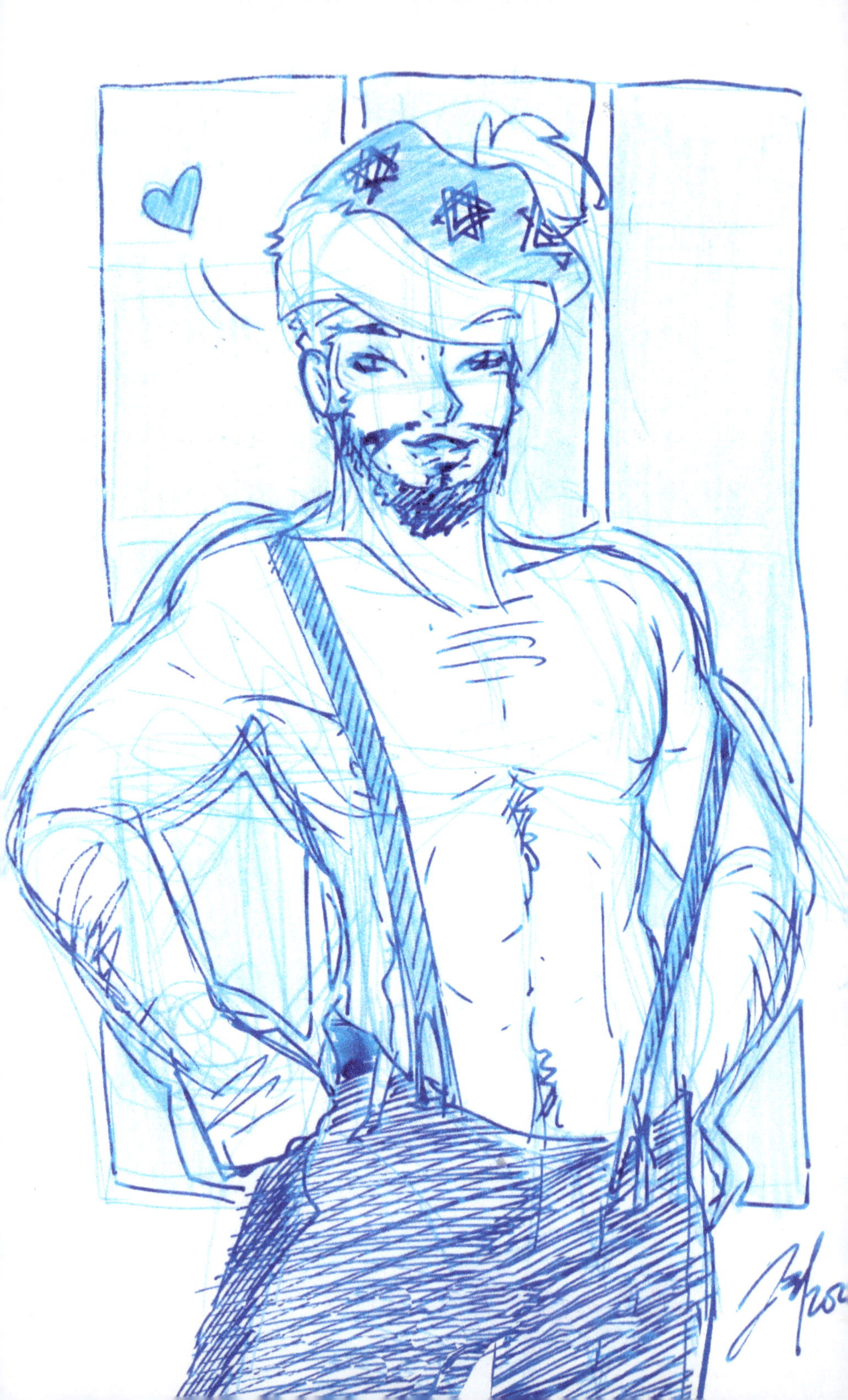

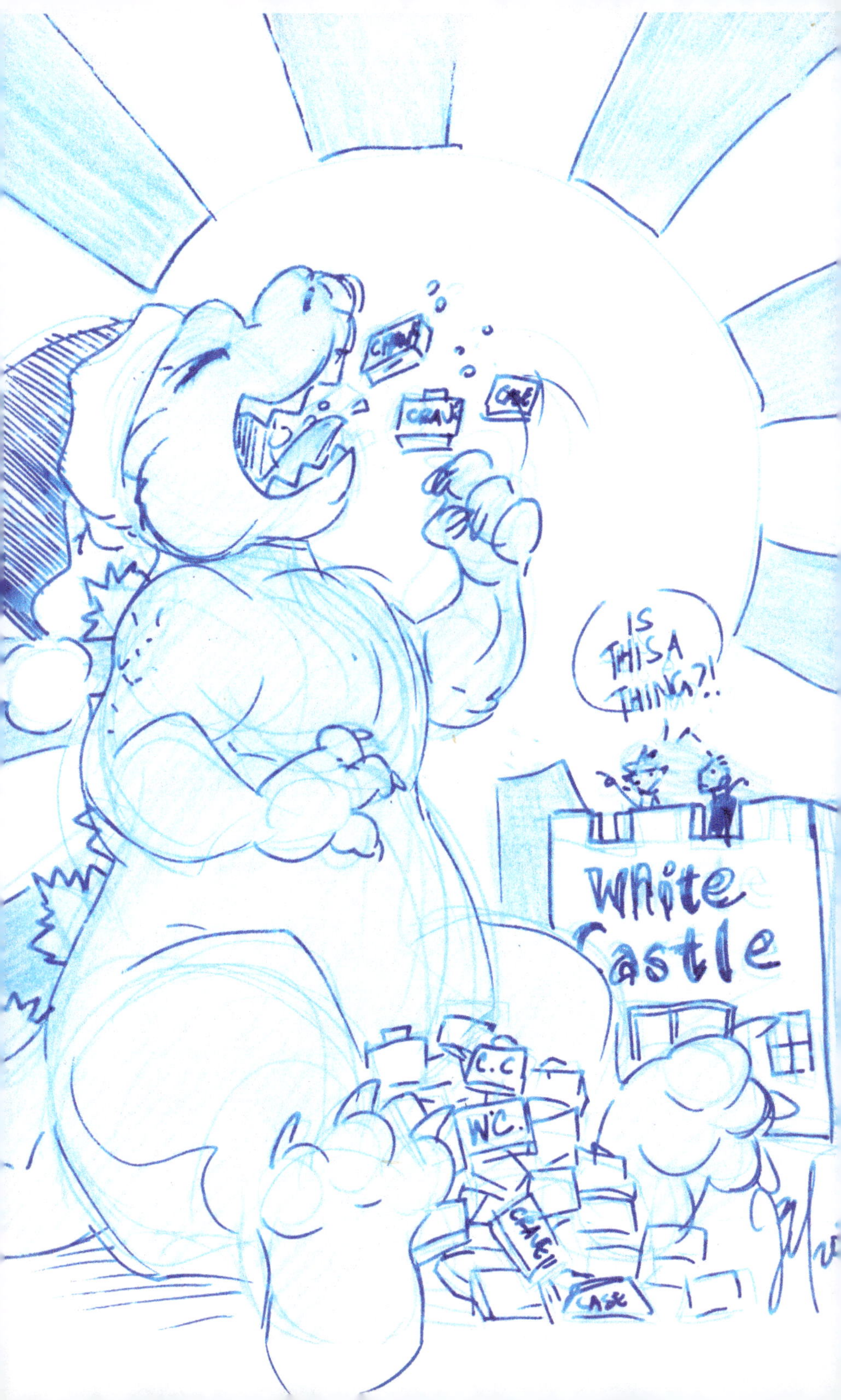
CRA!
CRA!
CRE!
IS THIS A THING?!
WHITE CASTLE
C..C
W'C.
CAKE!
CASE

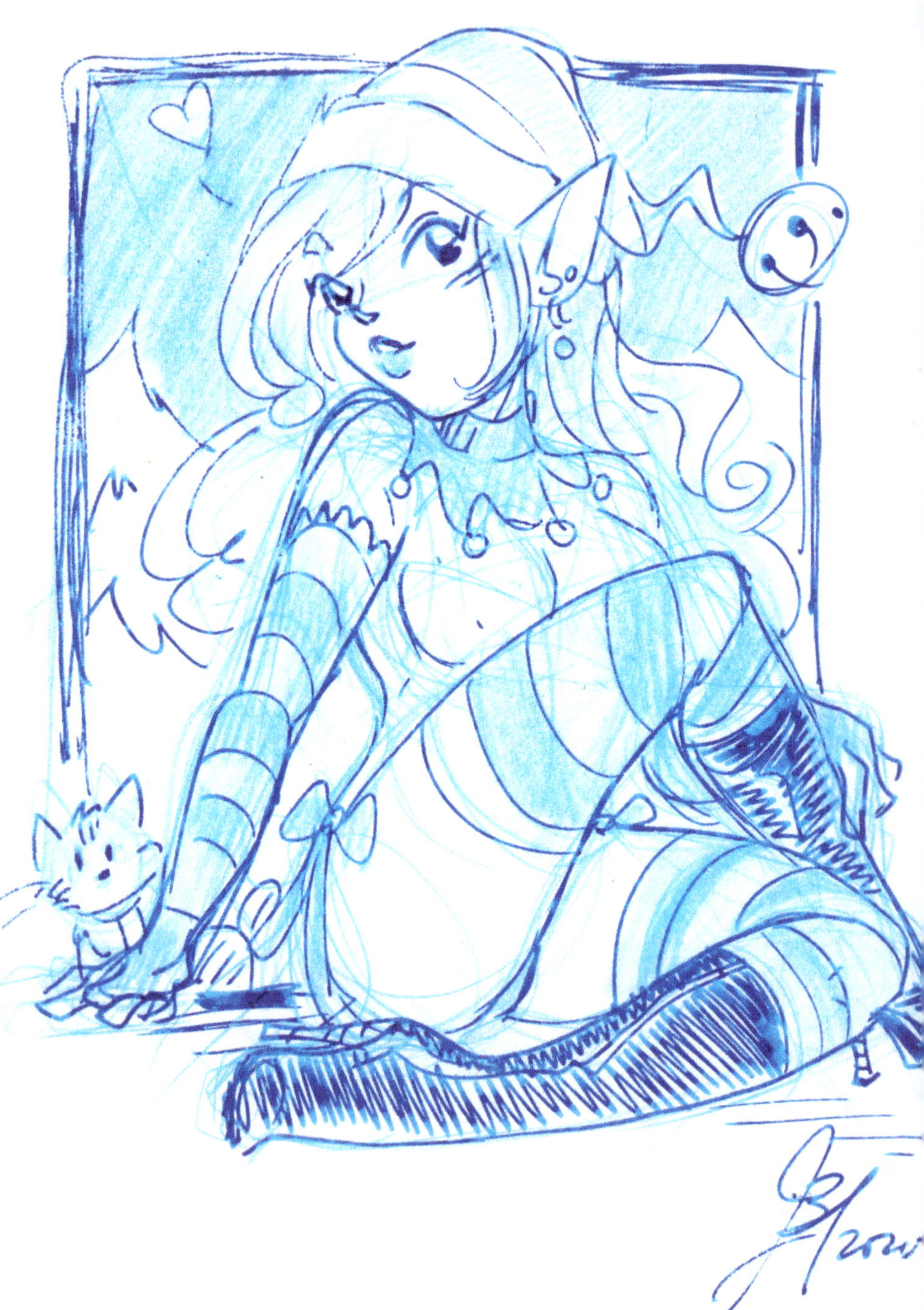

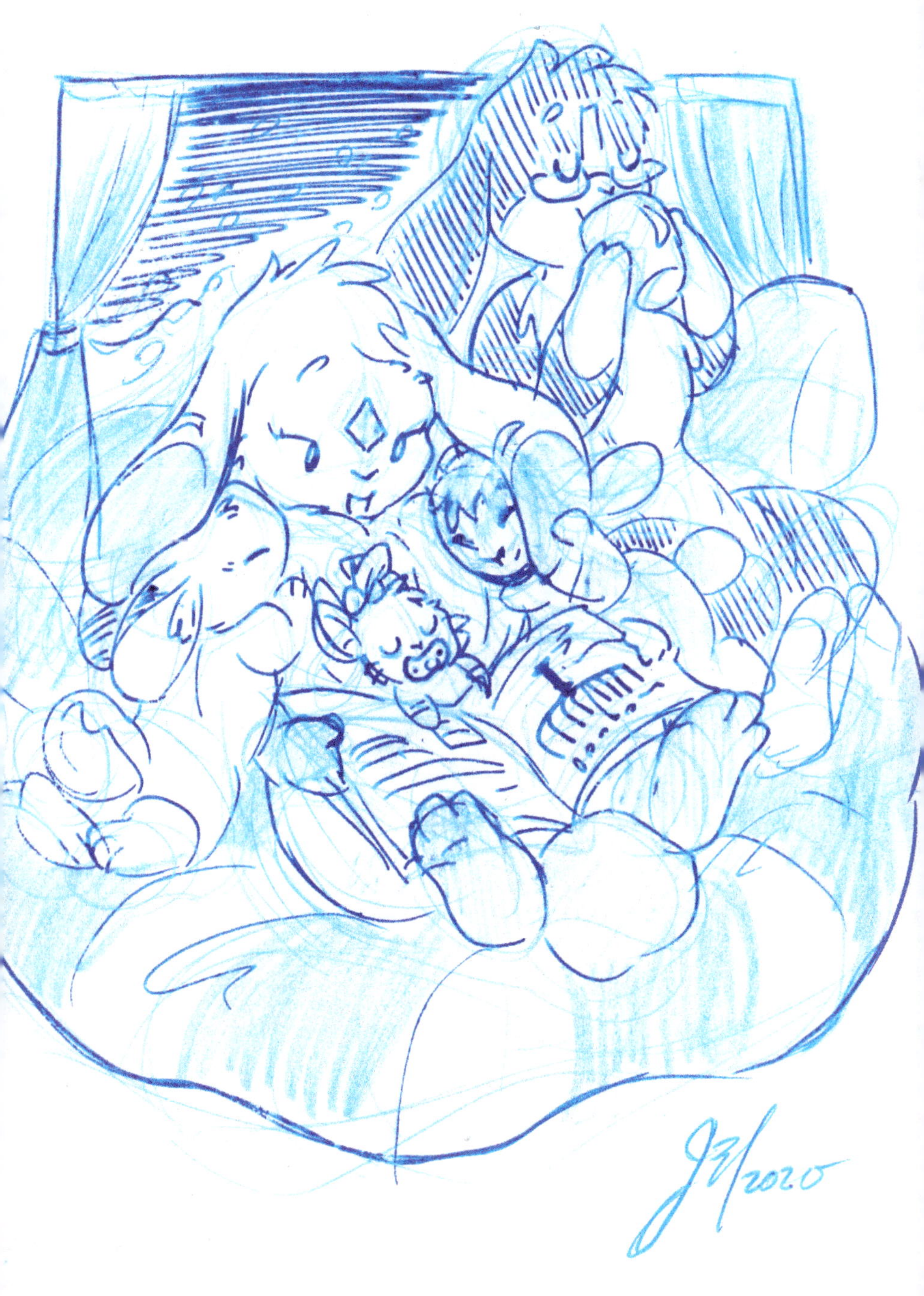

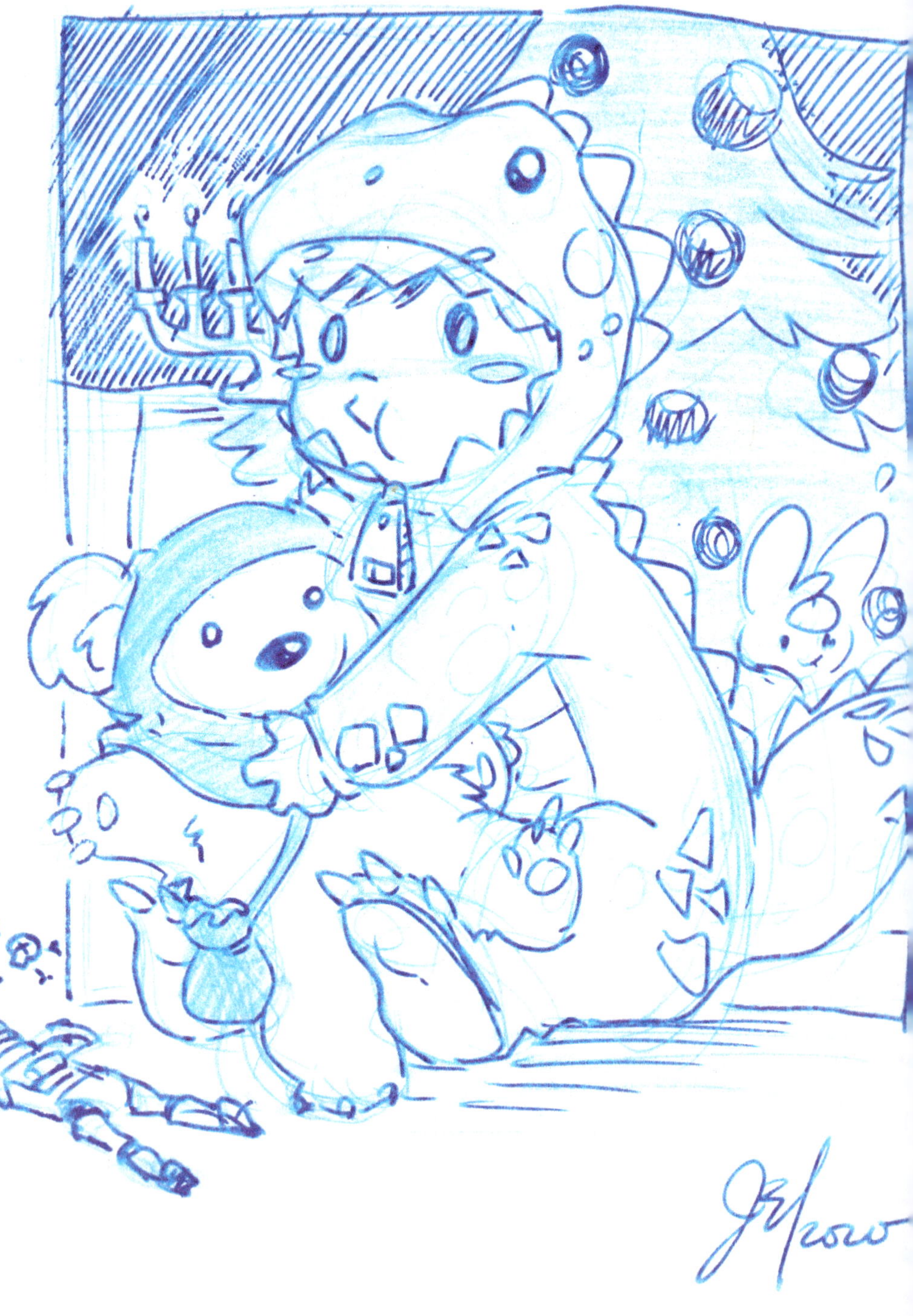

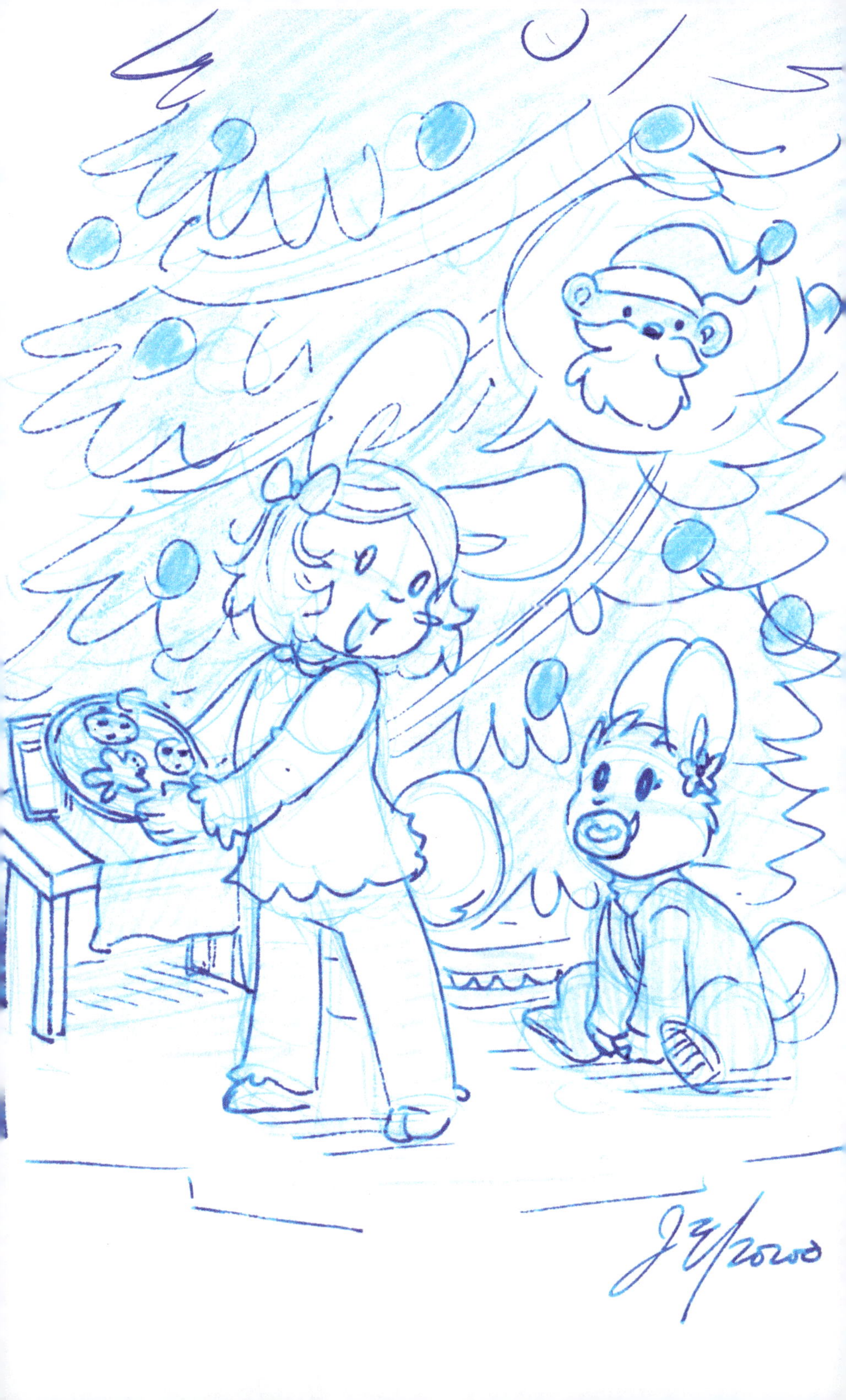

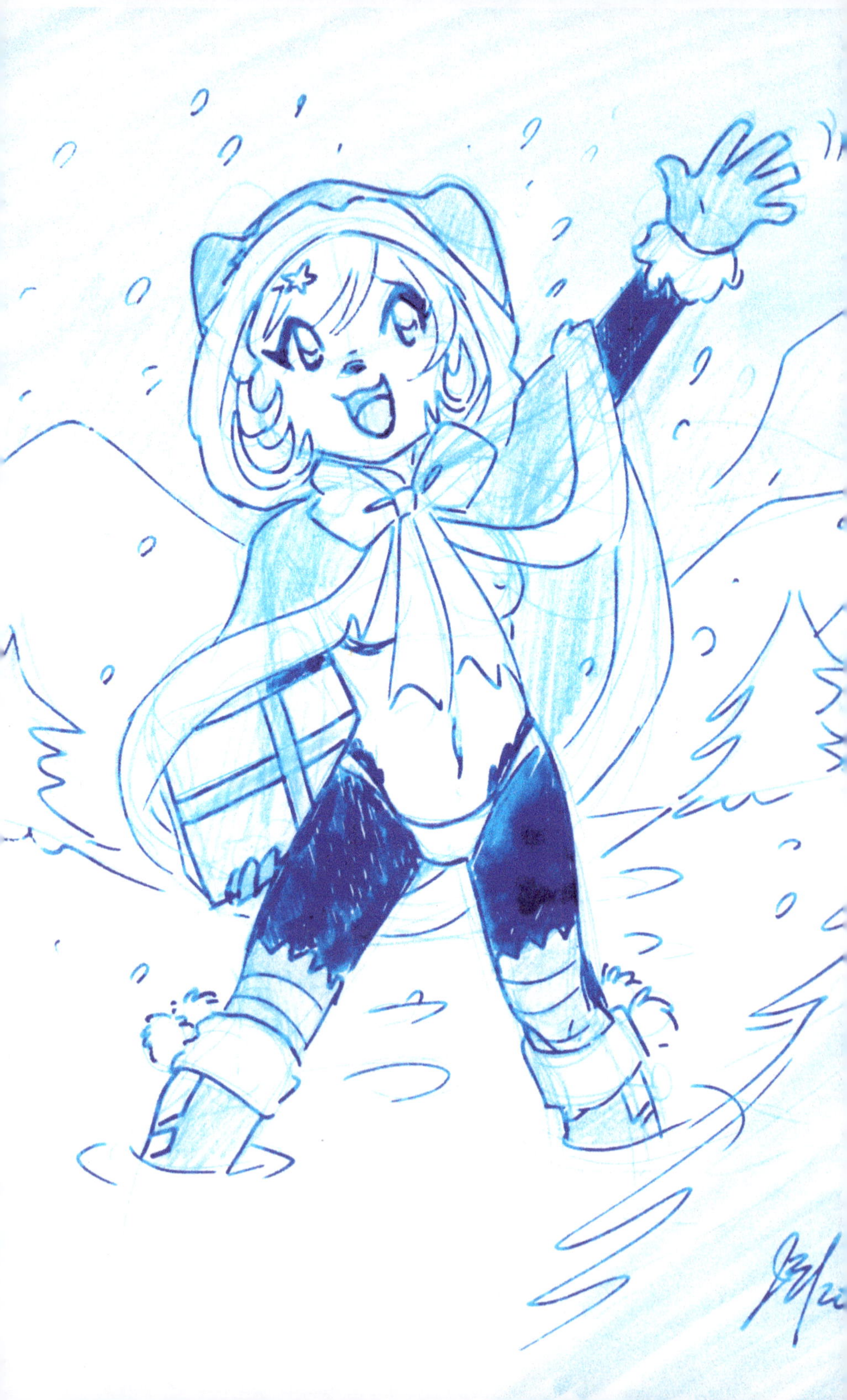

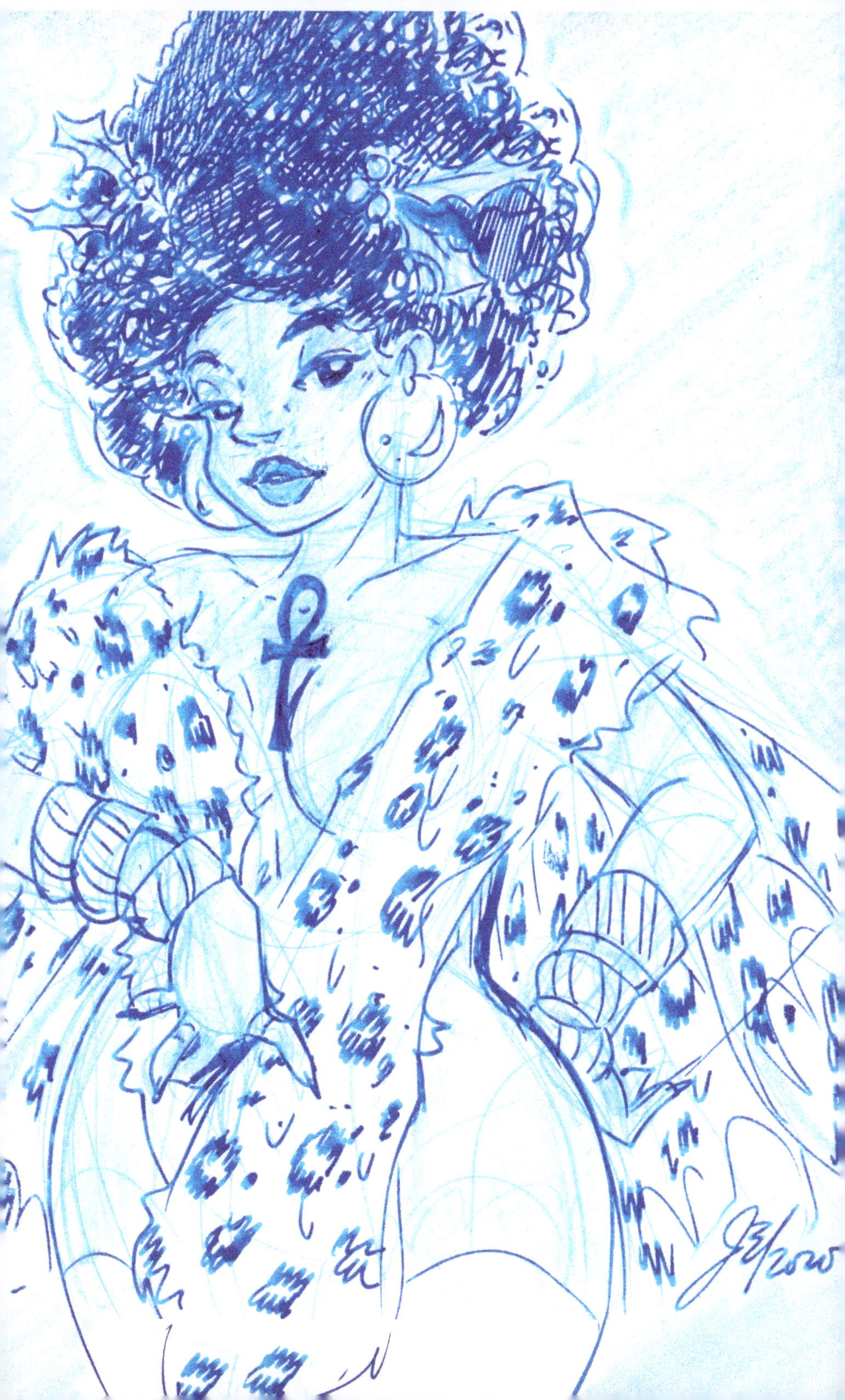

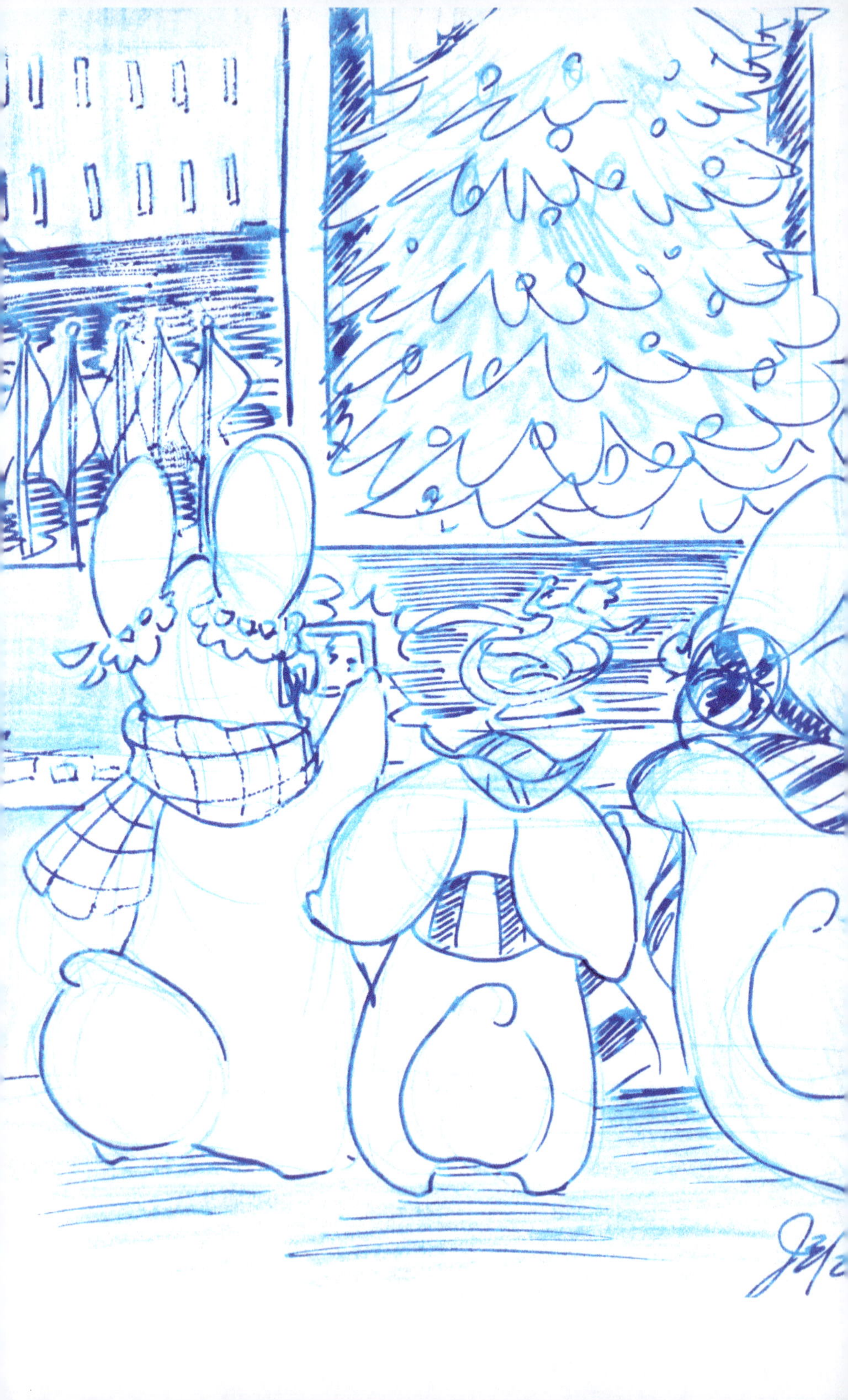

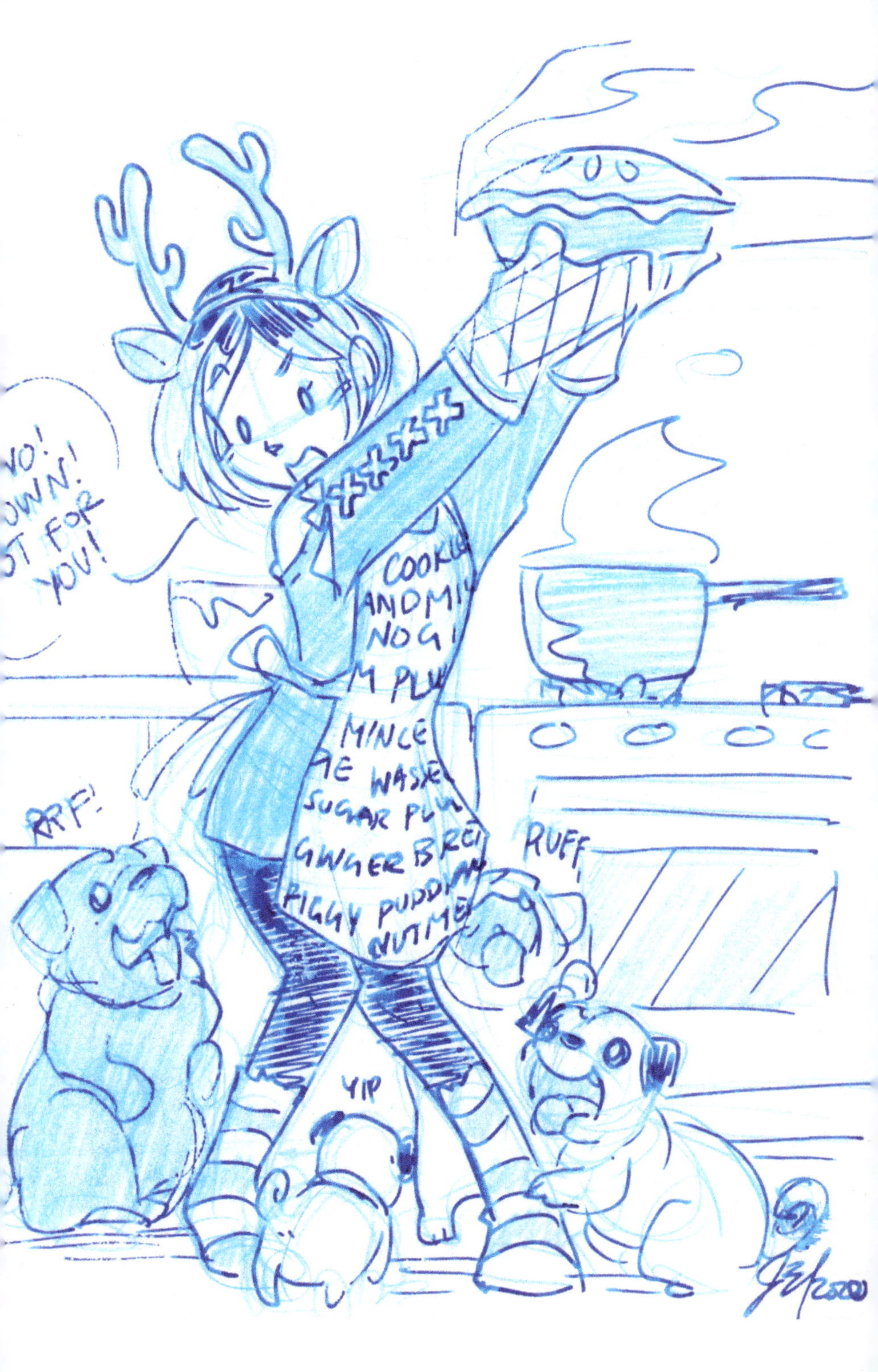

NO!
OWN!
OT FOR
YOU!
RRF!
RUFF
YIP
COOKI
AND MI
NO G
M PLU
MINCE
E WAS
SUGAR PLU
GINGER BREI
FIGGY PUDDIN
NUTMEG

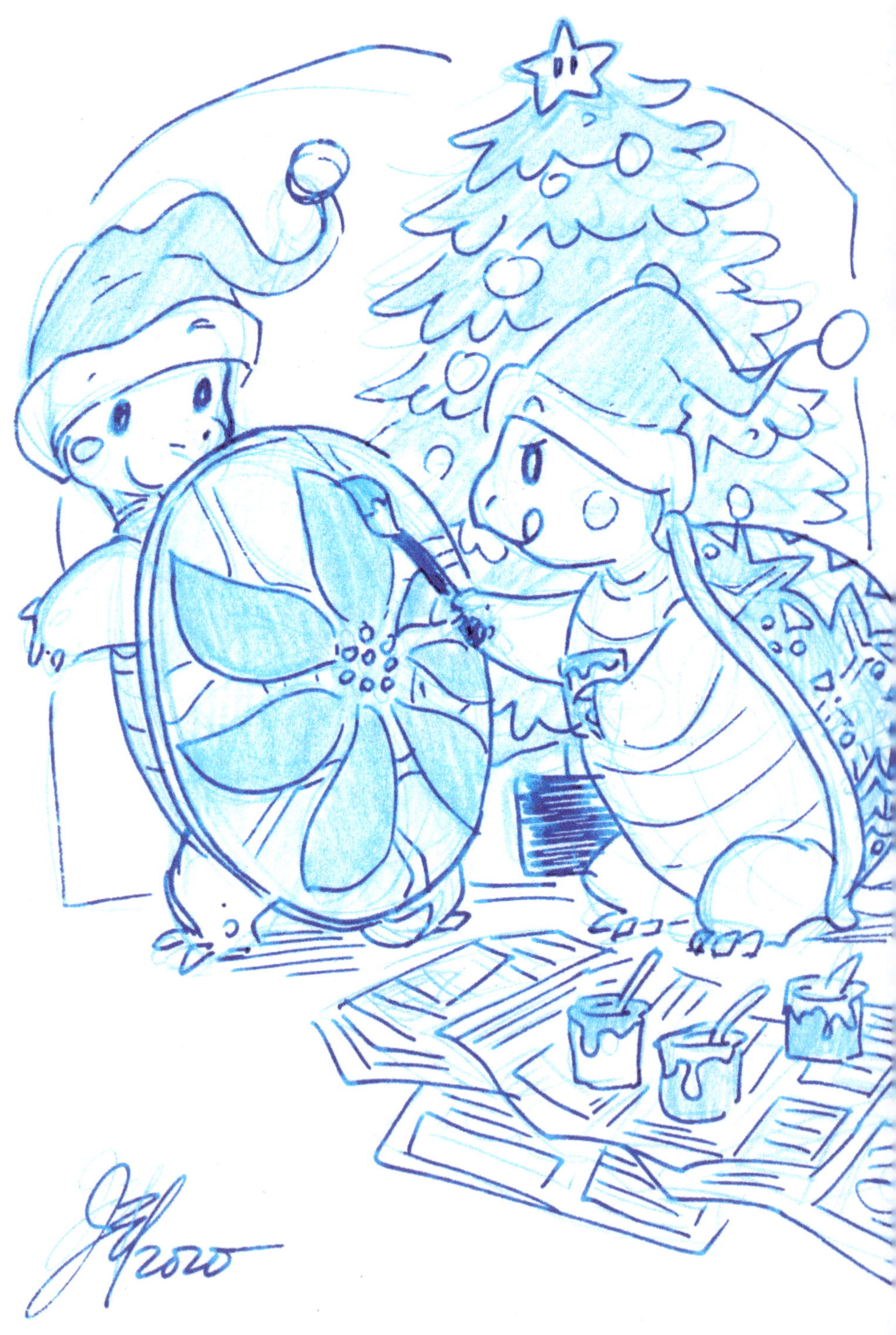

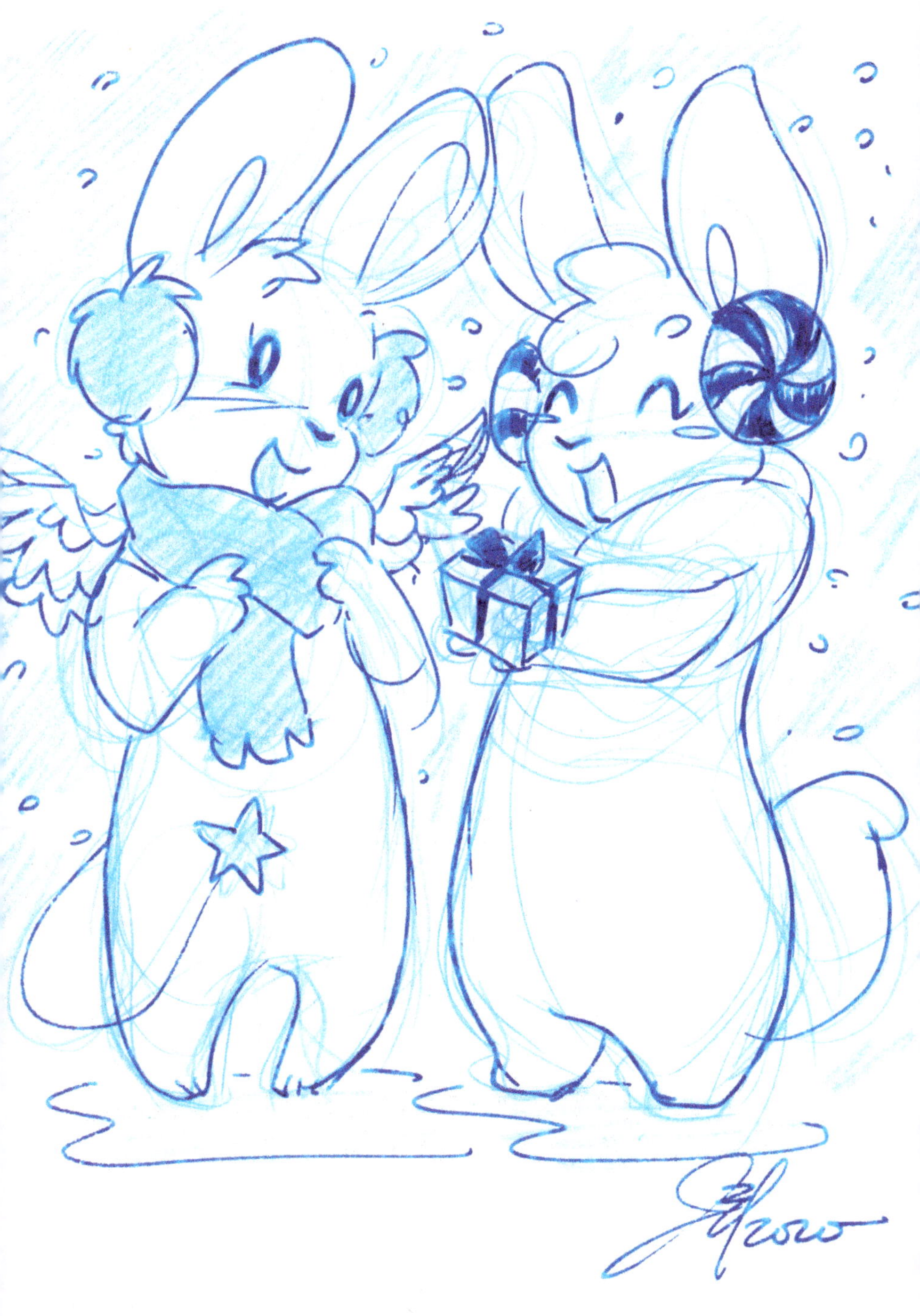

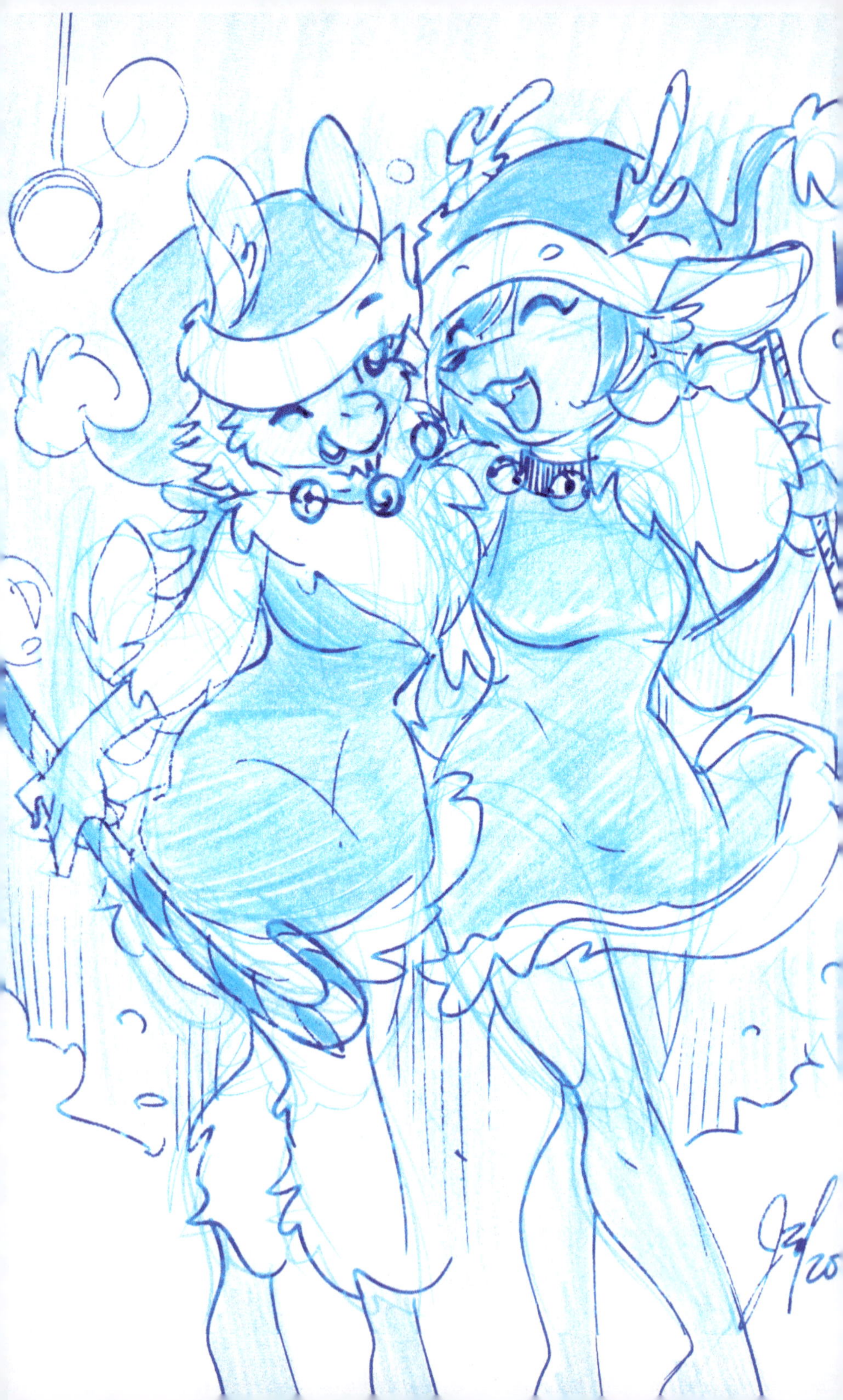

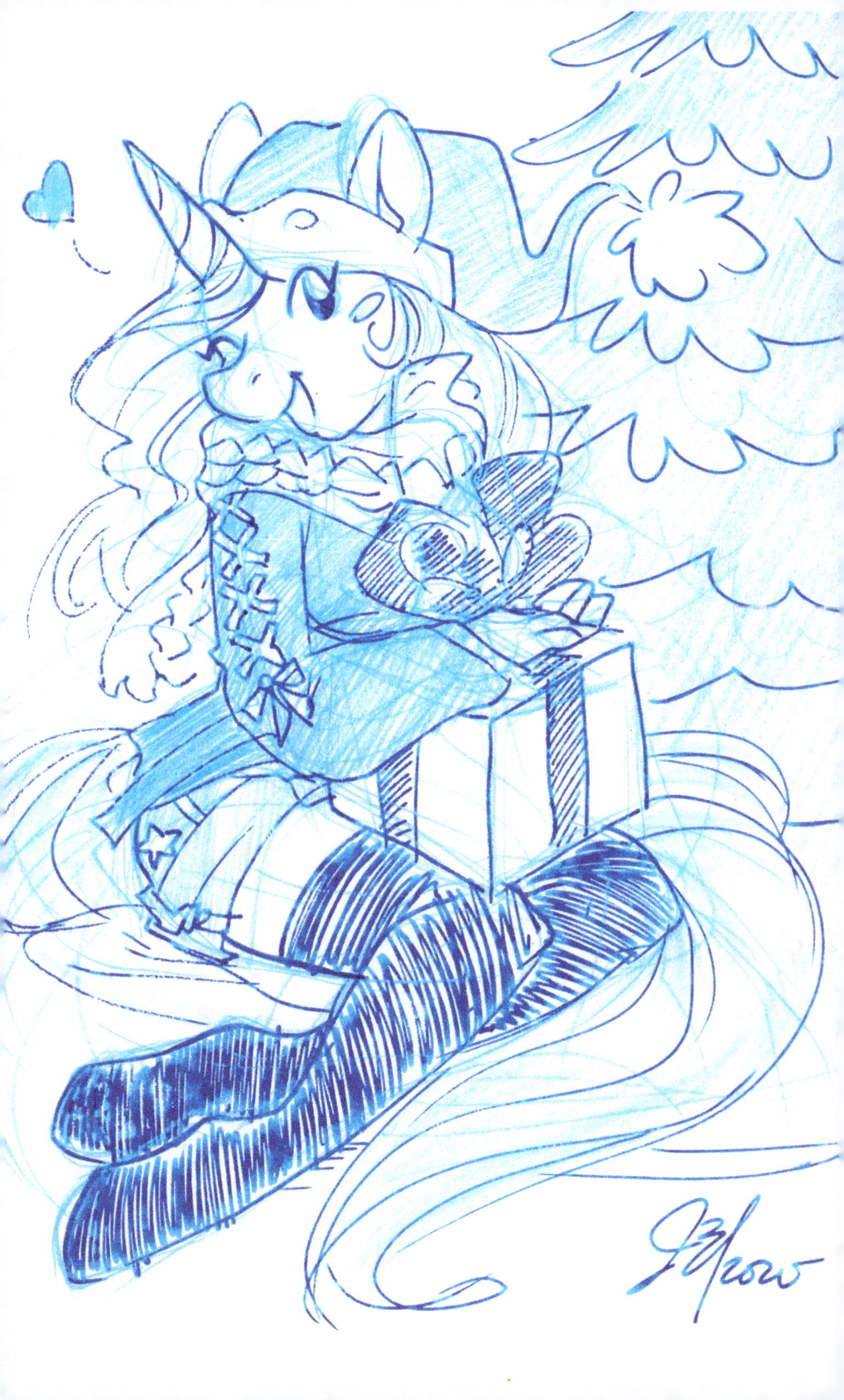

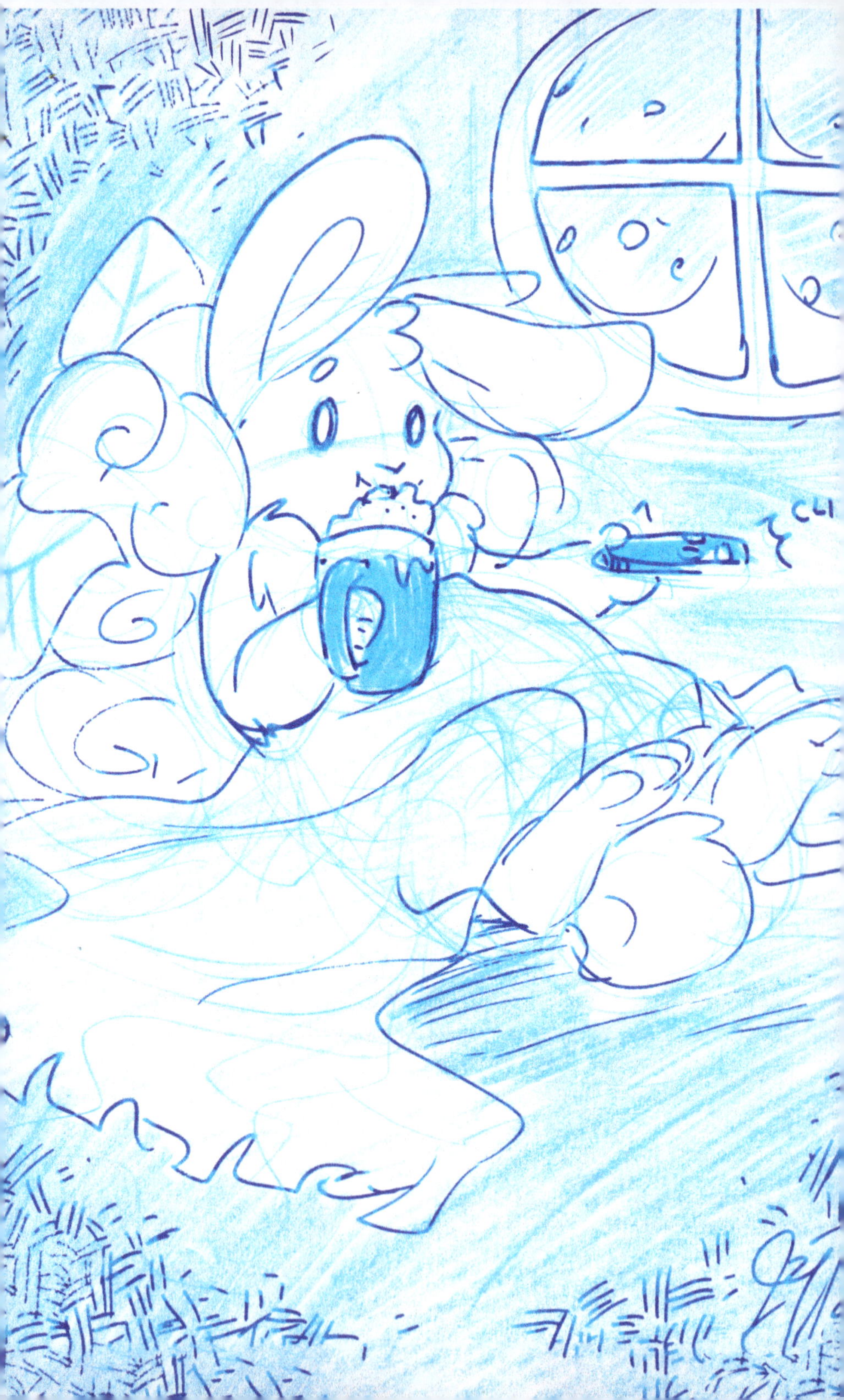

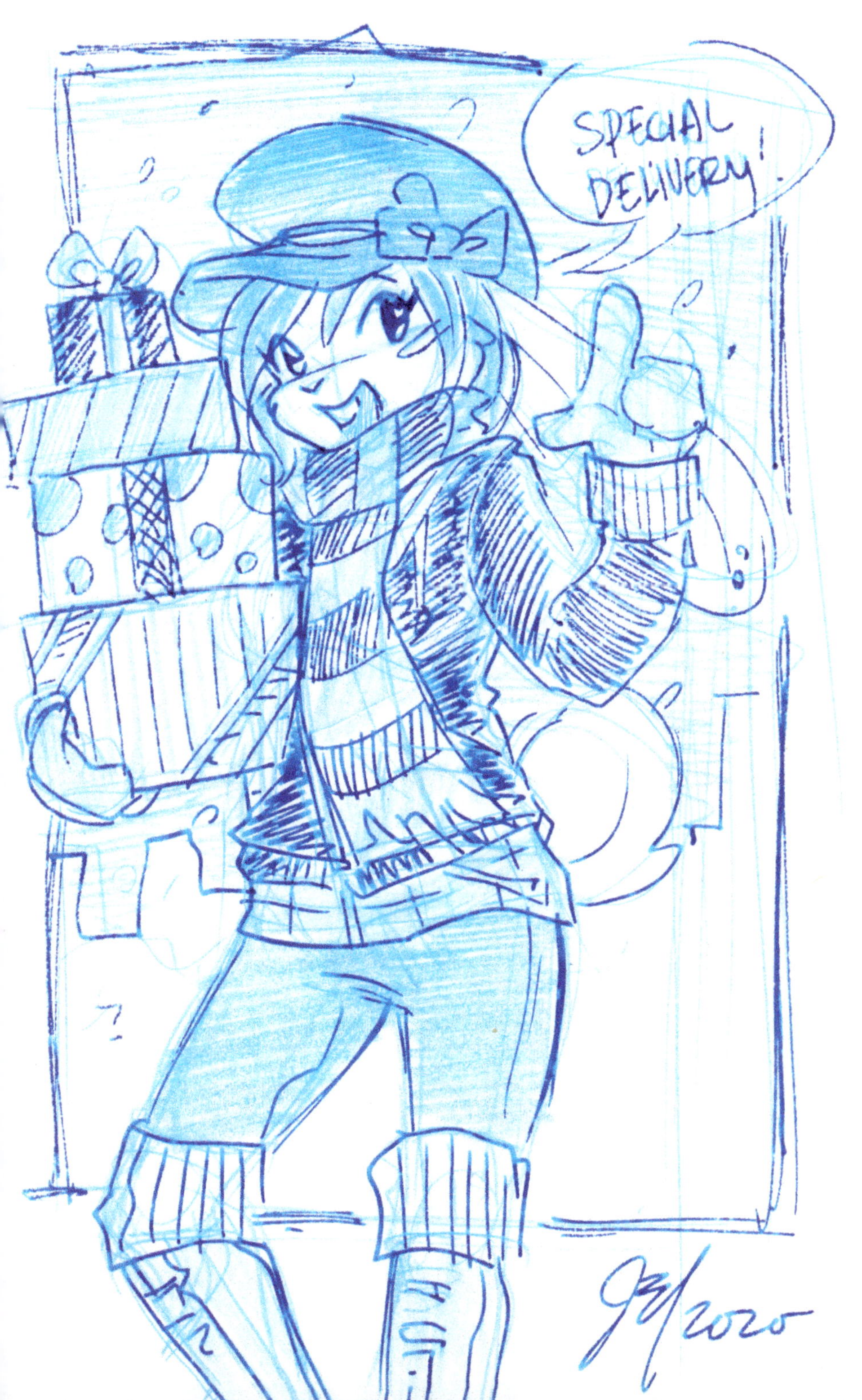

SPECIAL DELIVERY!

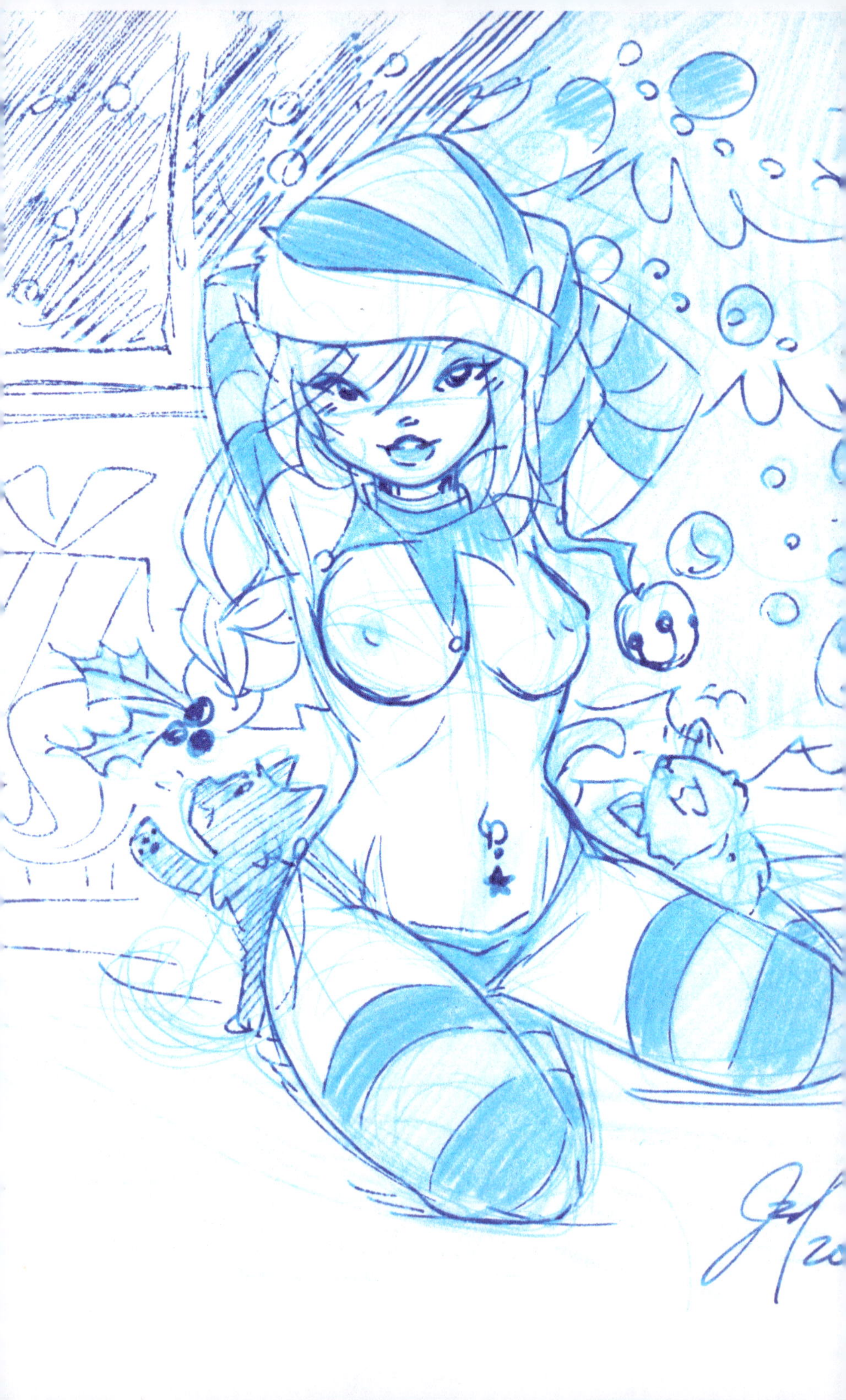

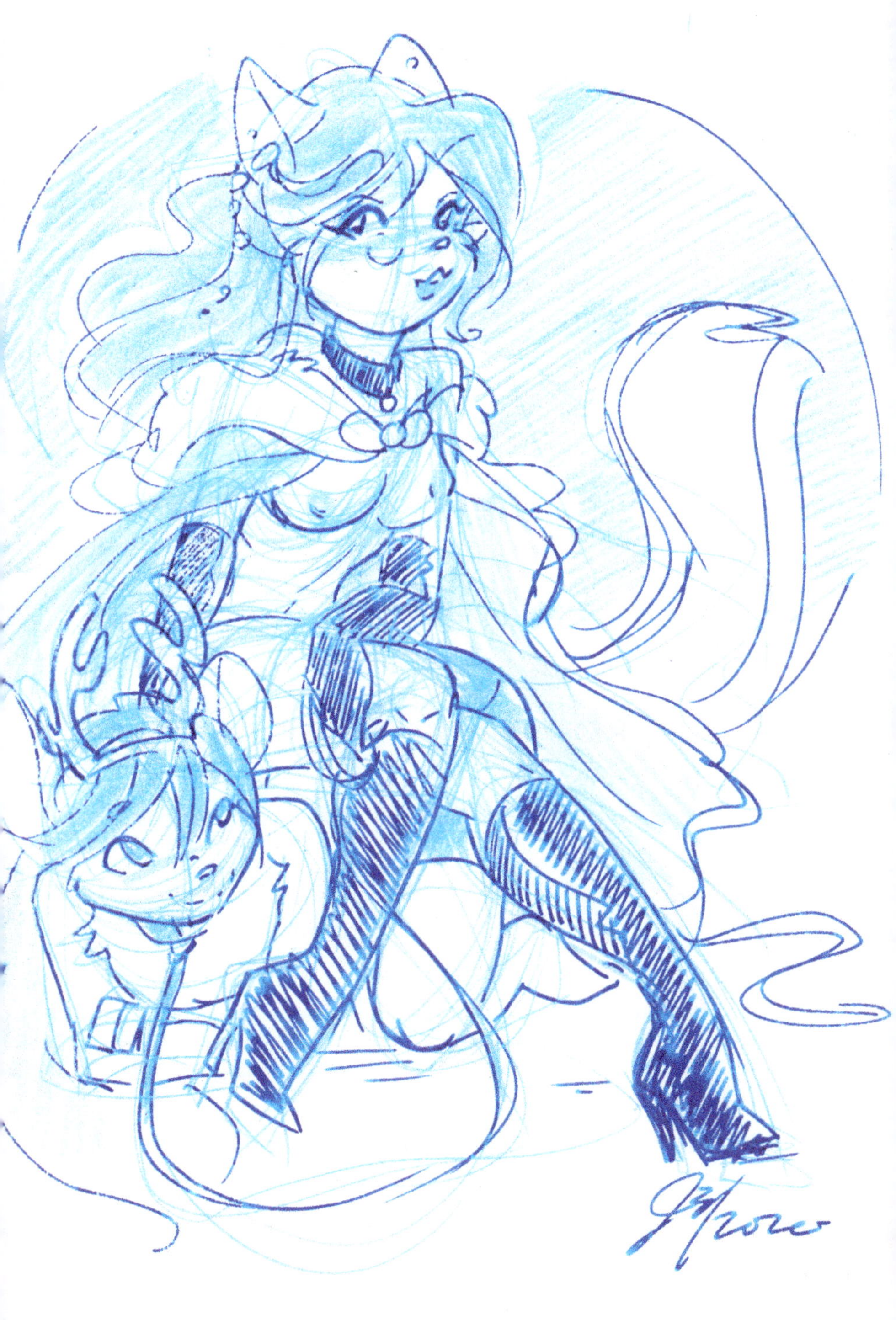

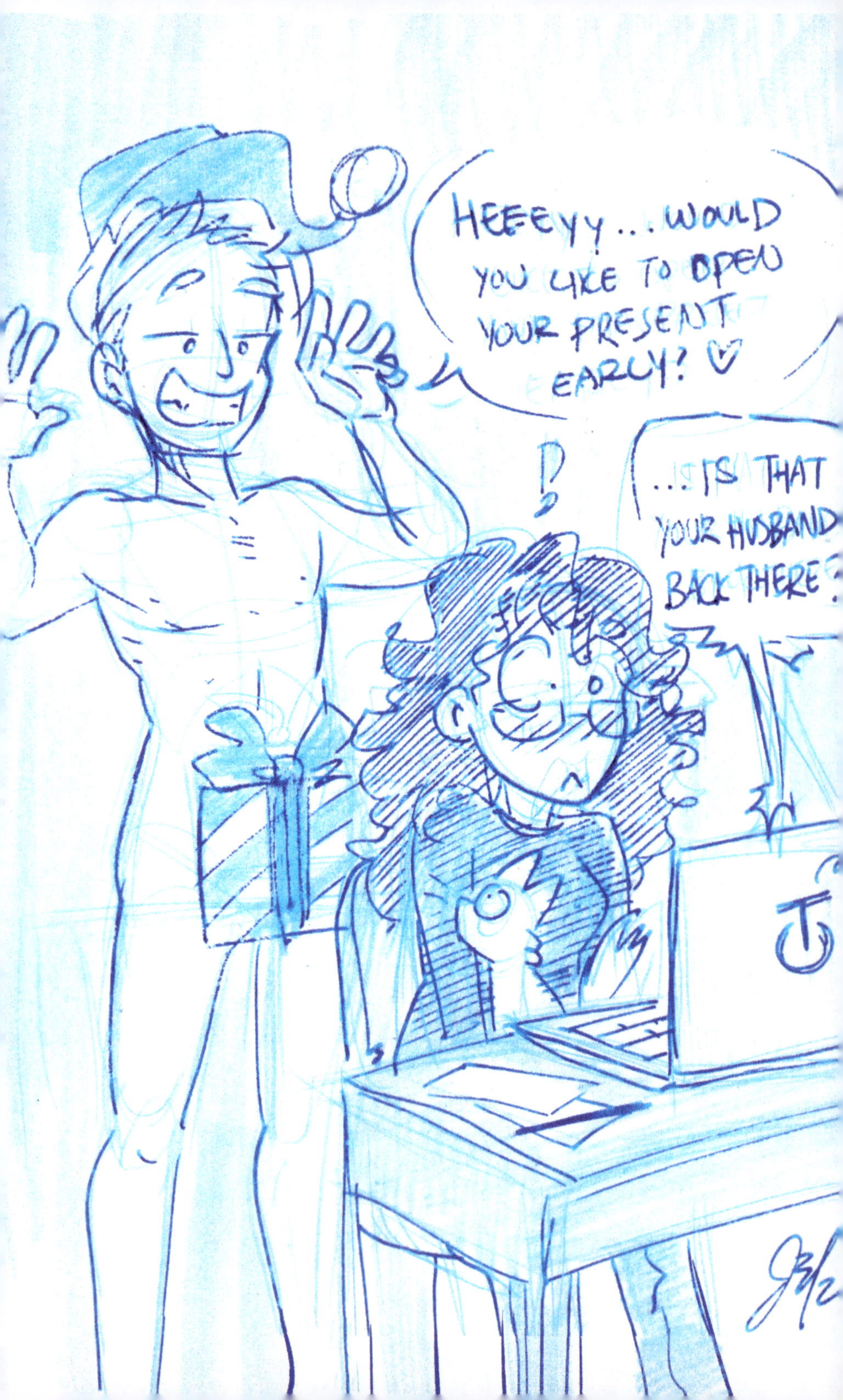

HEEEYY...WOULD YOU LIKE TO OPEN YOUR PRESENT EARLY?
...IS THAT YOUR HUSBAND BACK THERE?

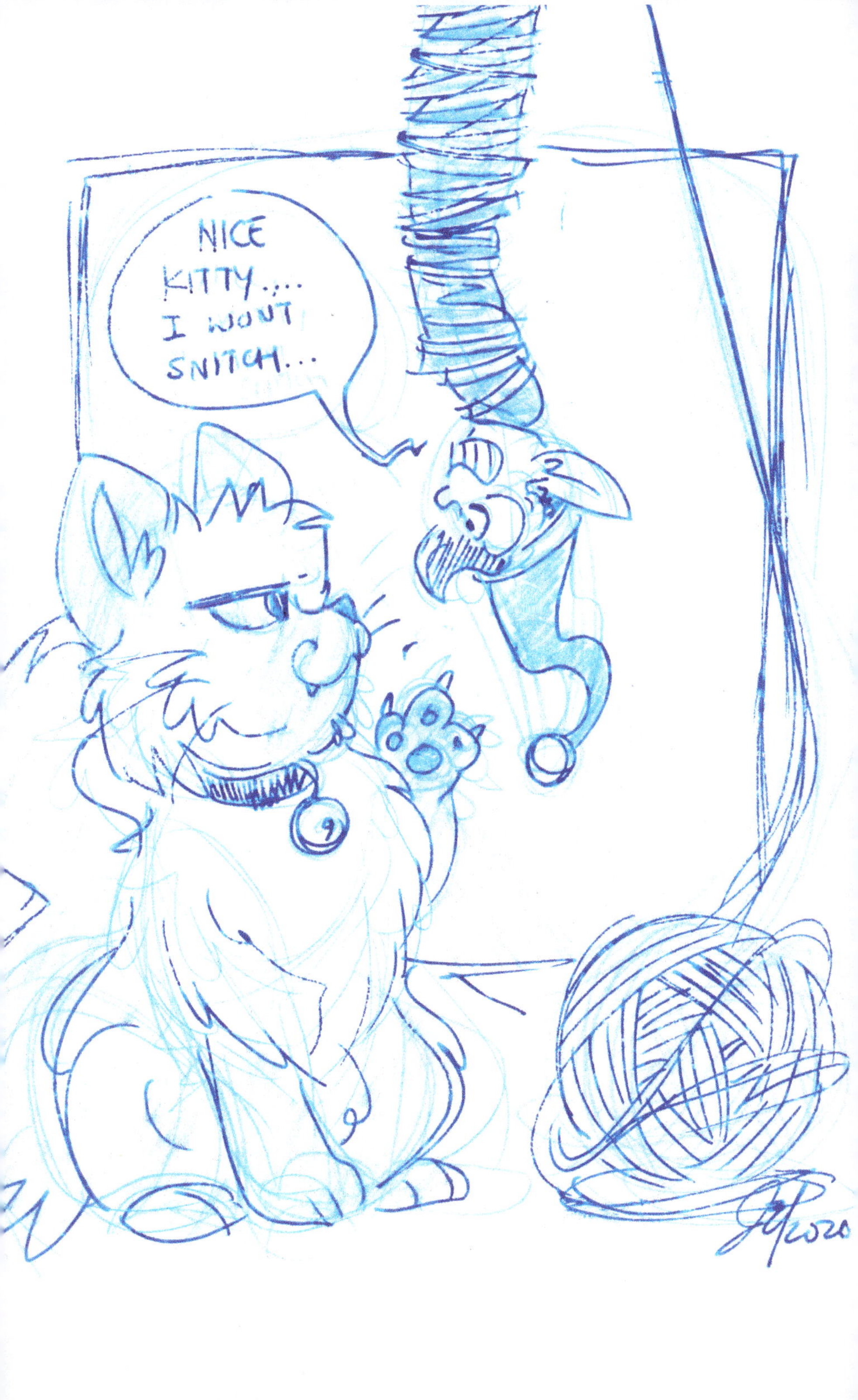
NICE KITTY....
I WONT SNITCH...

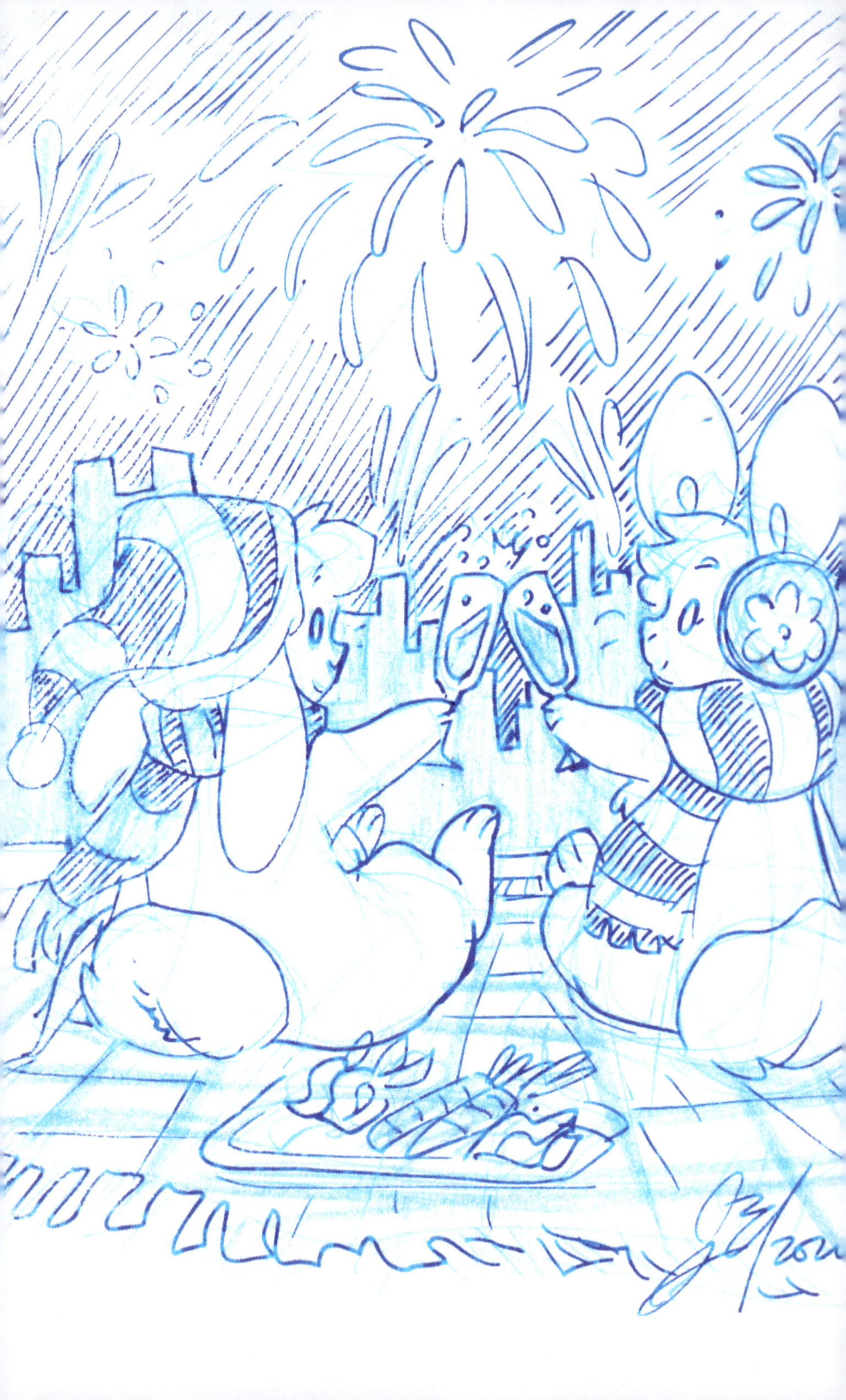

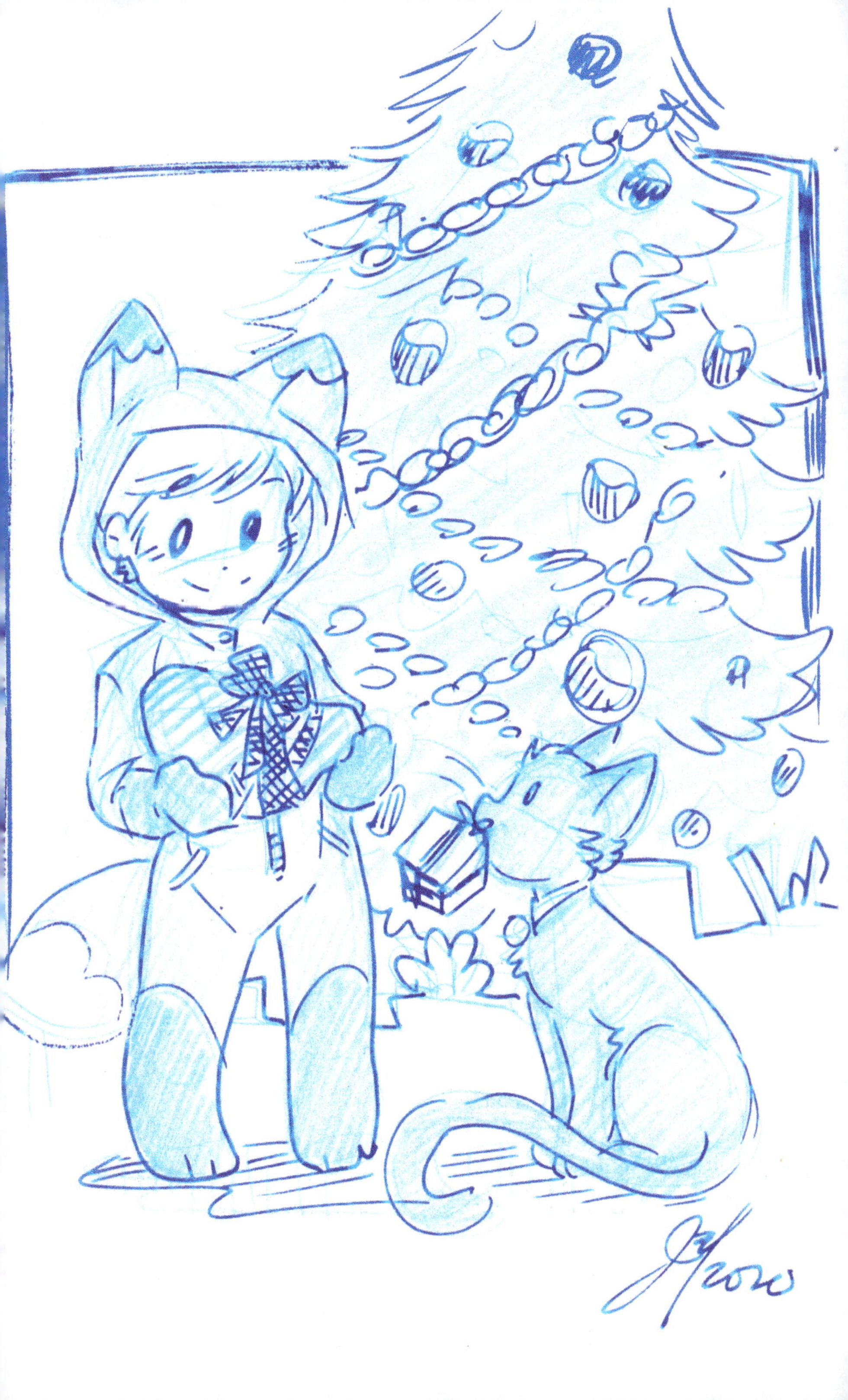

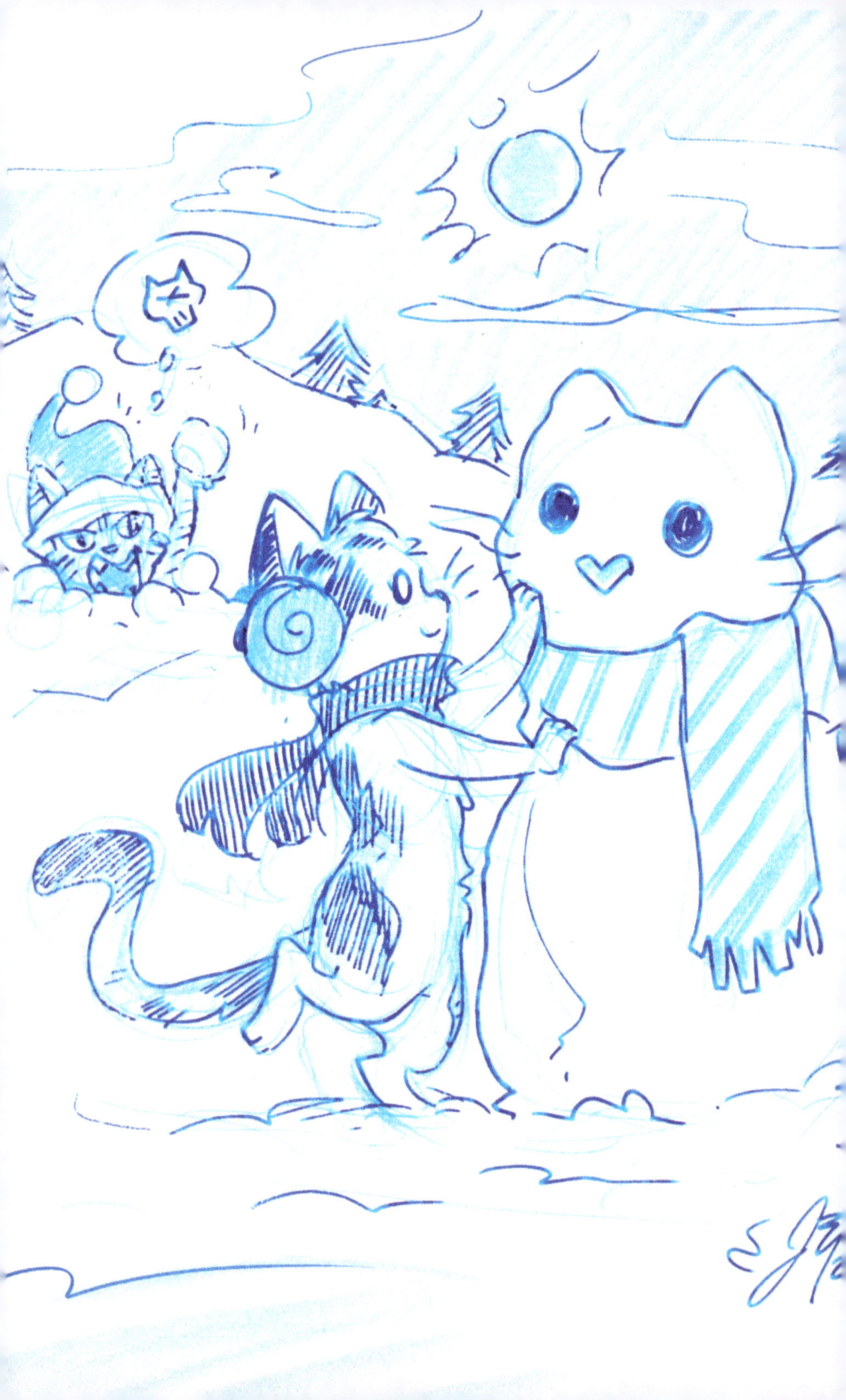

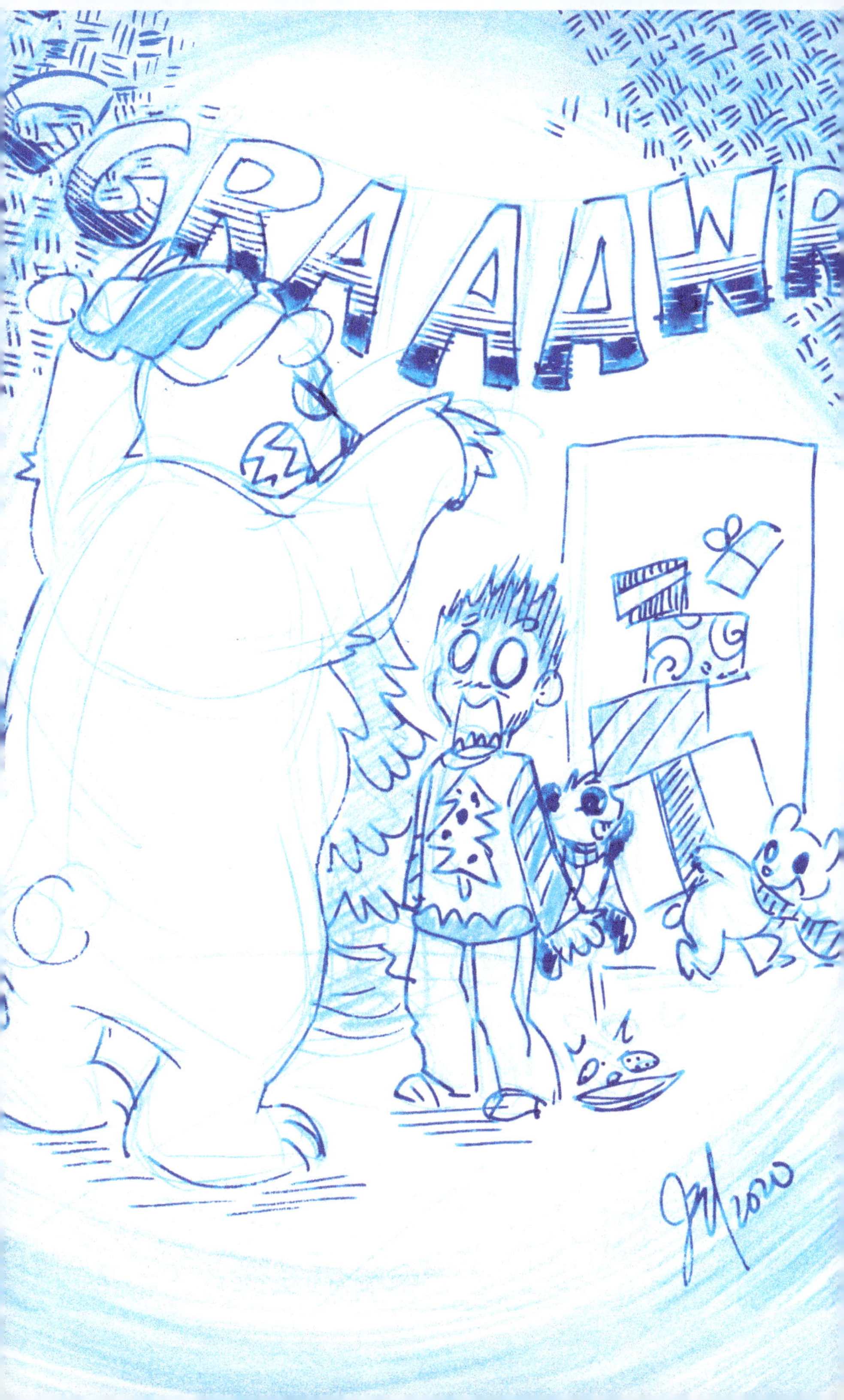

GRAAAWR

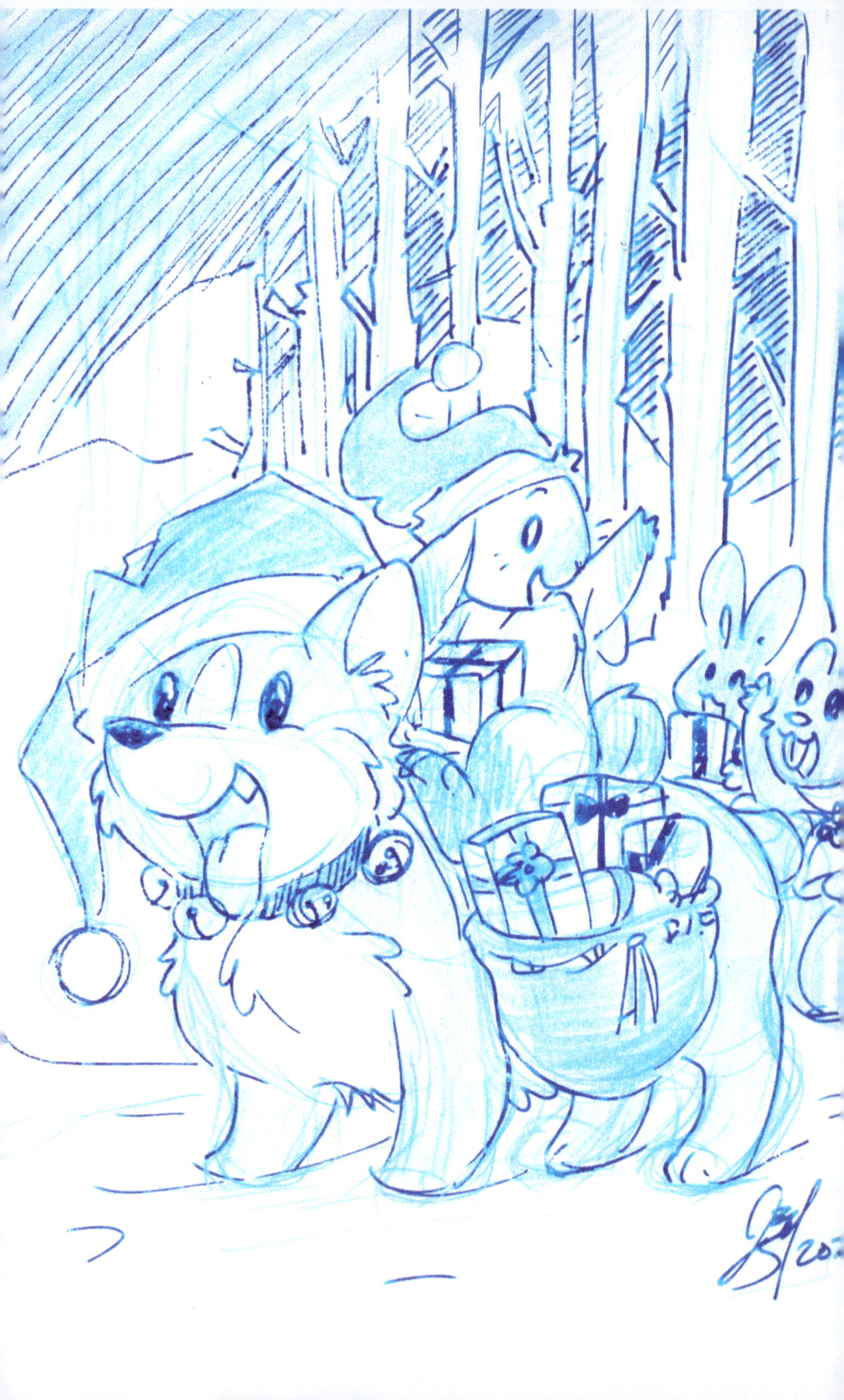

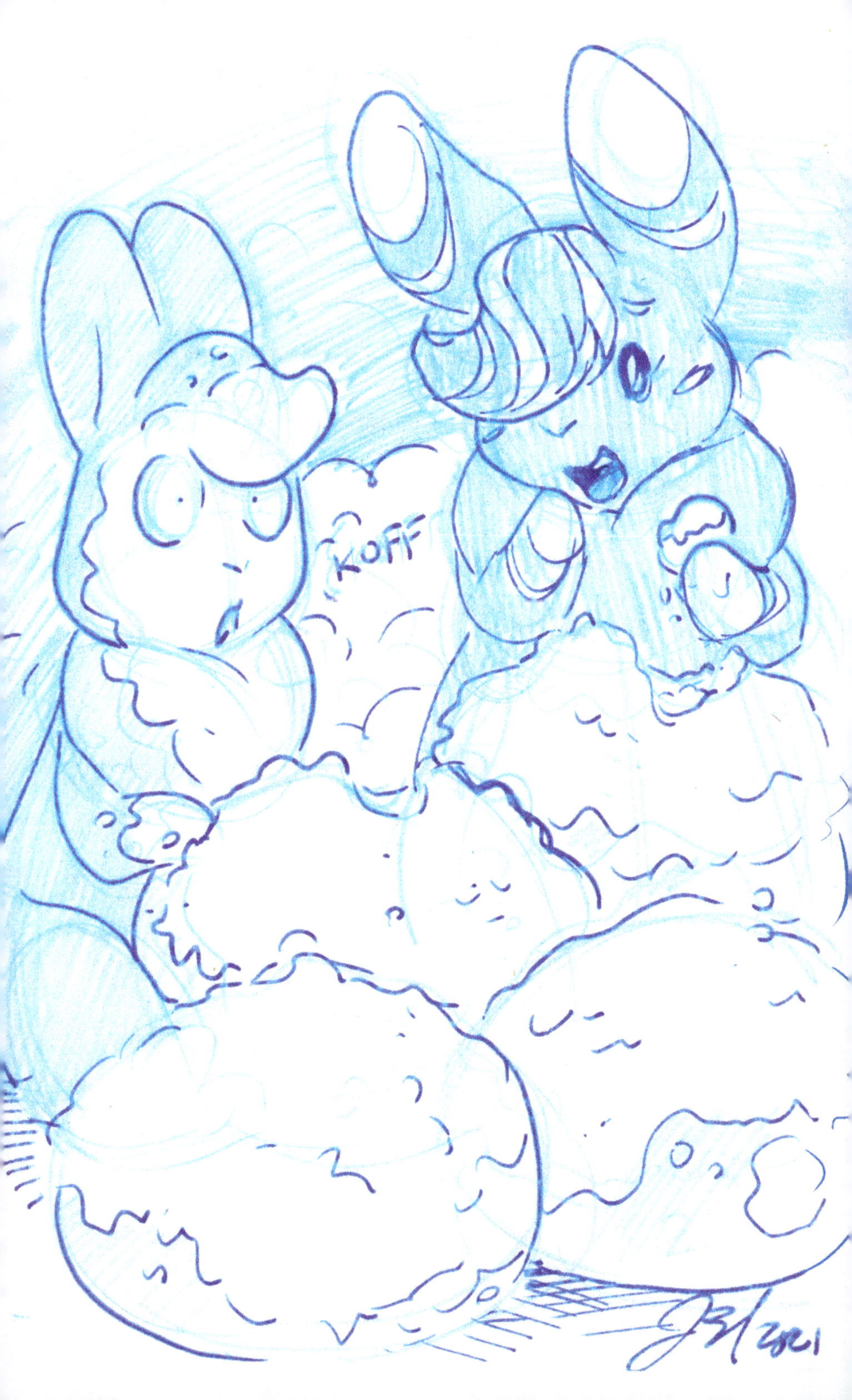
KOFF

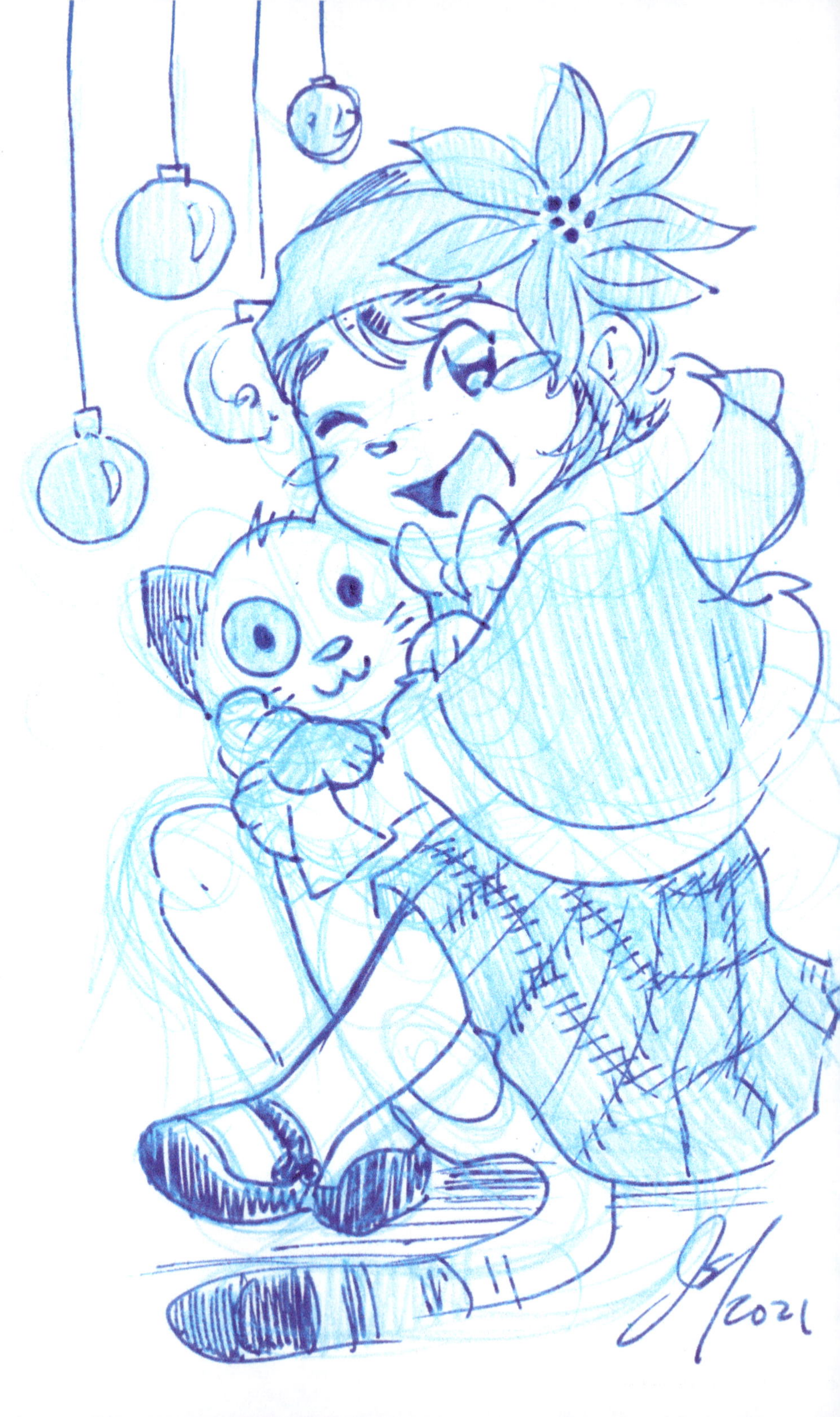

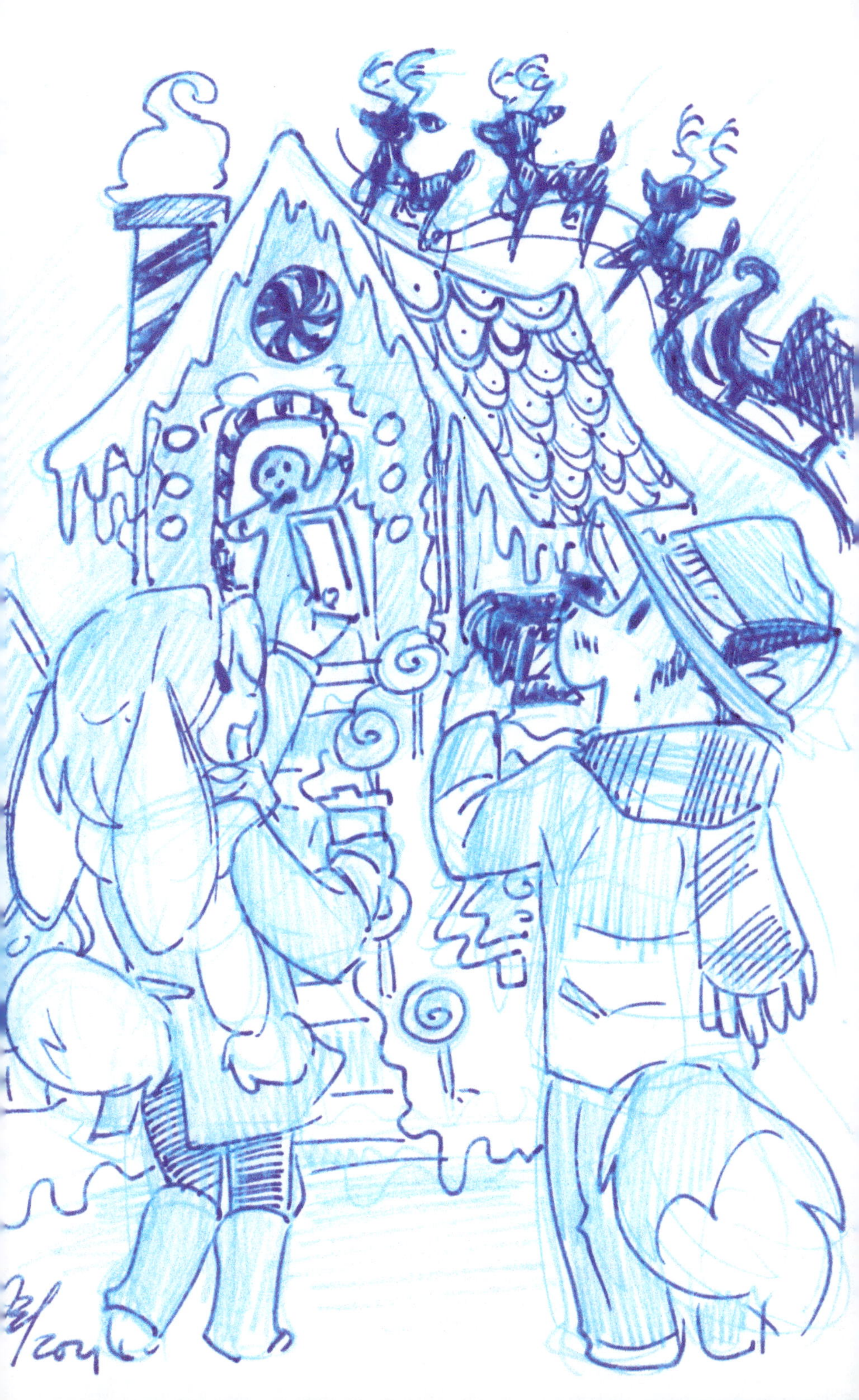

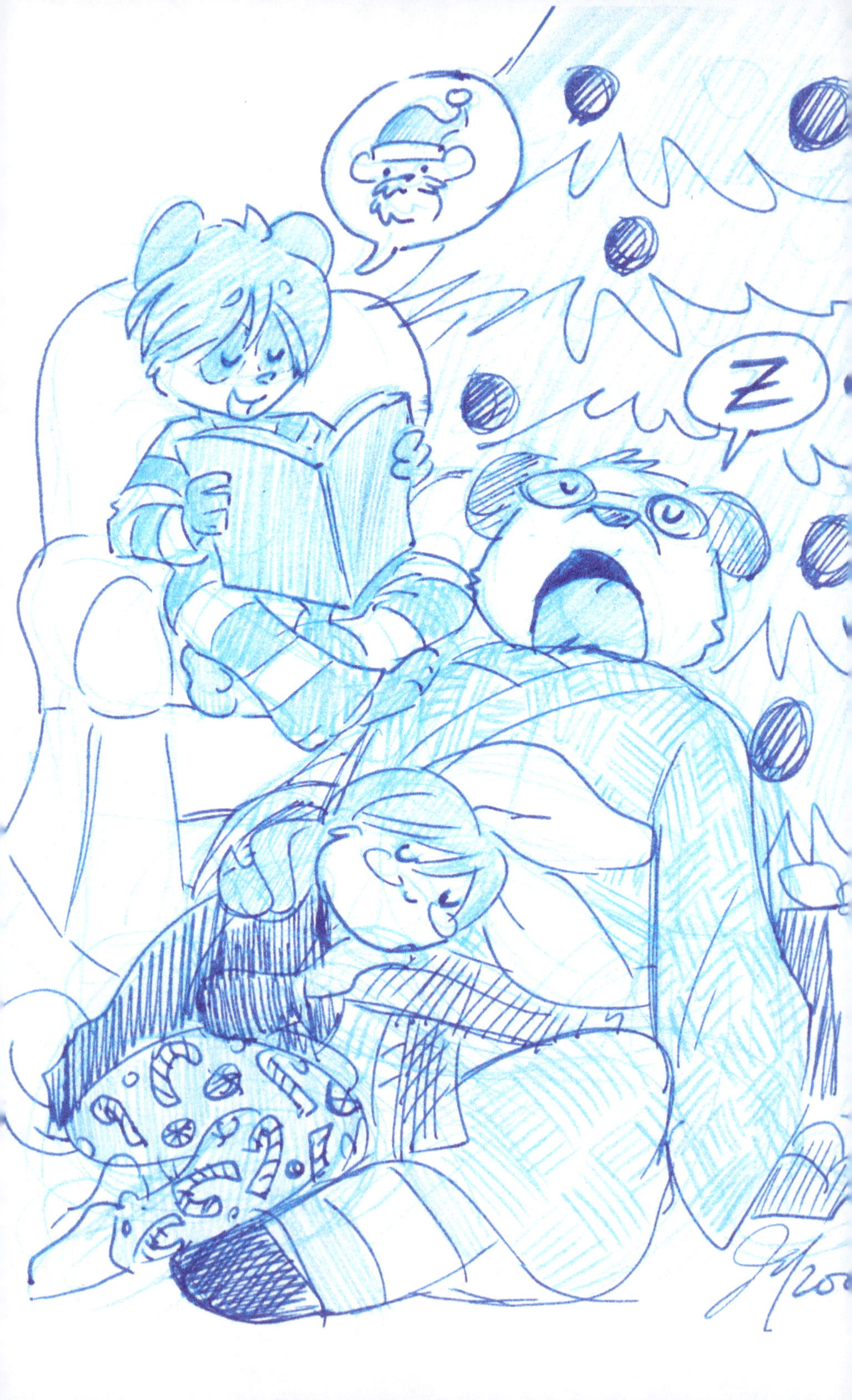
Z

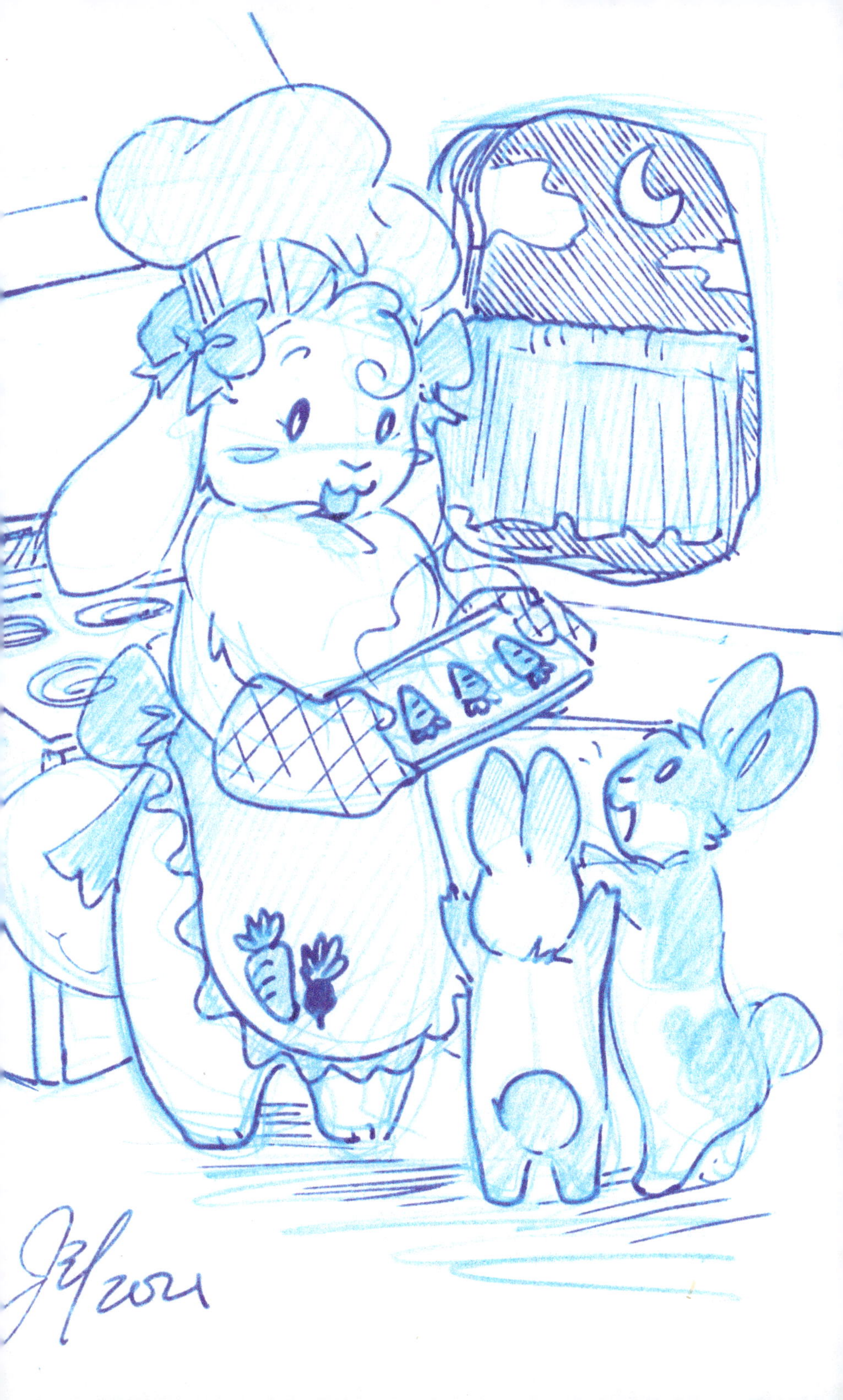

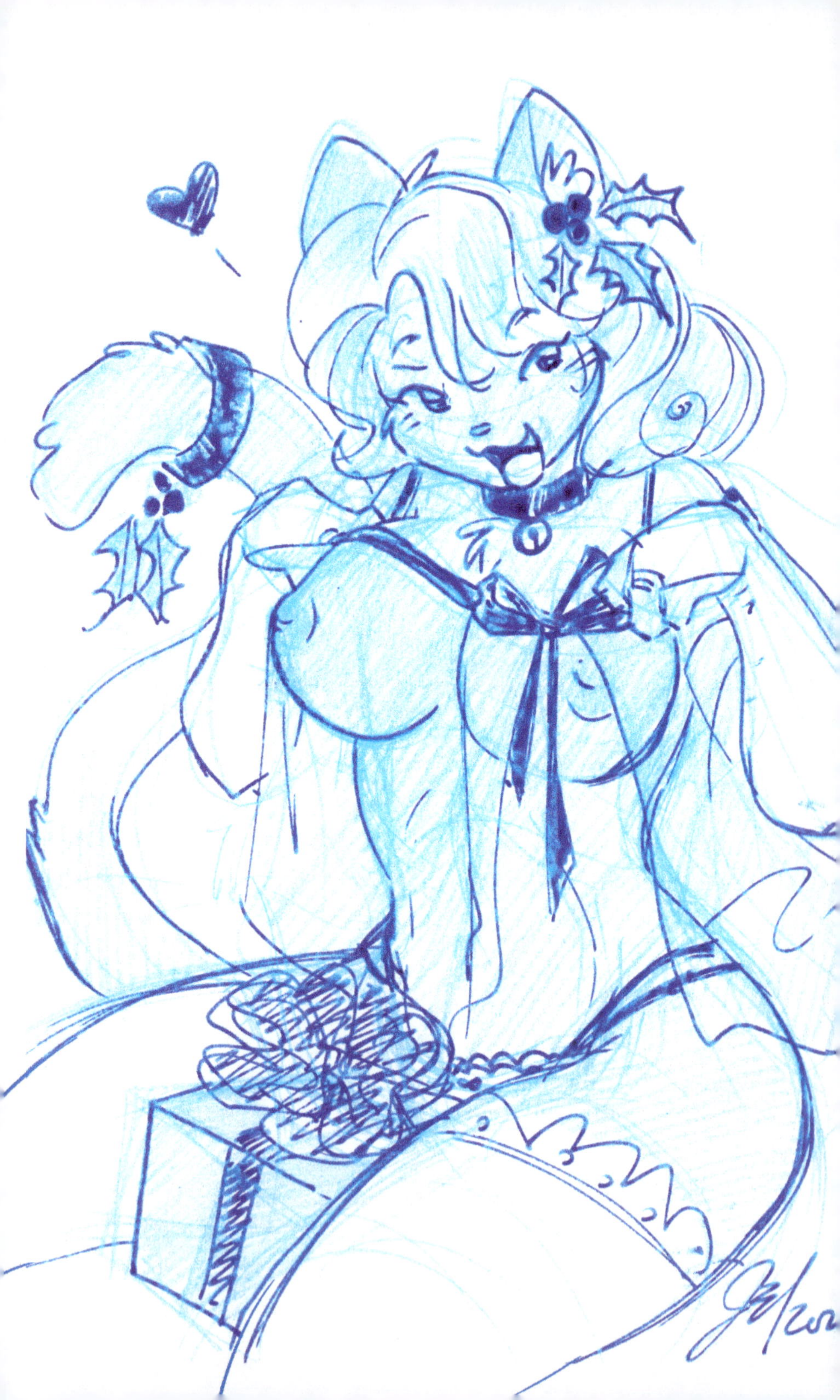

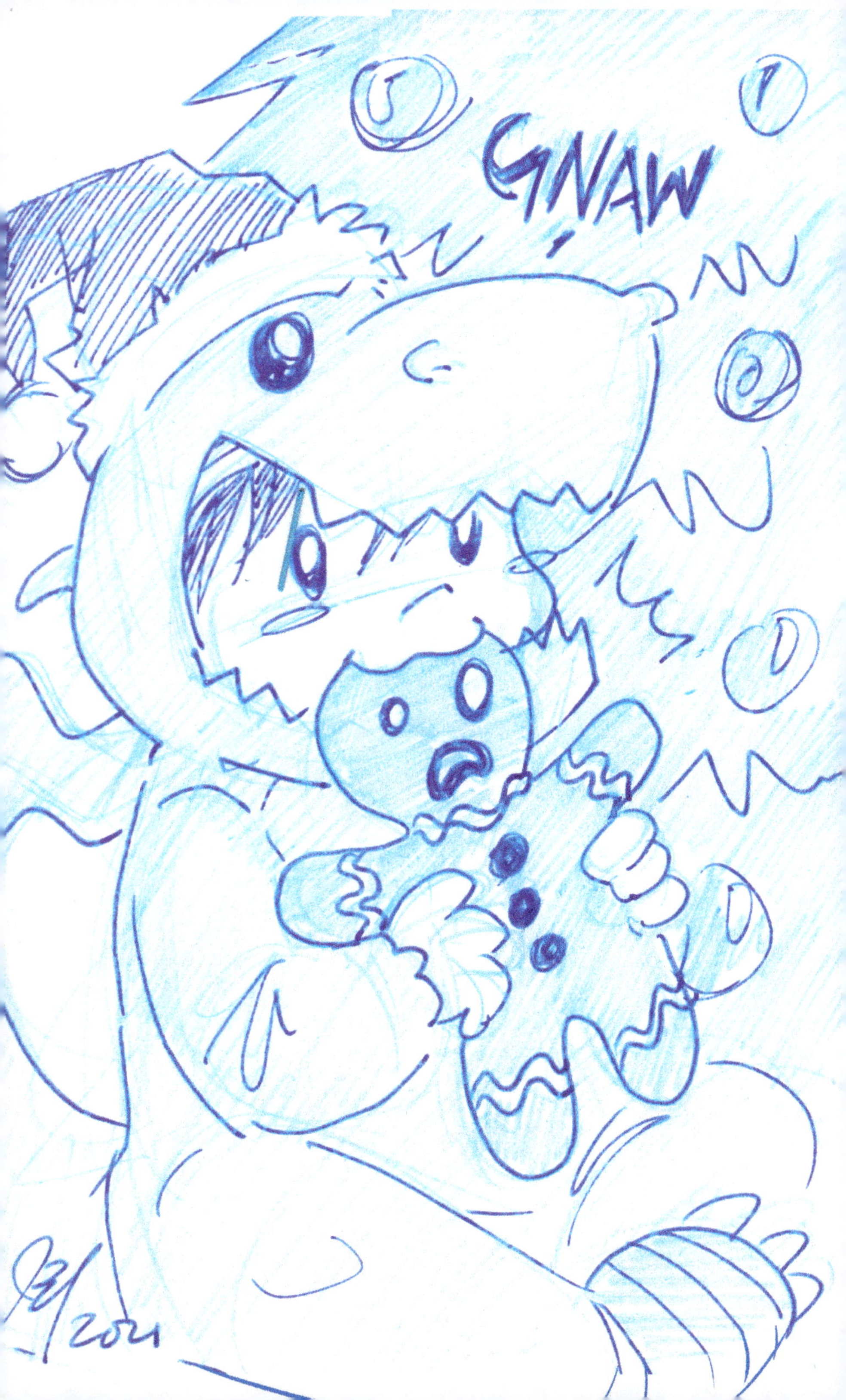
GNAW

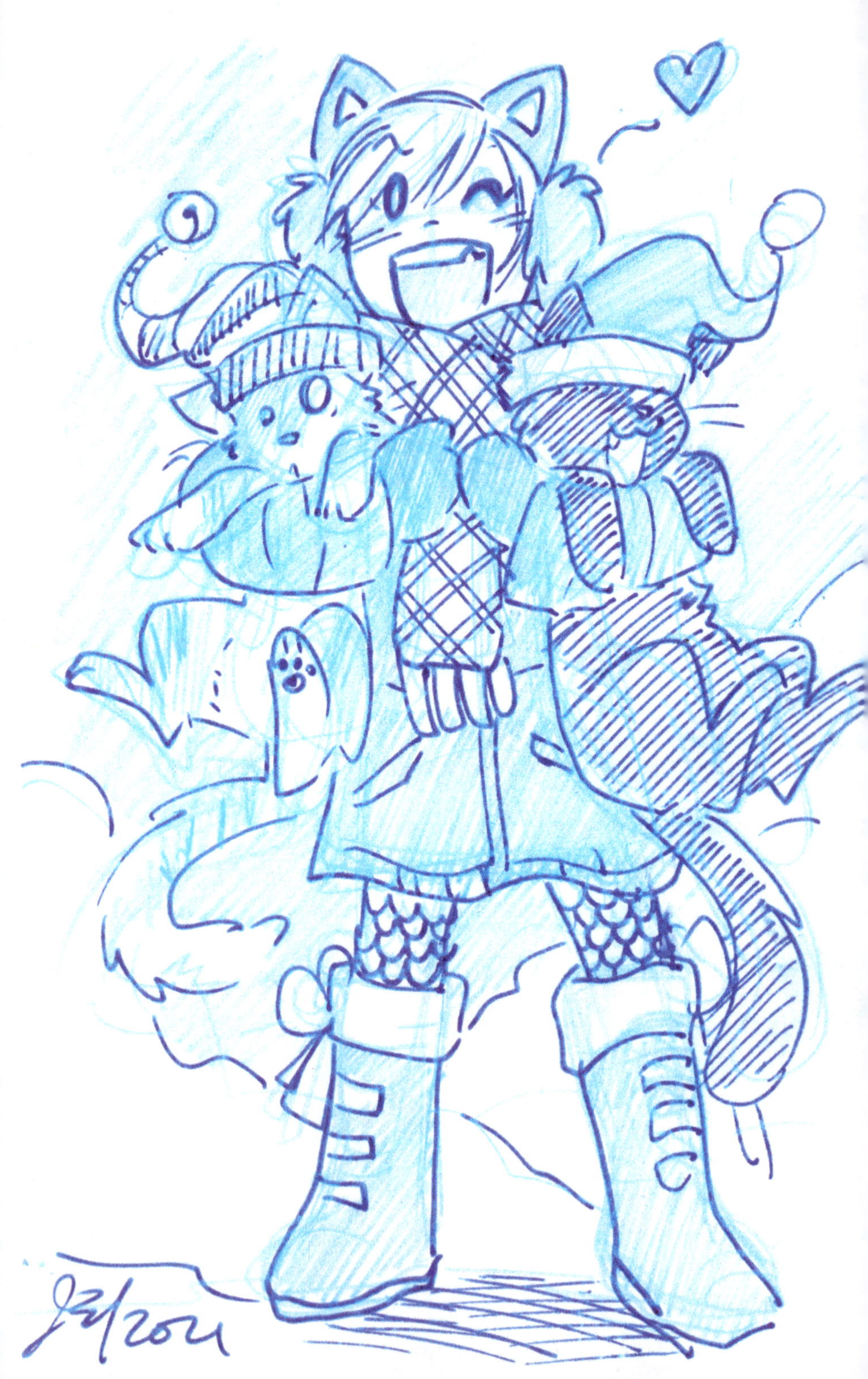

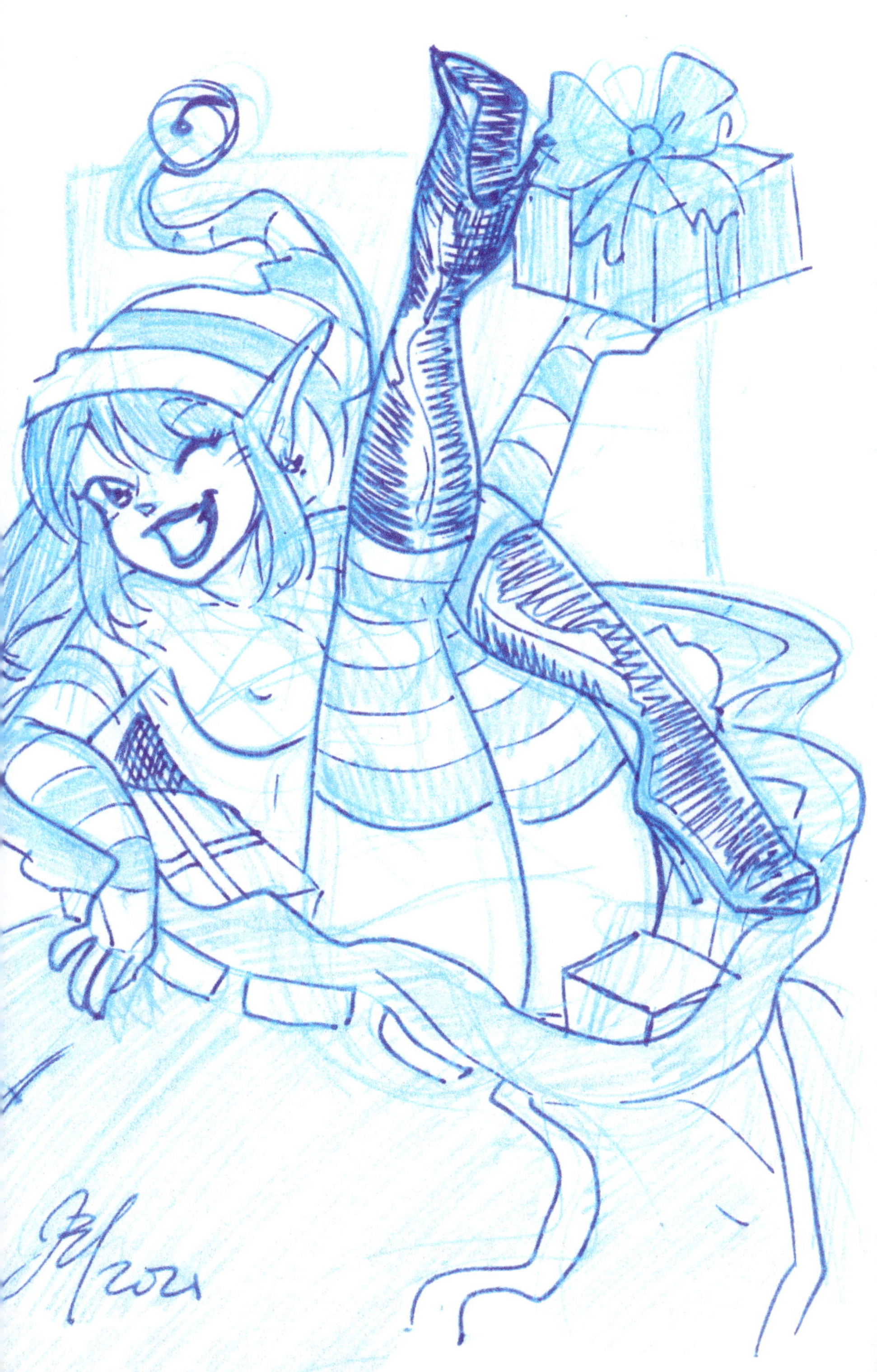

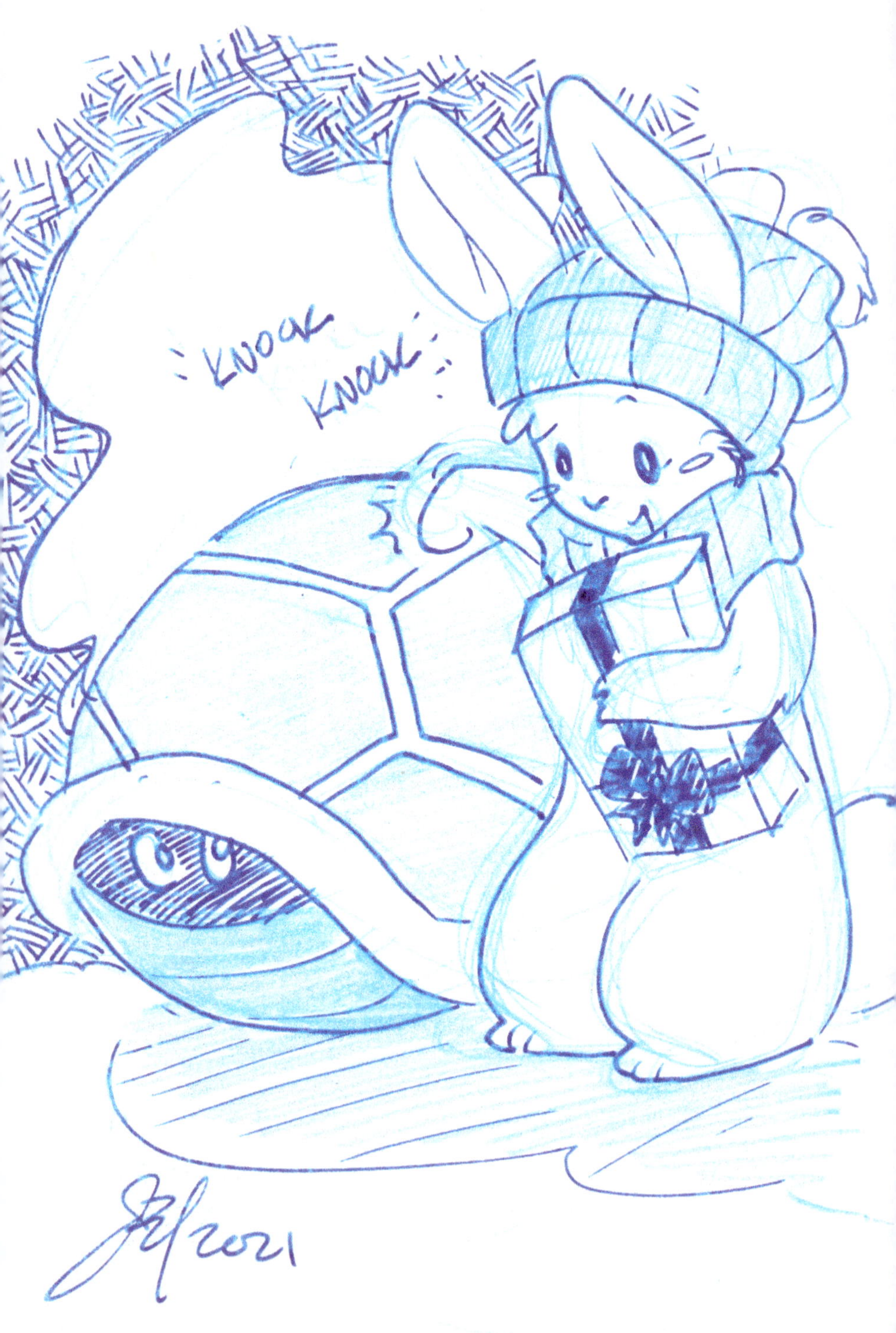

KNOCK
KNOCK

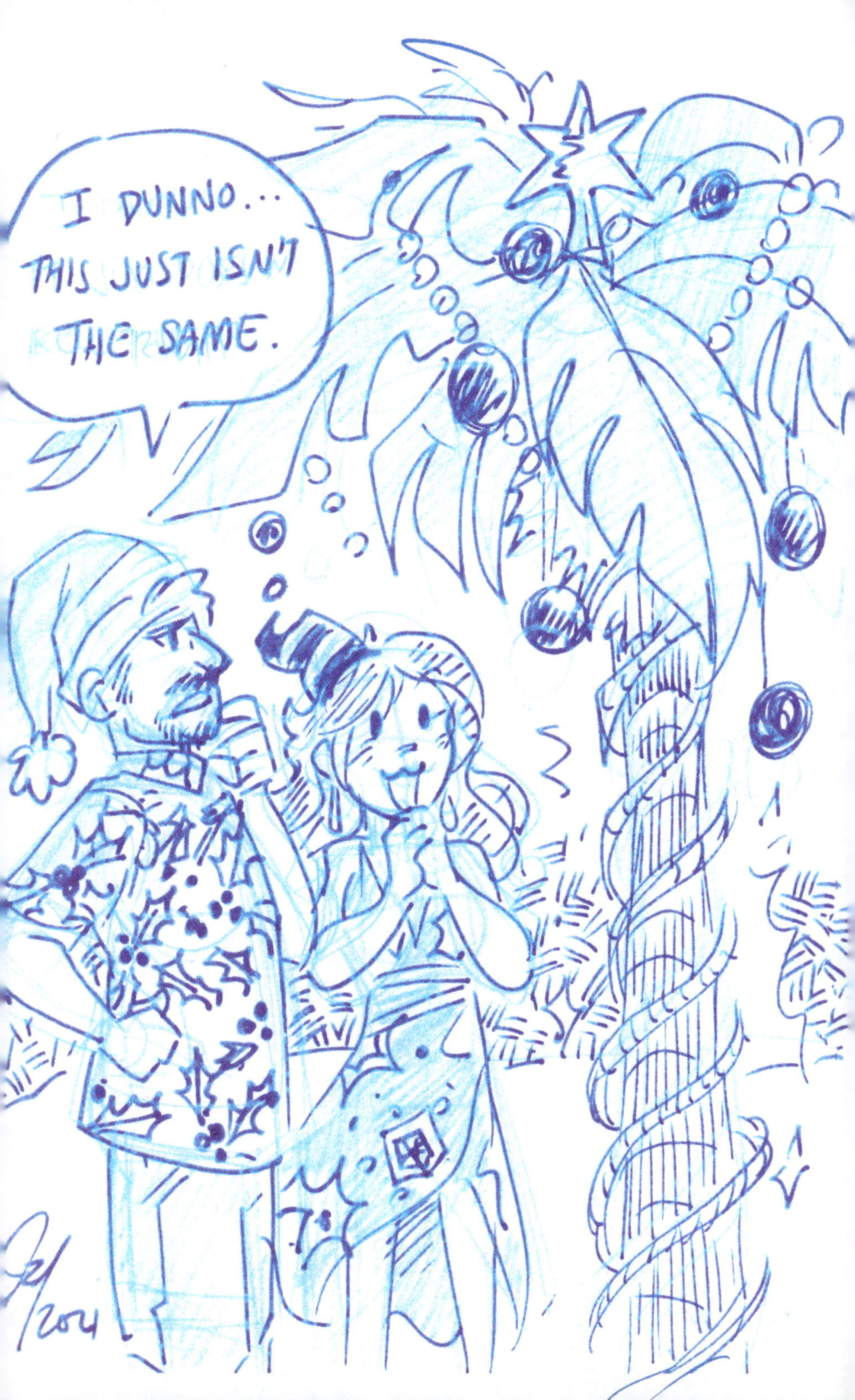

I DUNNO...
THIS JUST ISN'T
THE SAME.

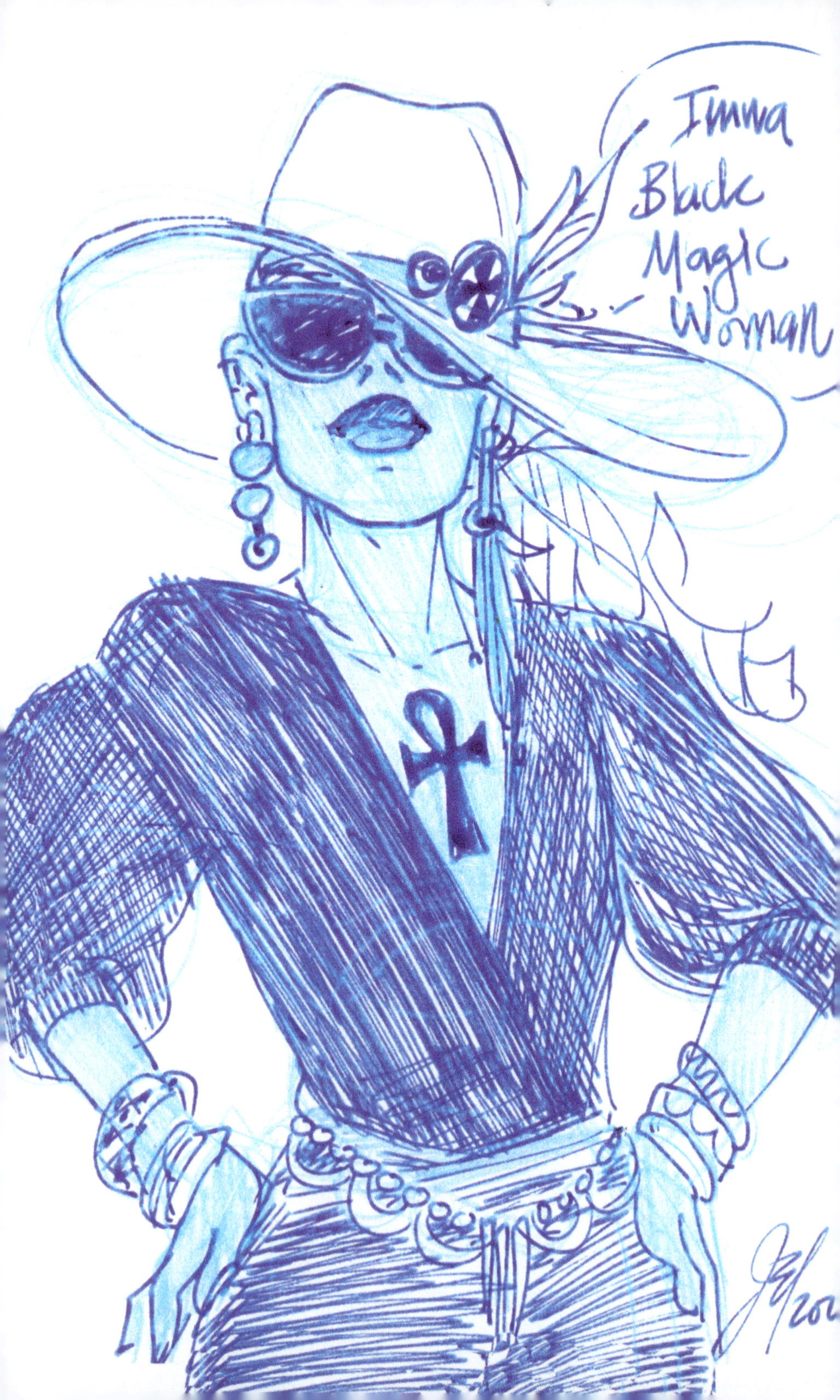

Imma
Black
Magic
Woman

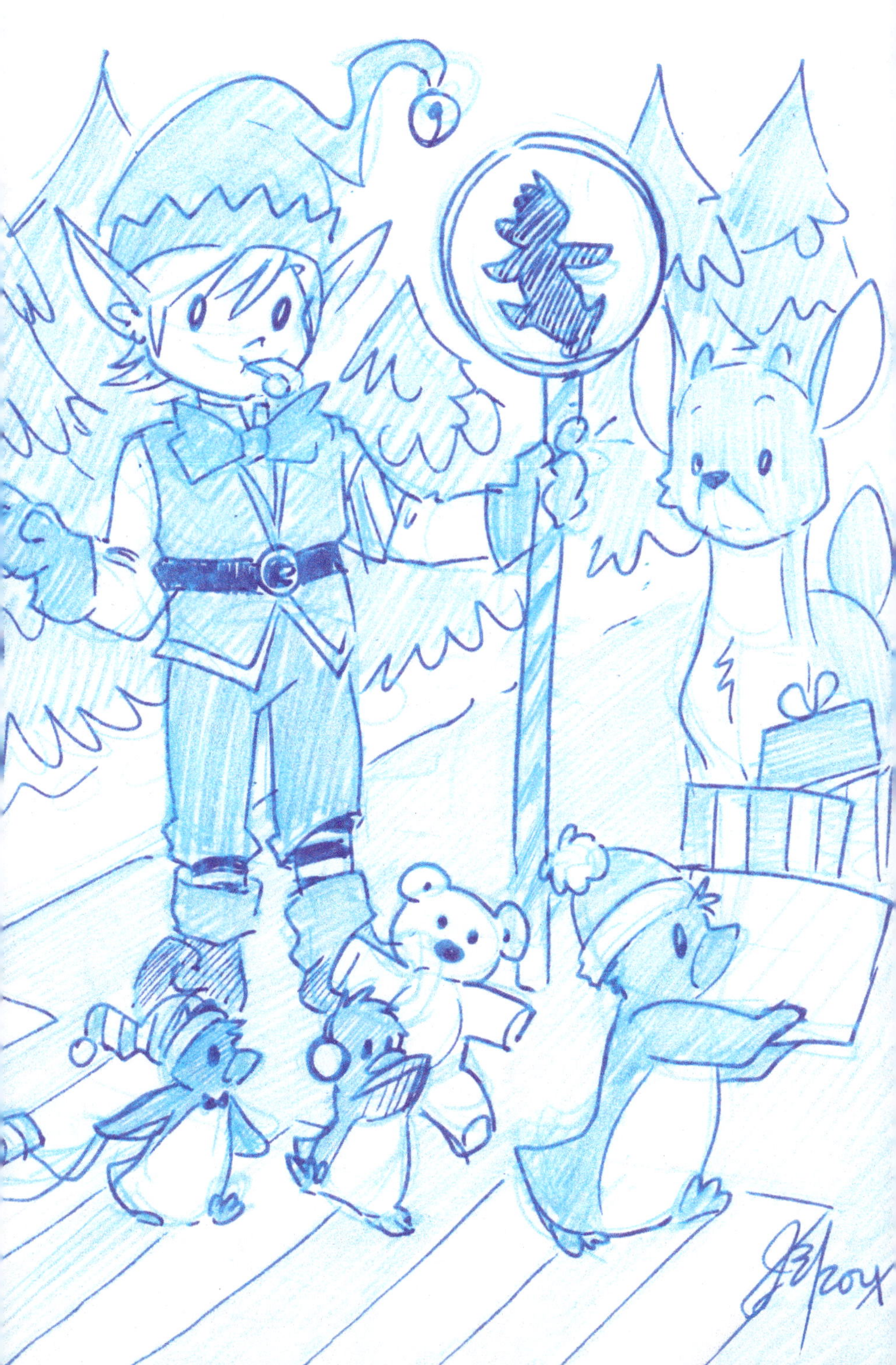

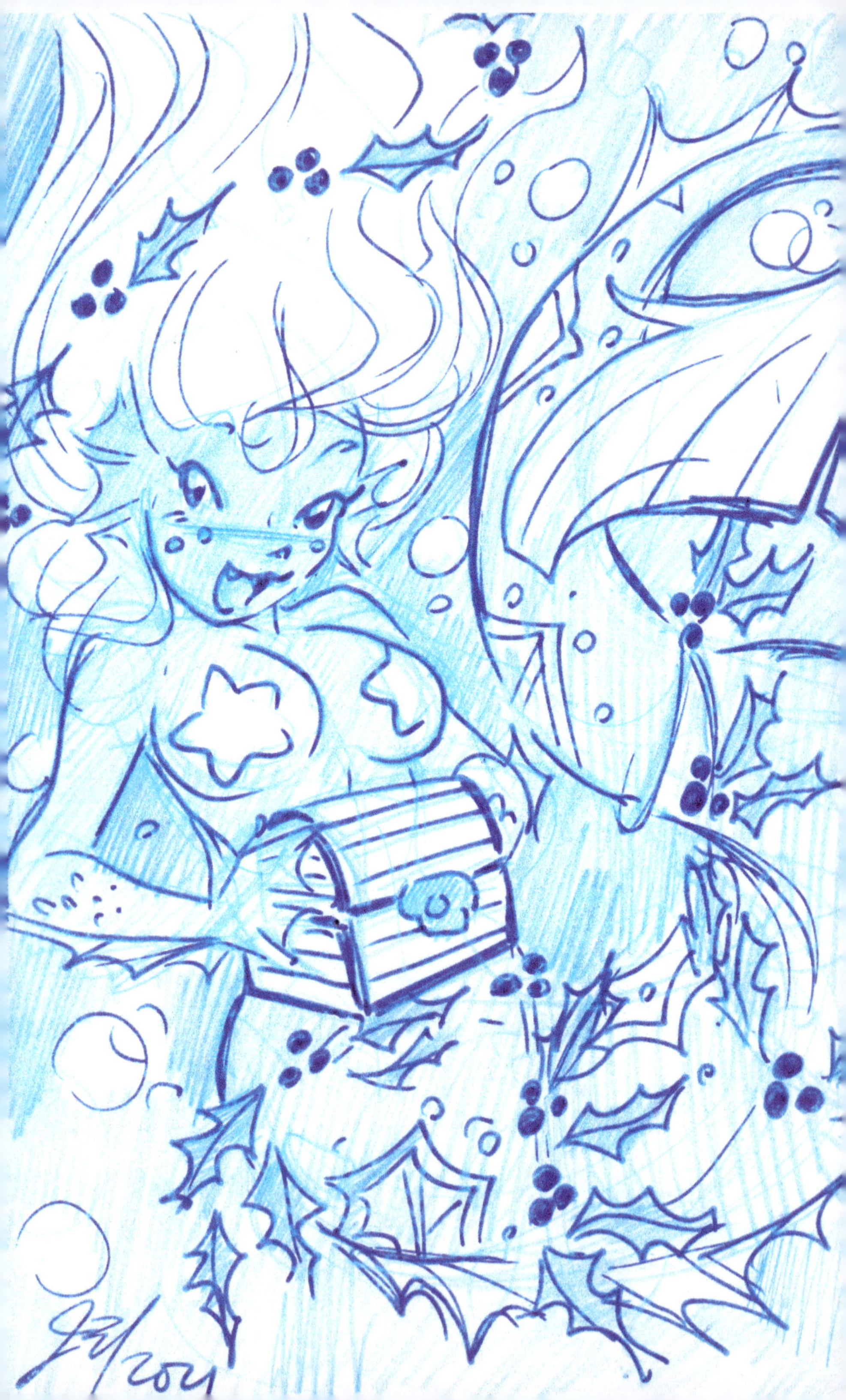

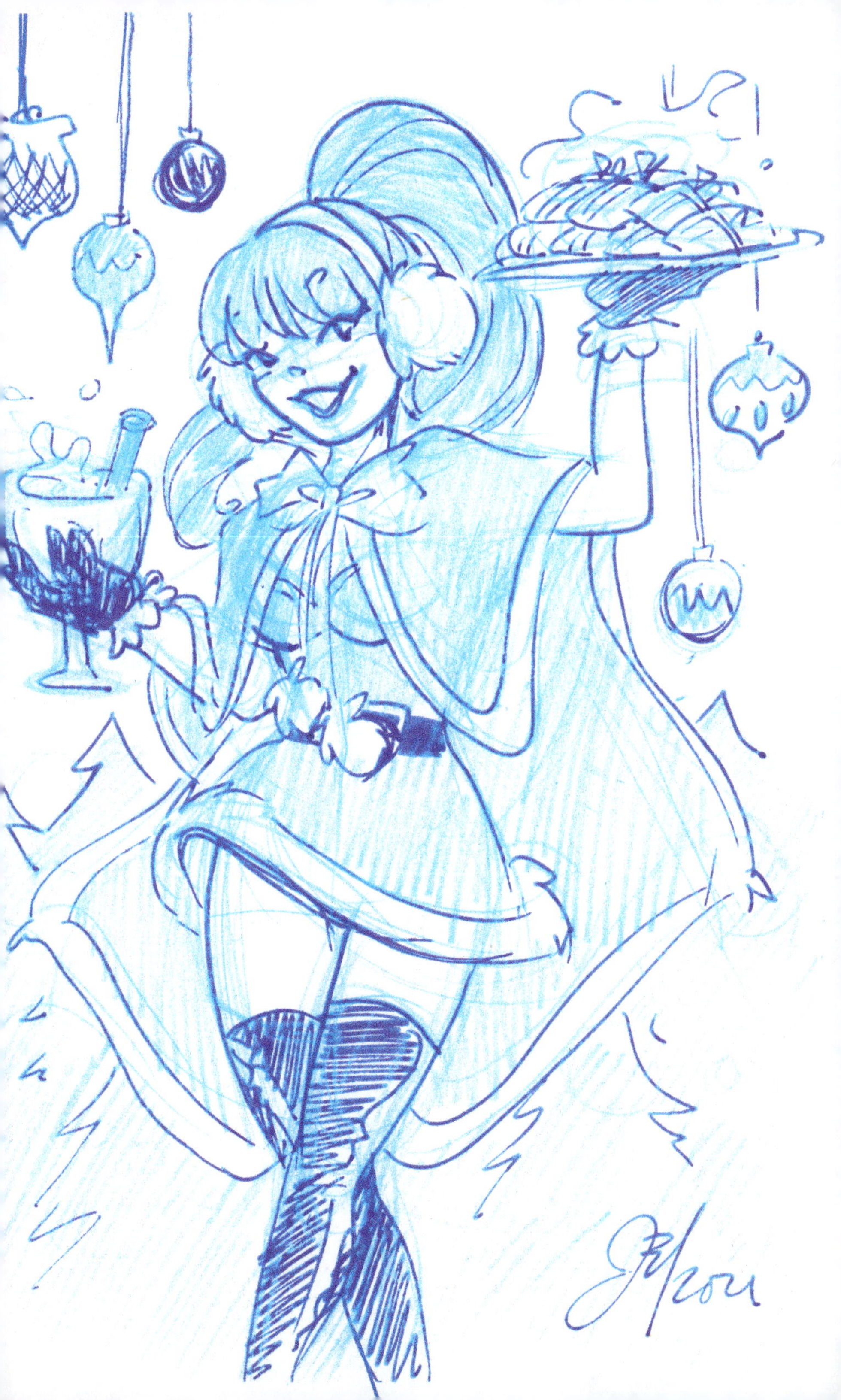

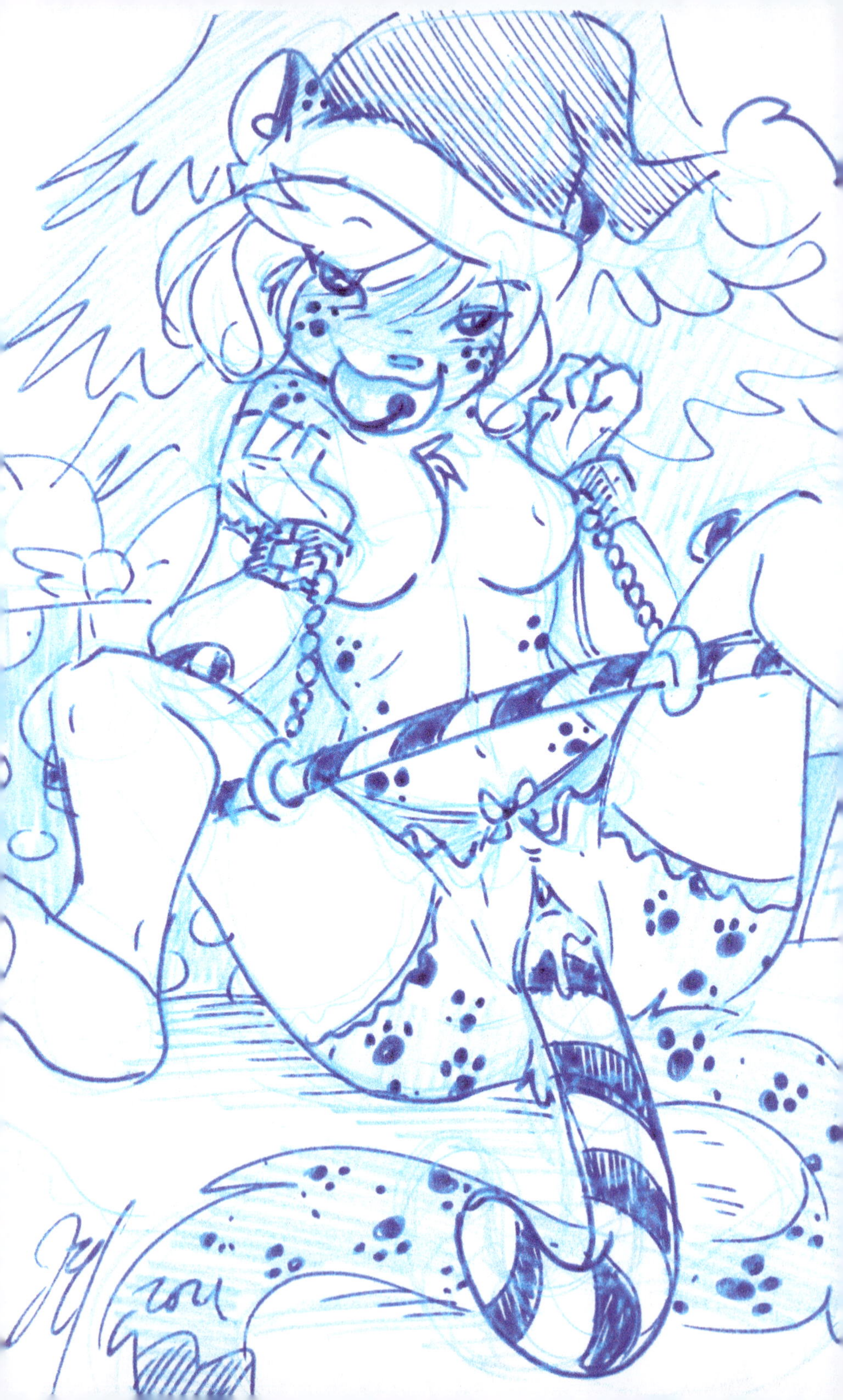

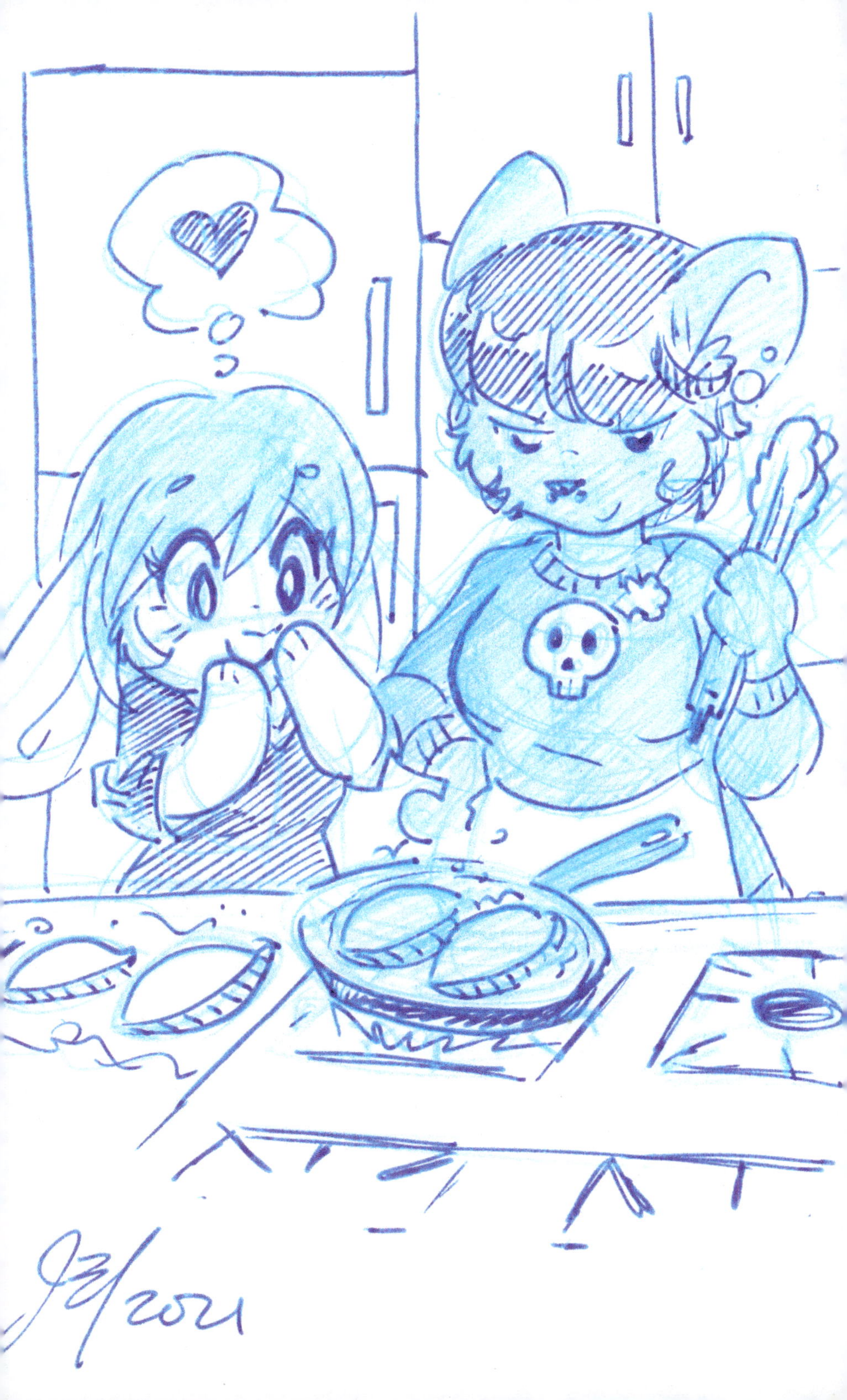

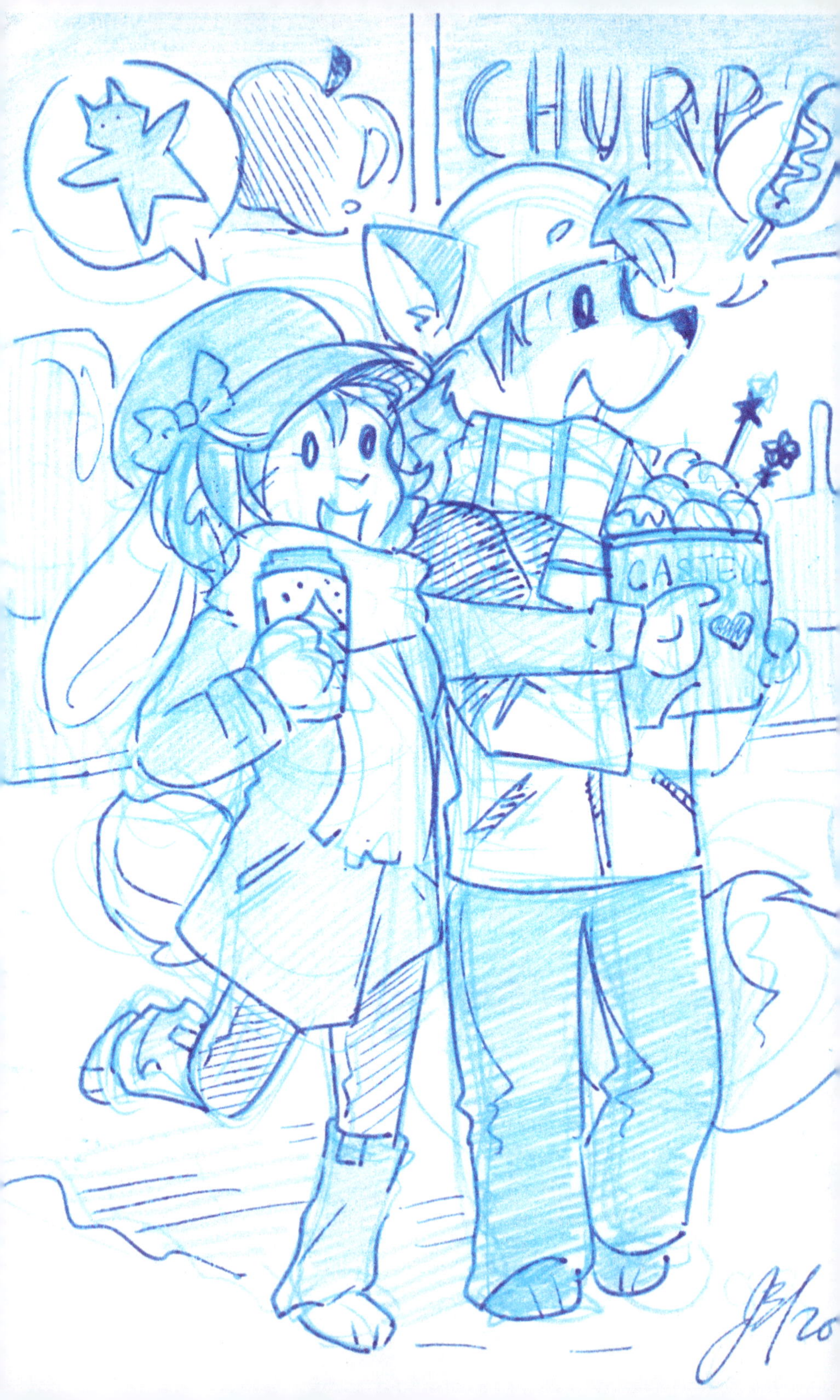
CHURR
CASTELL

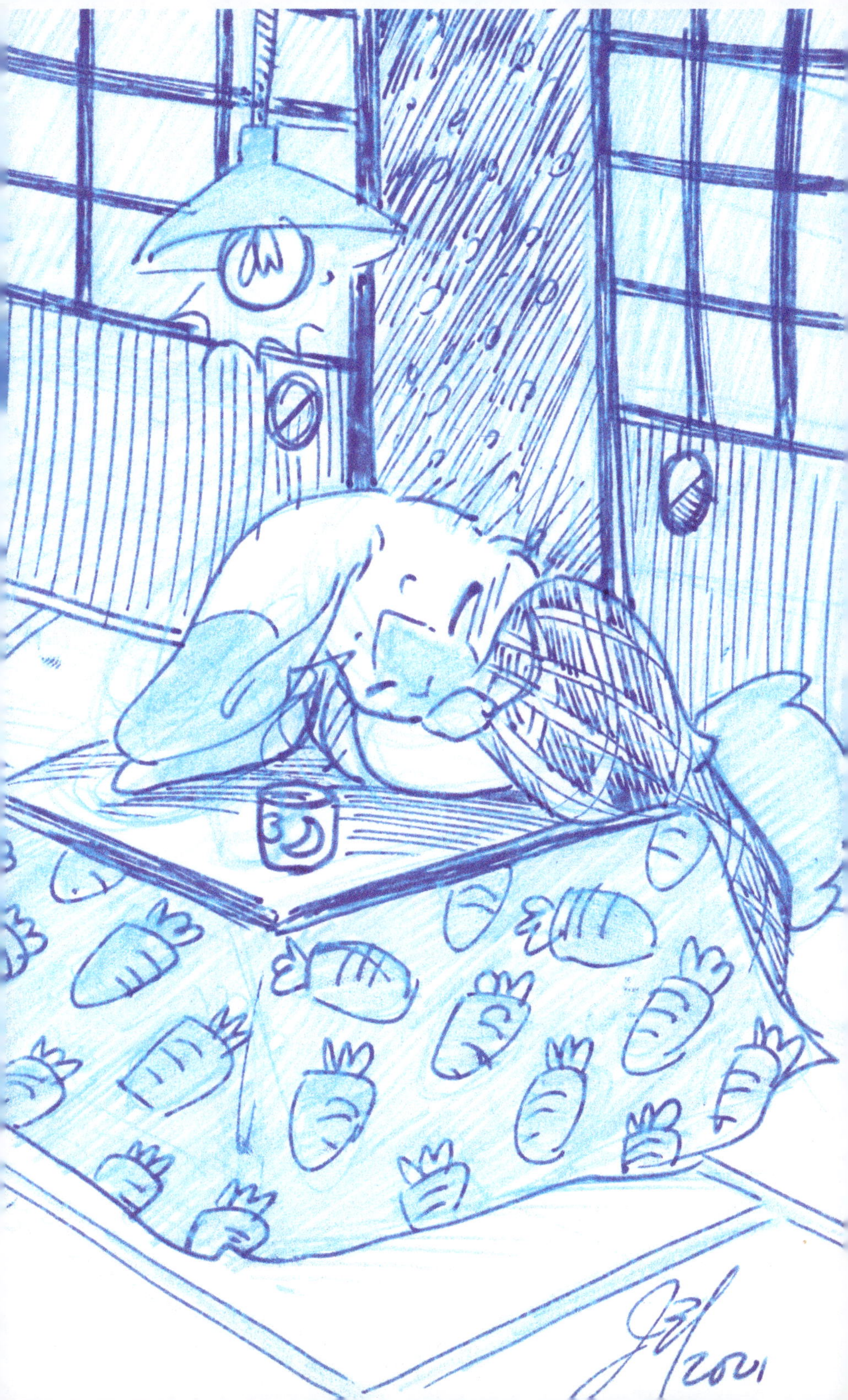

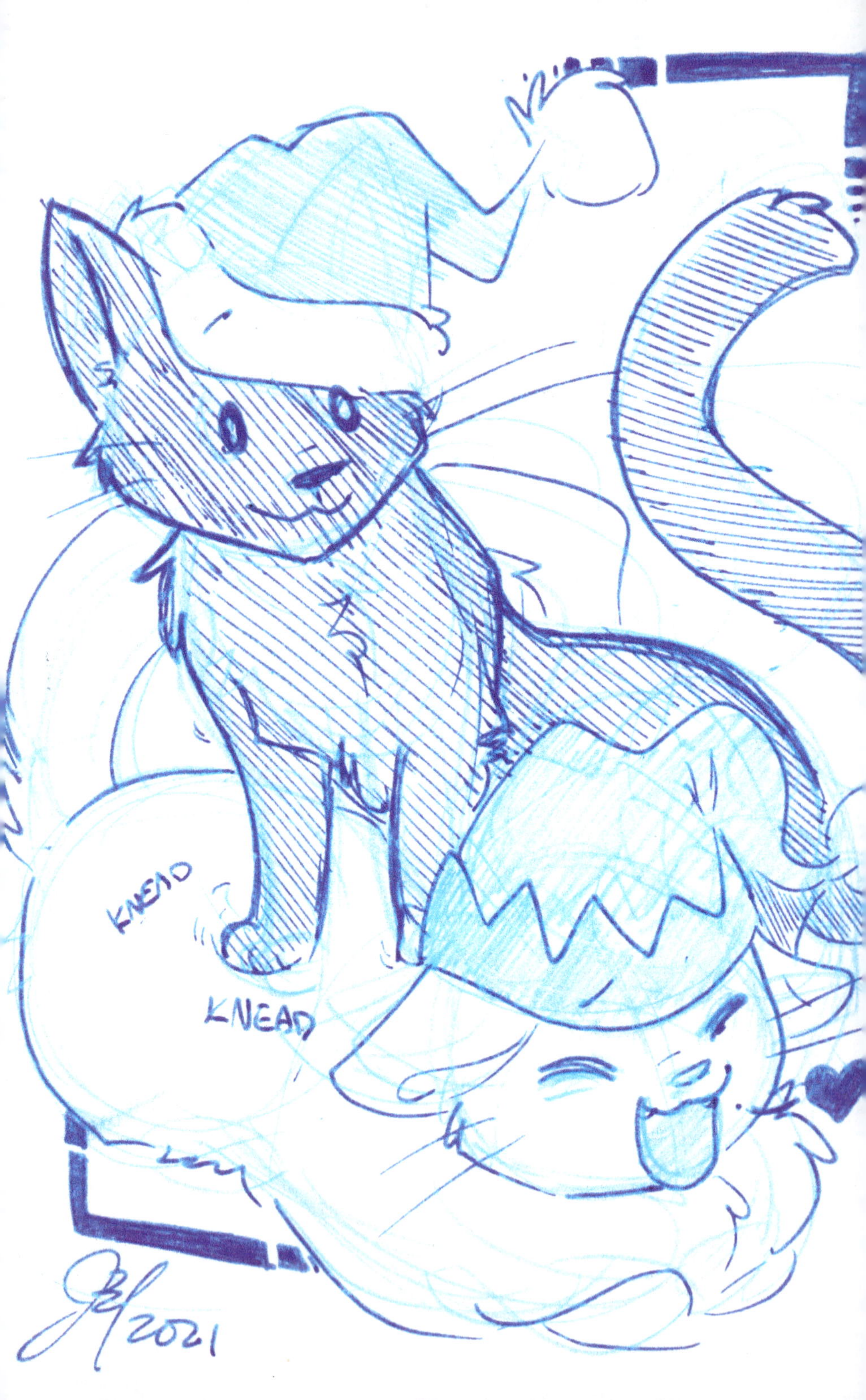

KNEAD
KNEAD
2021

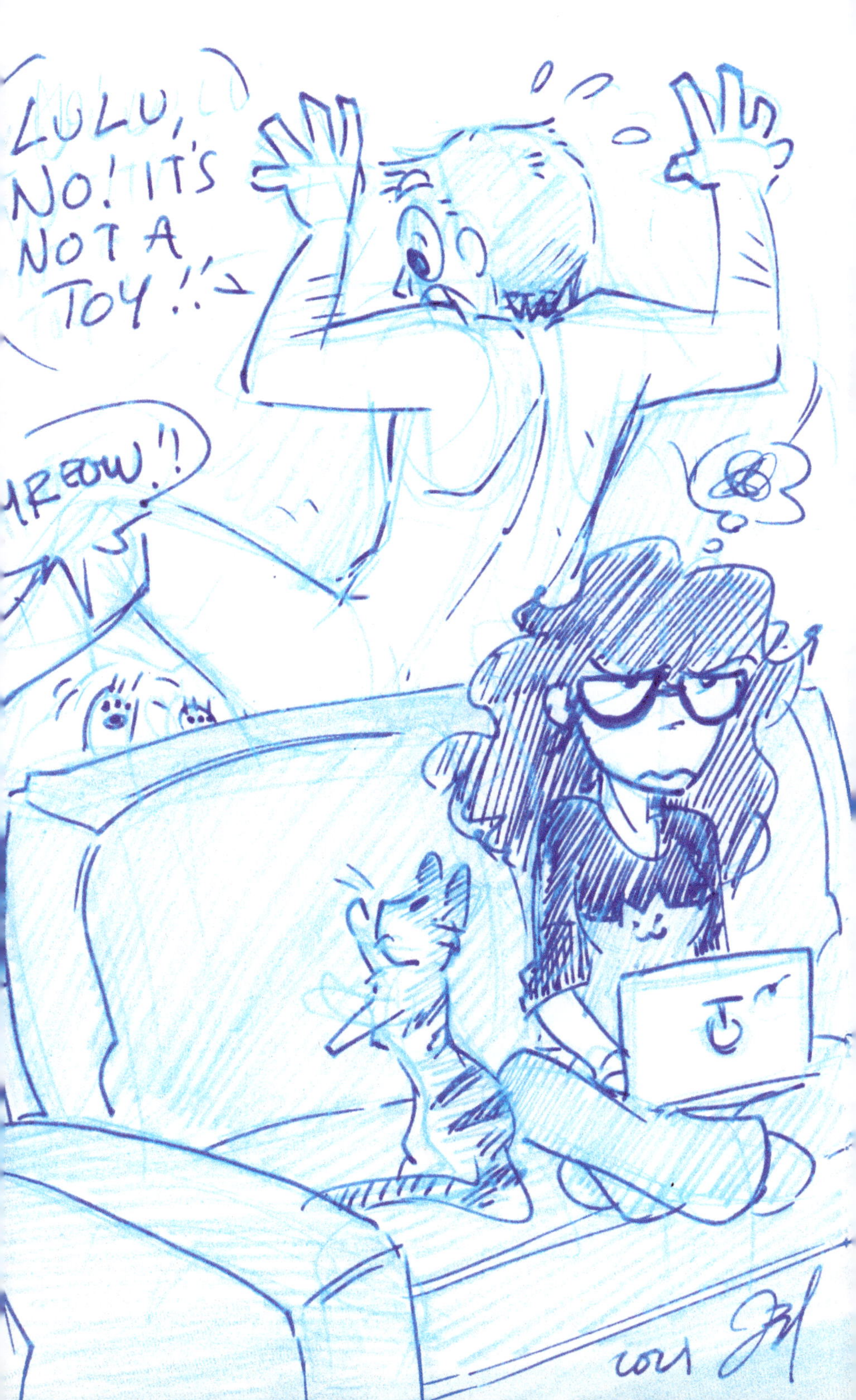

LULU, NO! IT'S NOT A TOY!!
MREOW!!

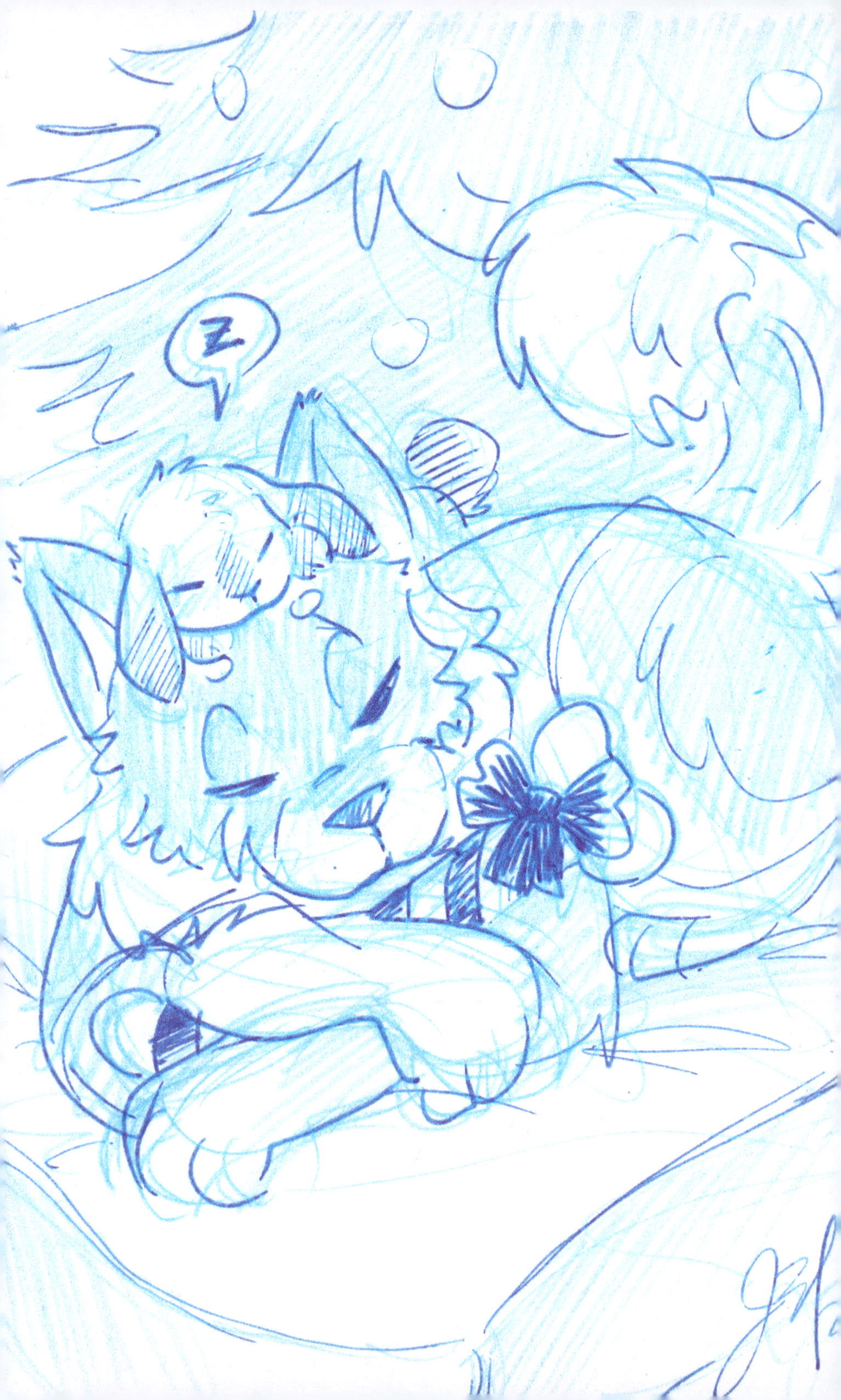

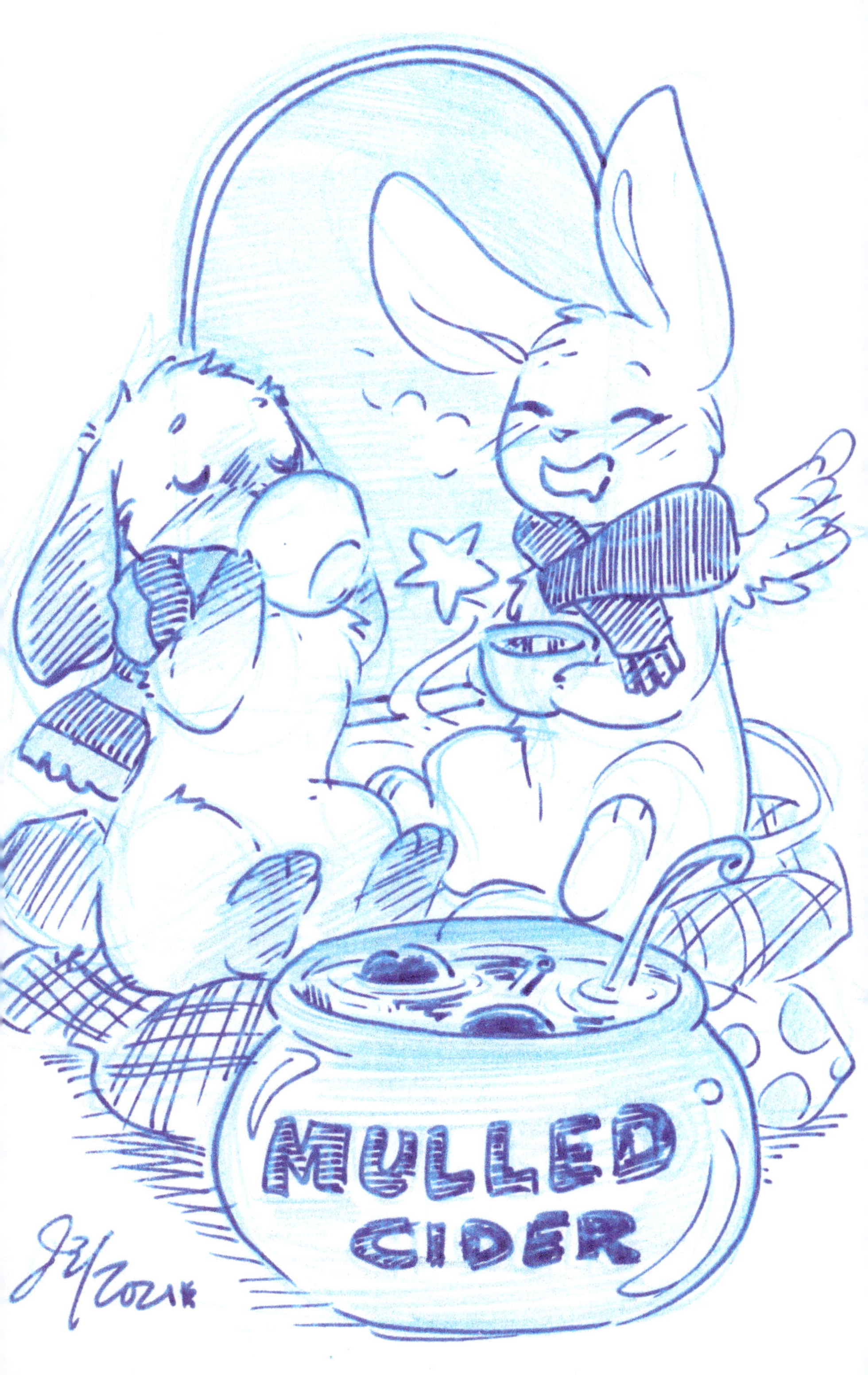

MULLED
CIDER

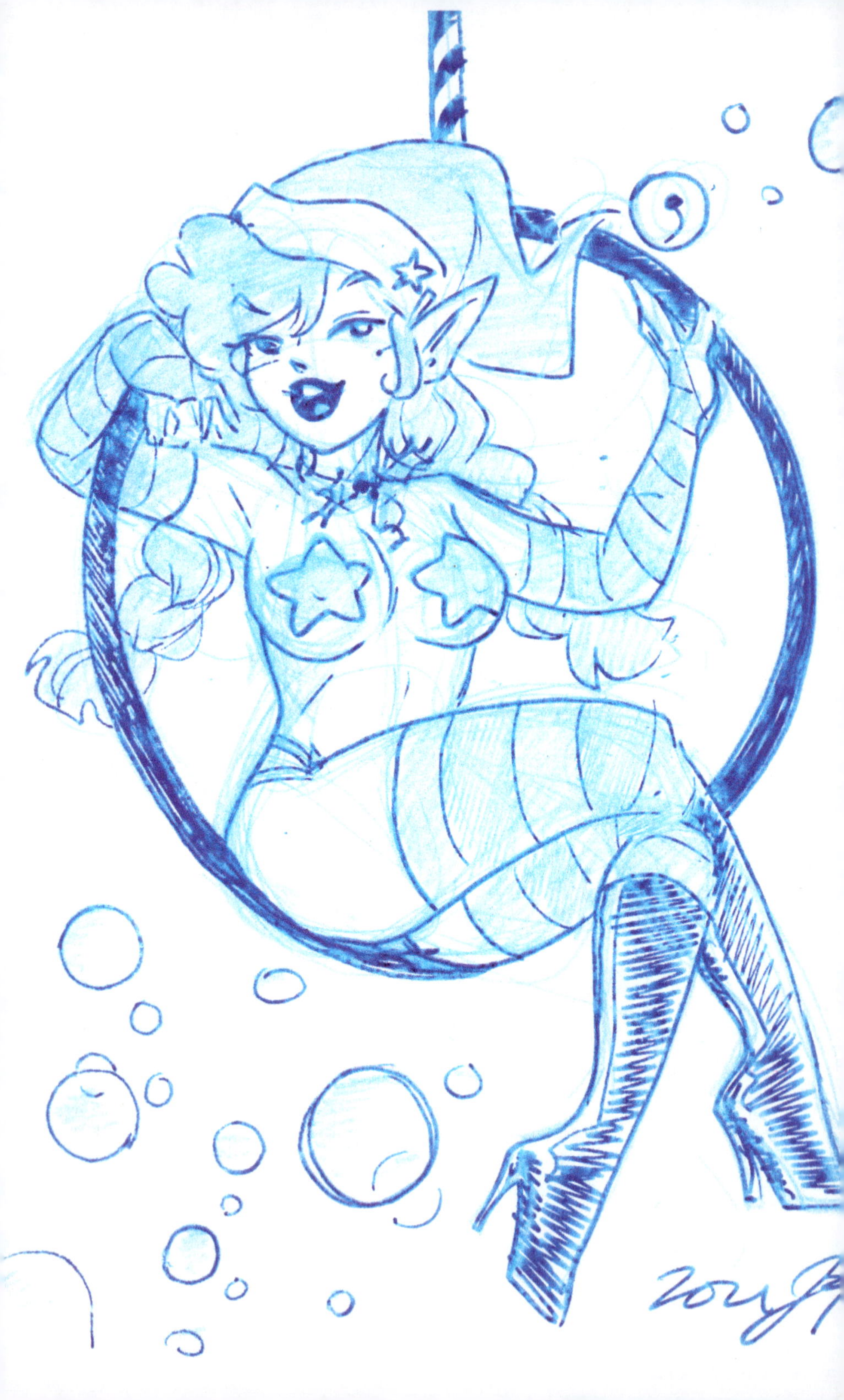

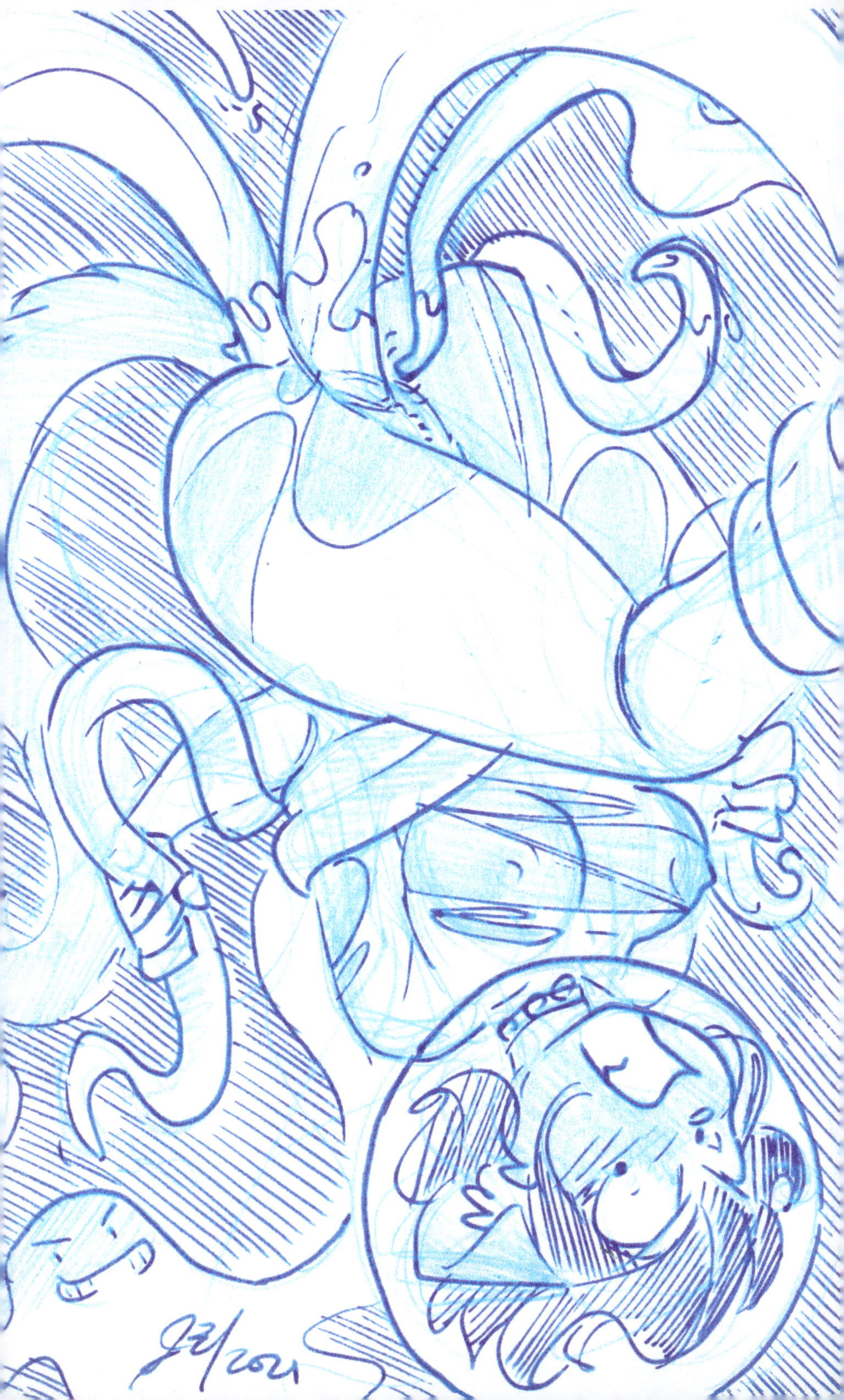

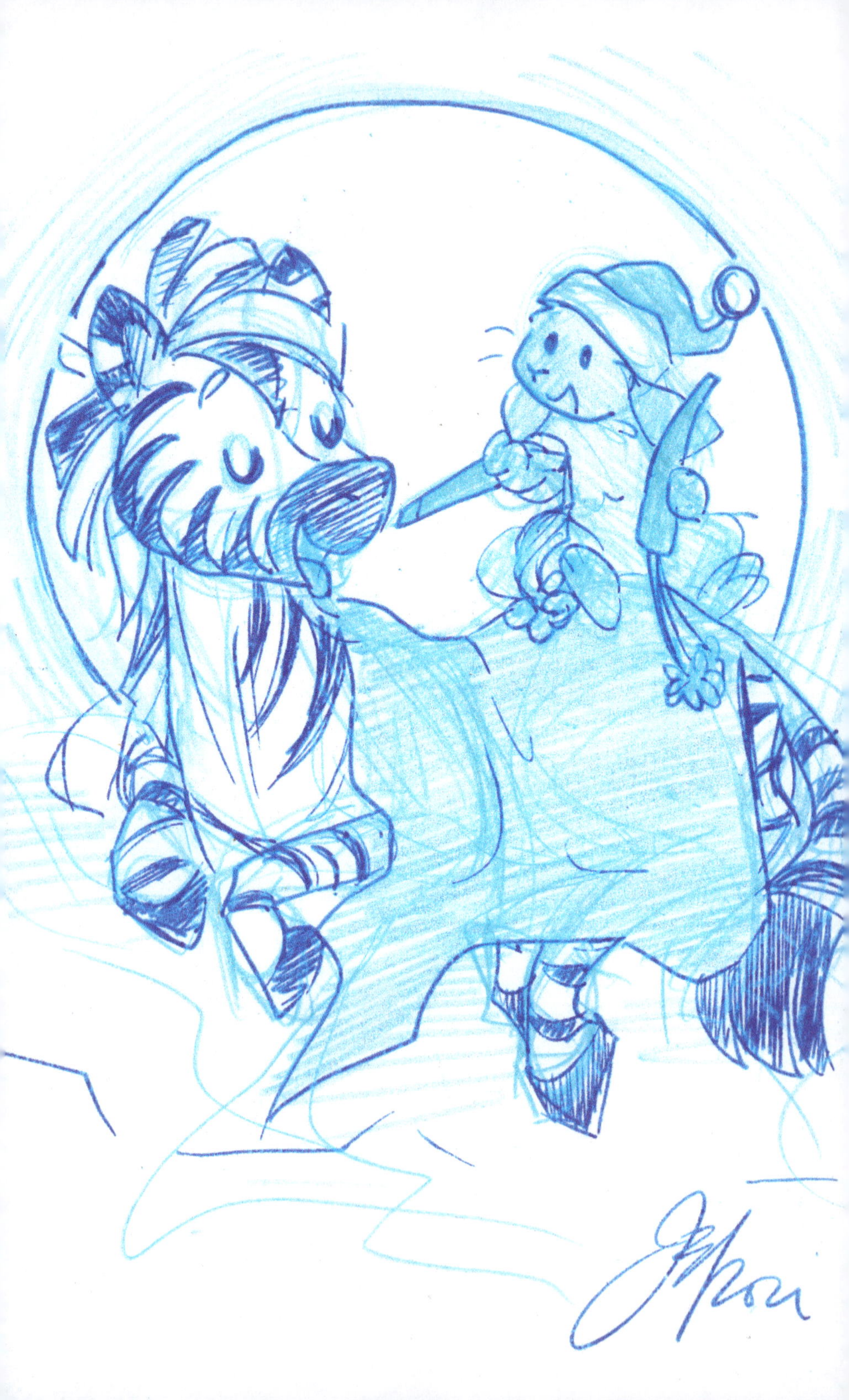

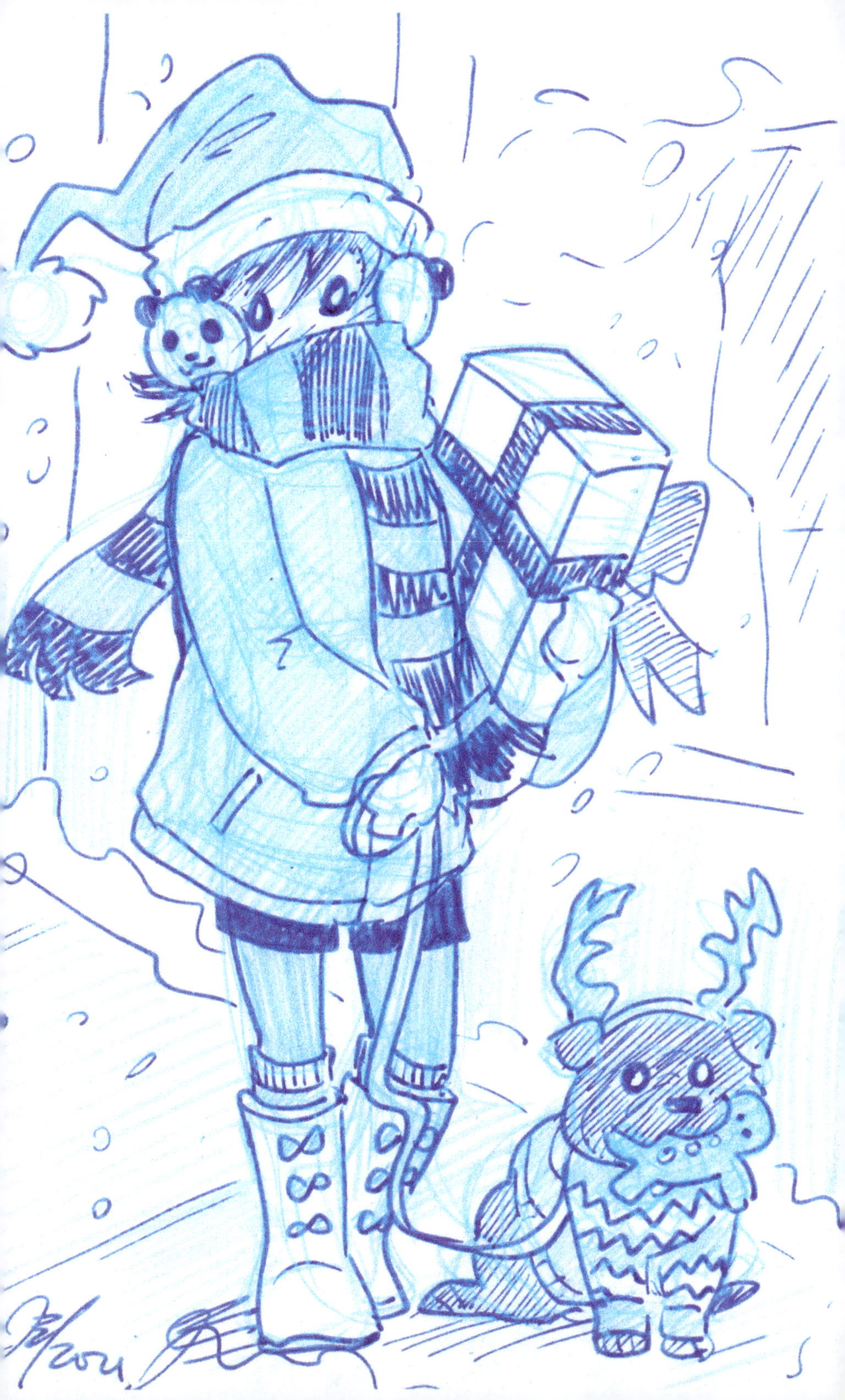

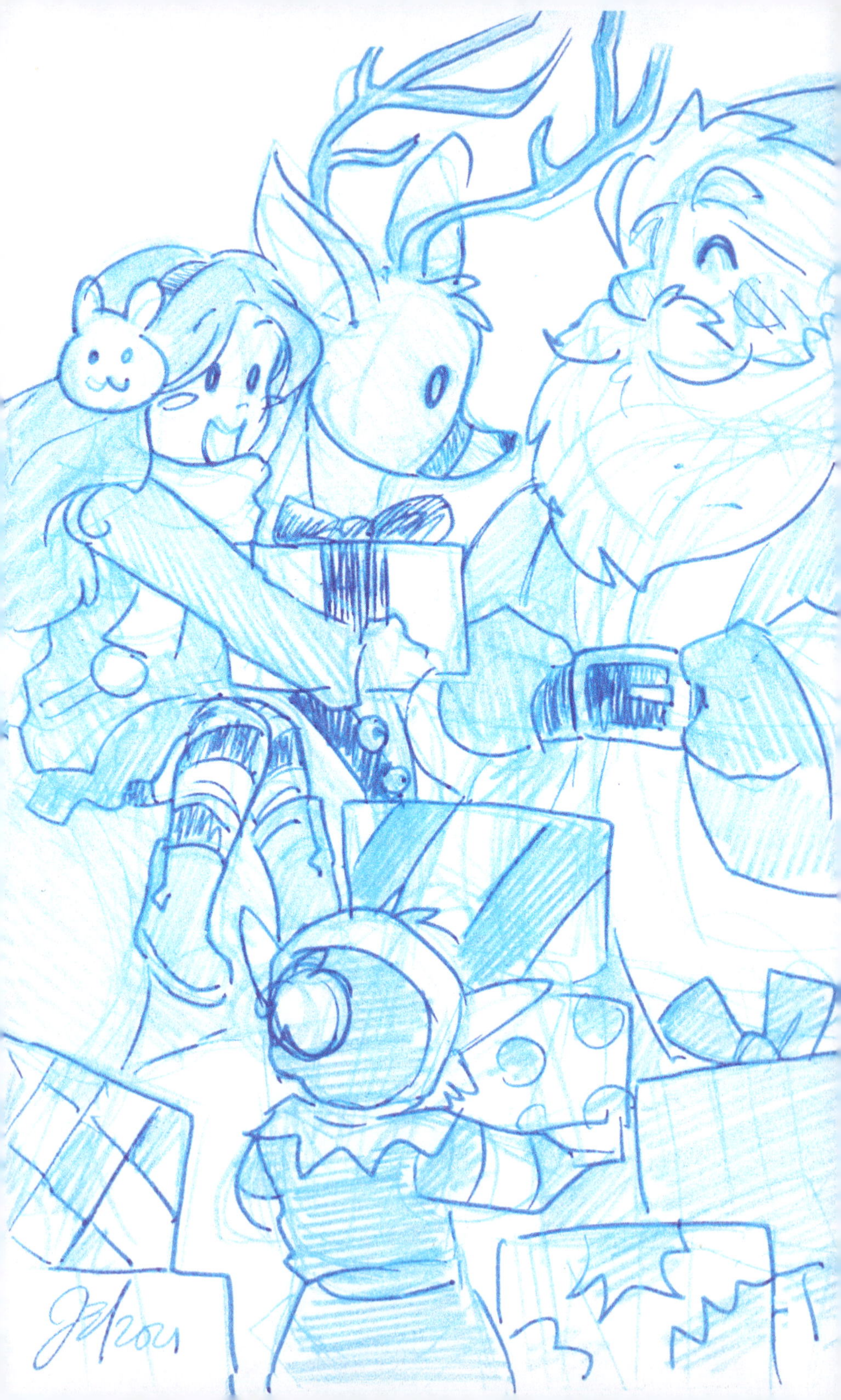

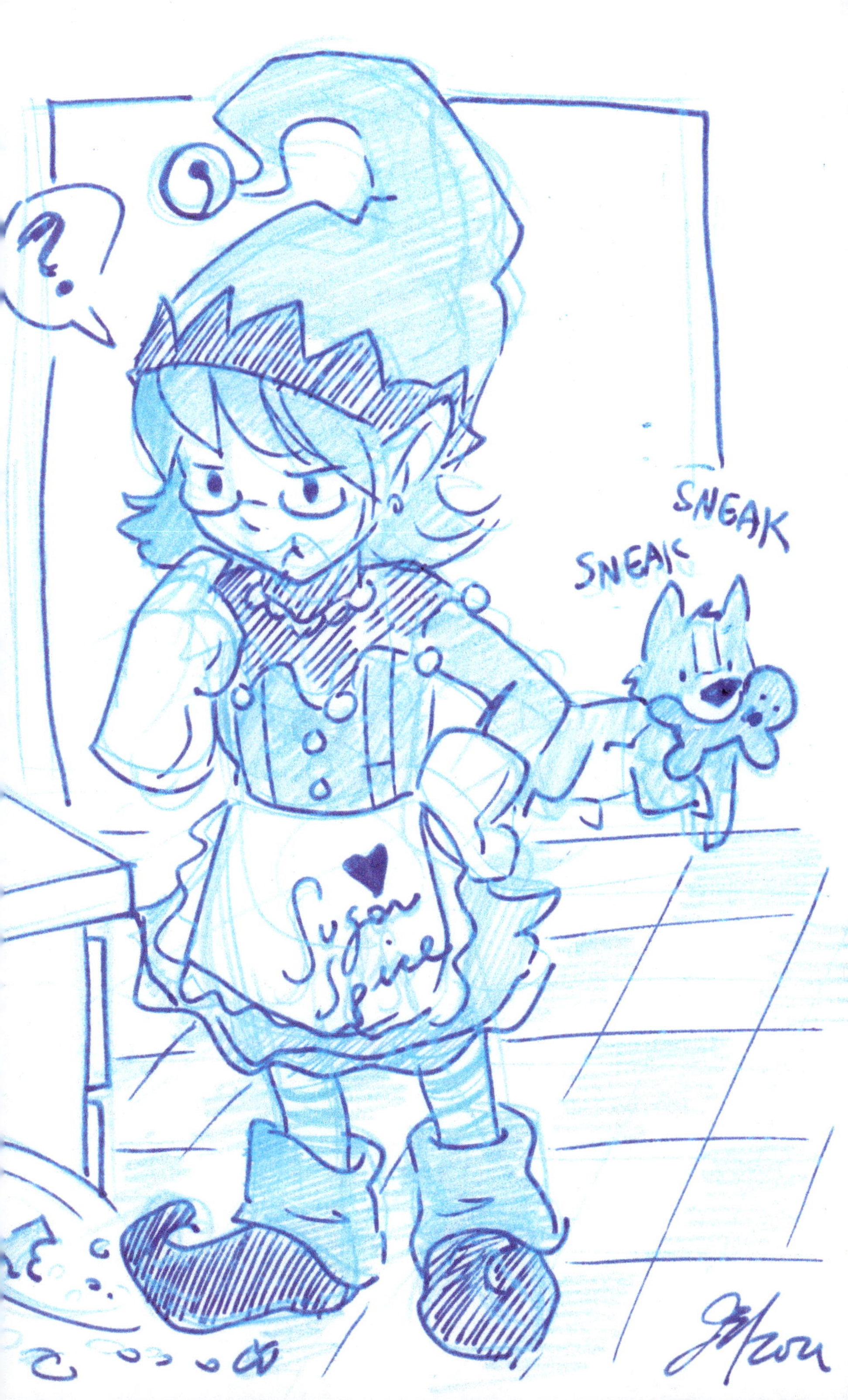

?
SNEAK
SNEAK
Sugar Spice

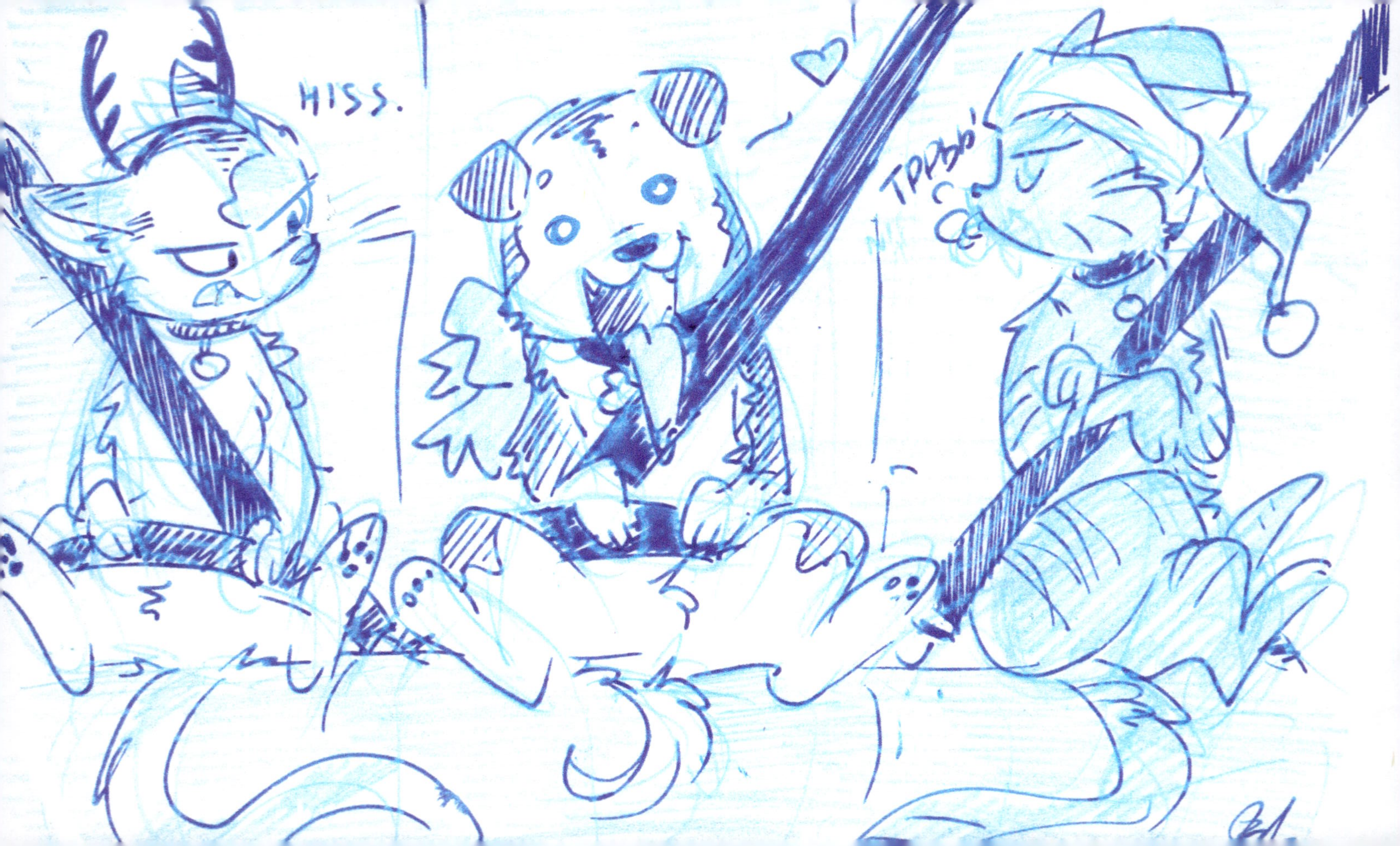
HISS.
TPPbb'

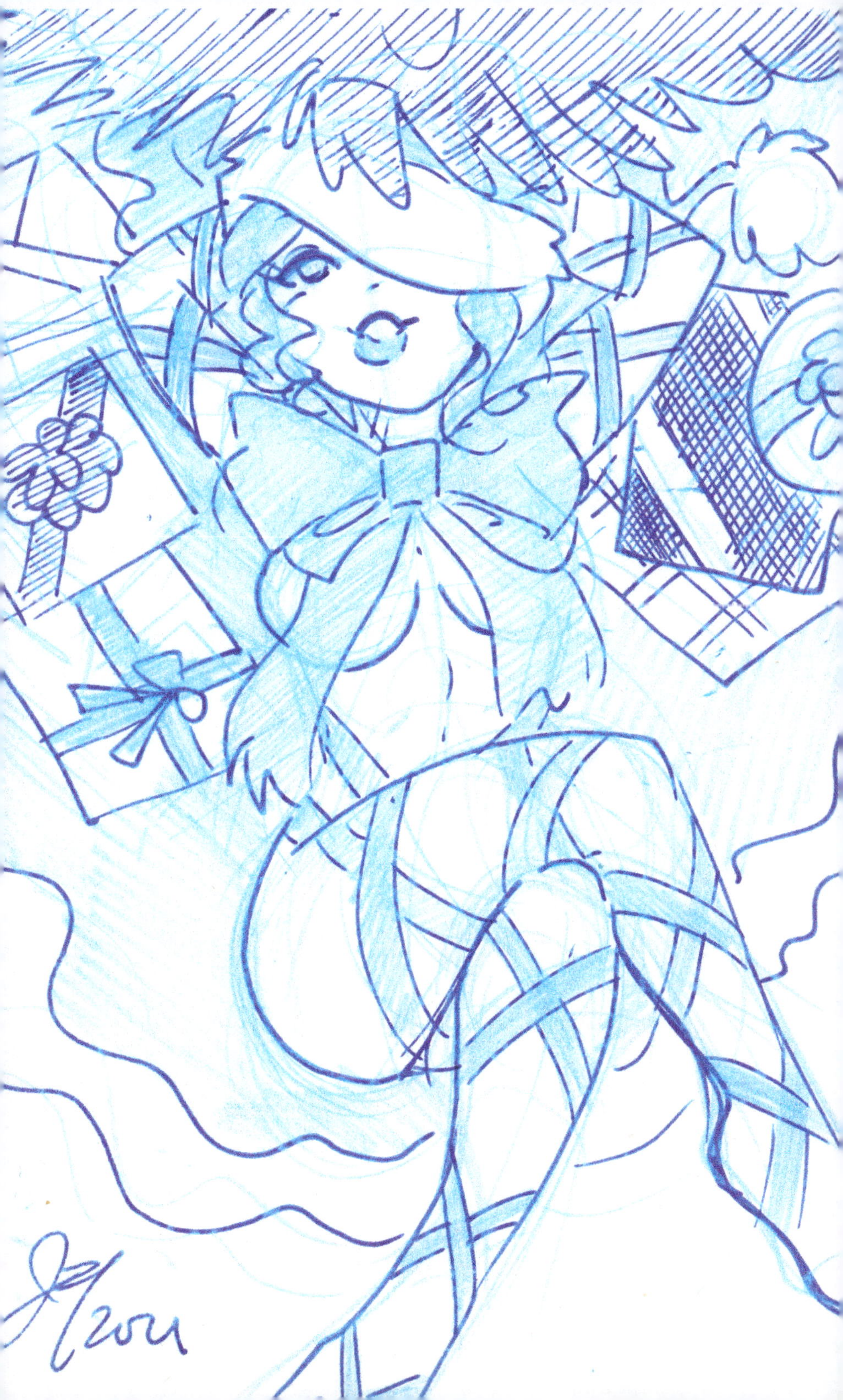

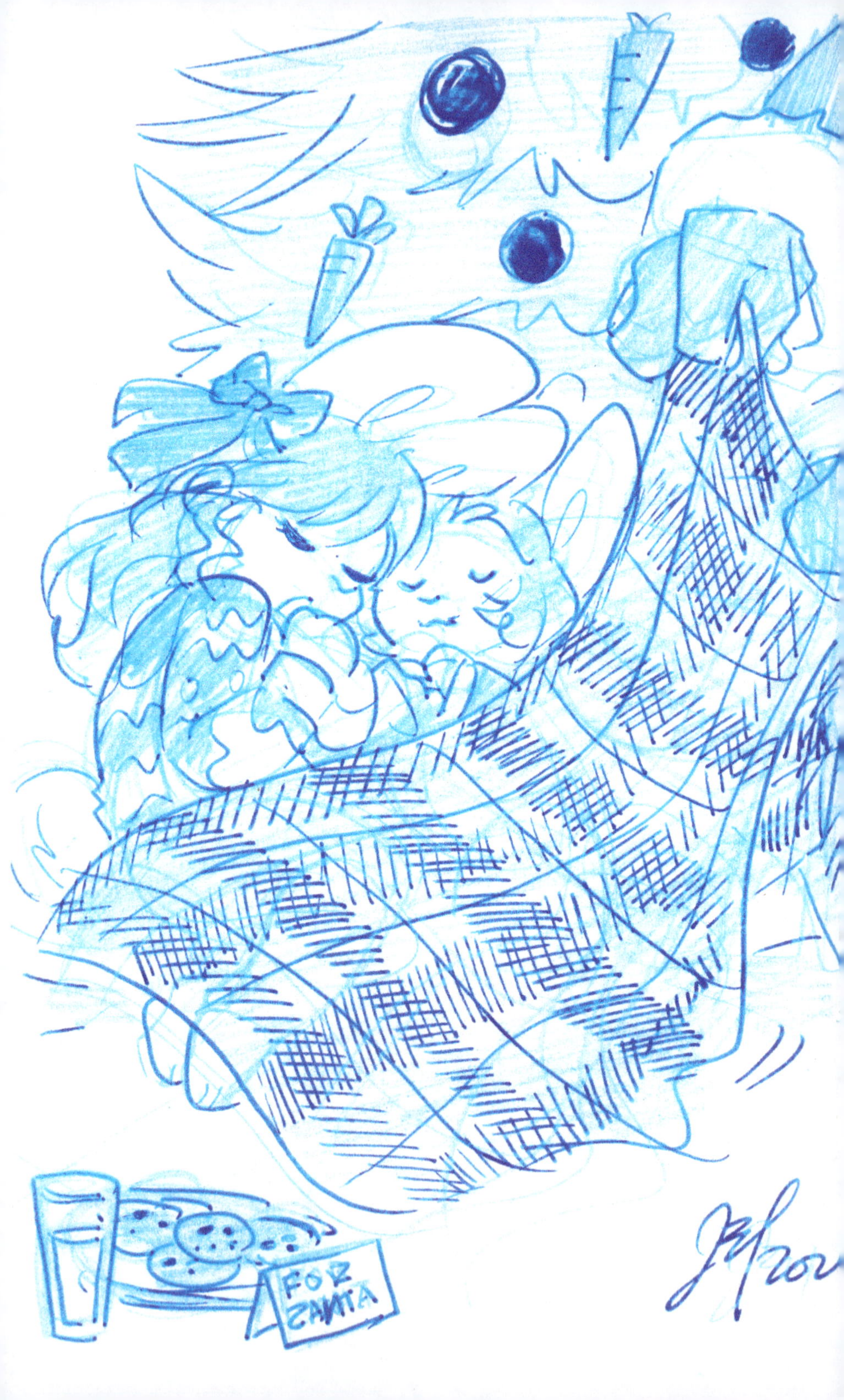

FOR
SANTA

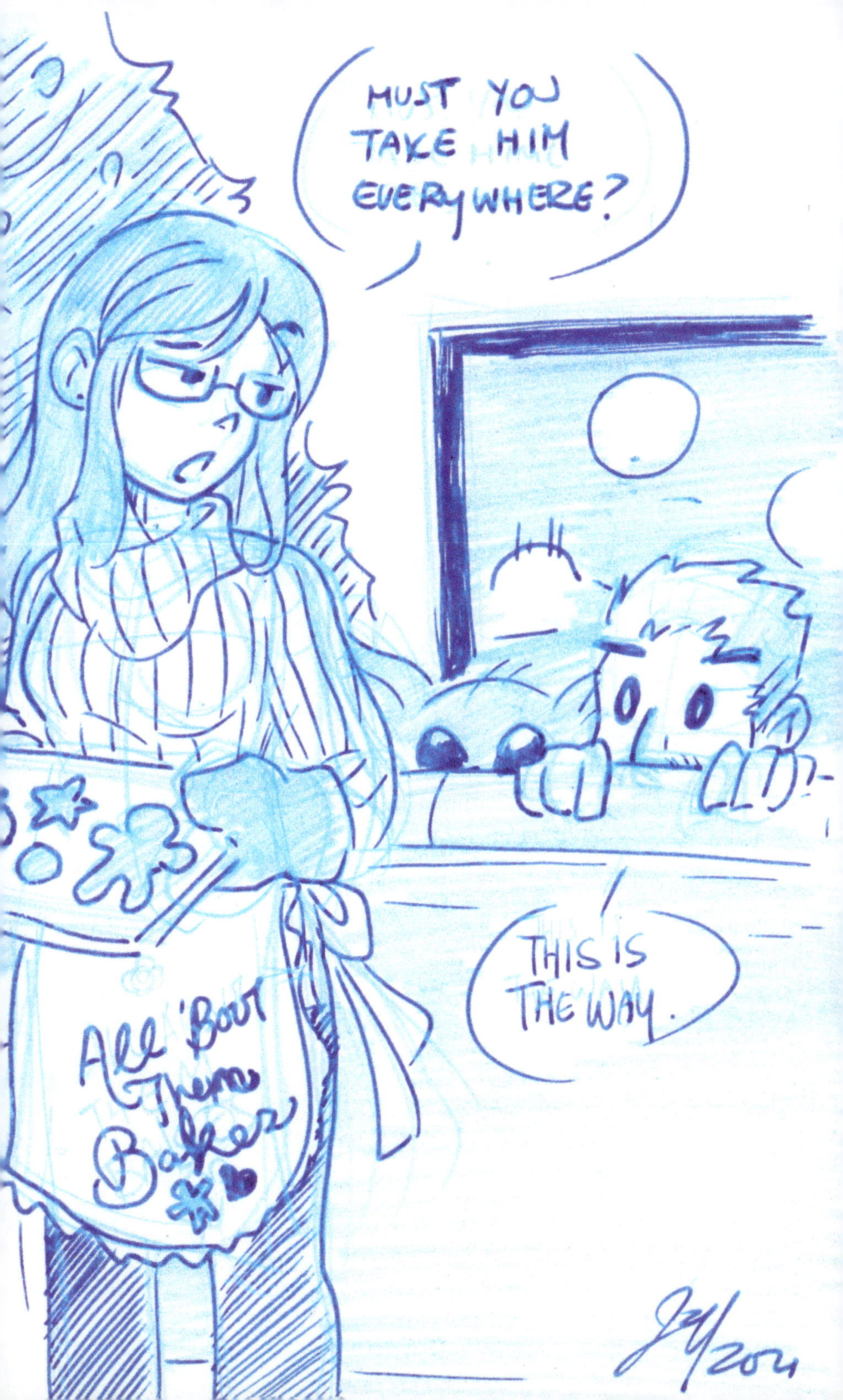

MUST YOU TAKE HIM EVERYWHERE?
THIS IS THE WAY.
ALL 'BOUT THEM BAKES

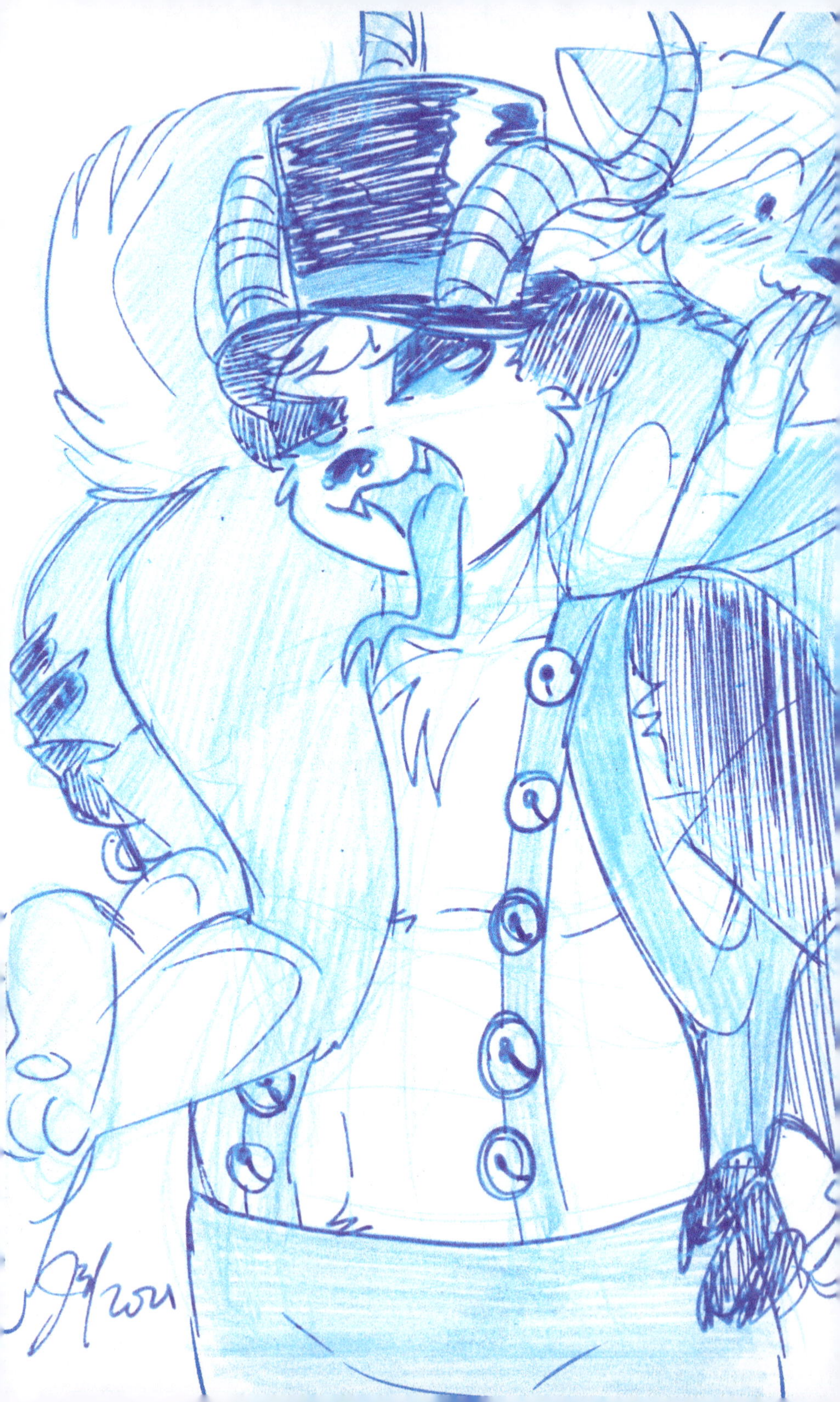

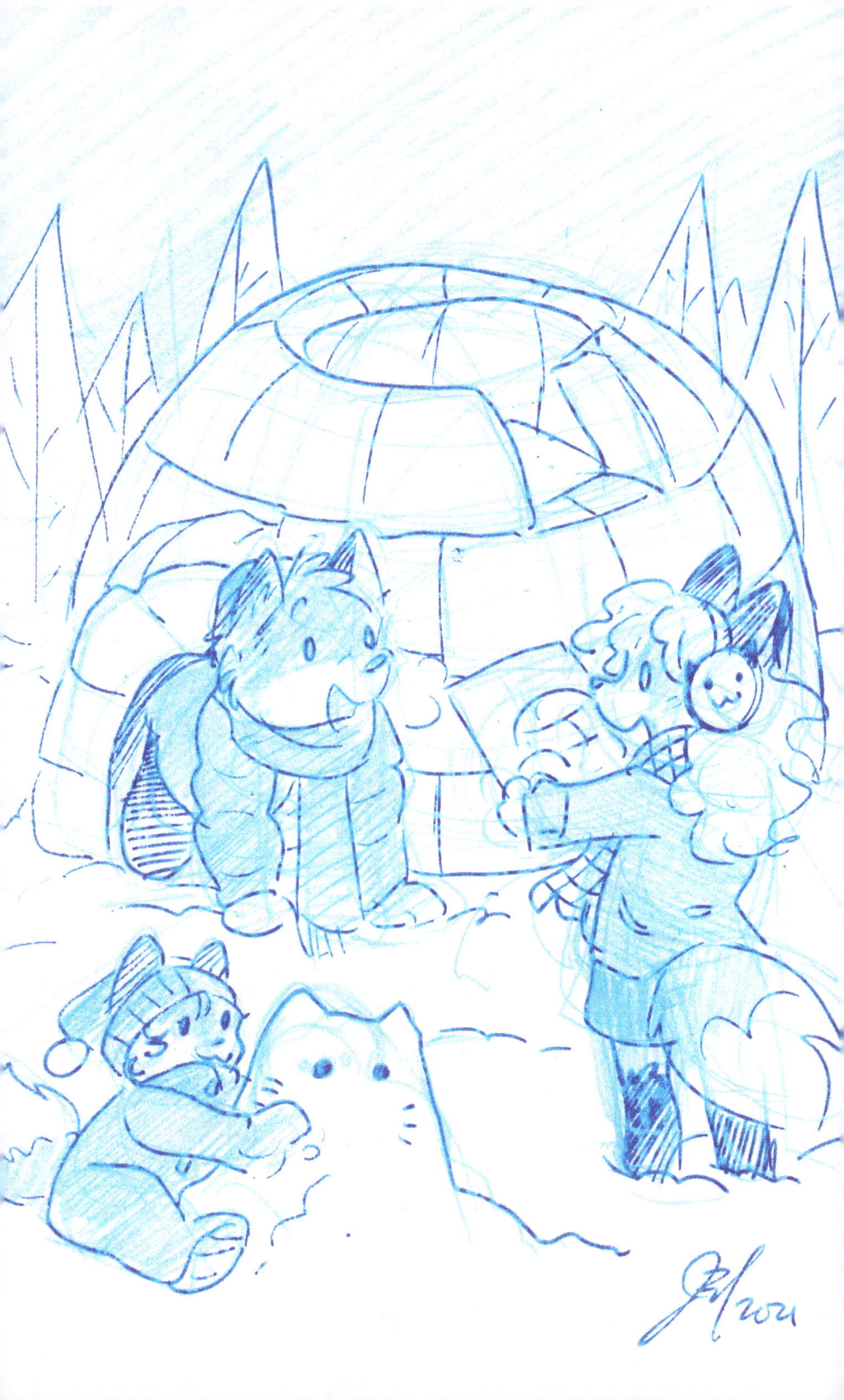

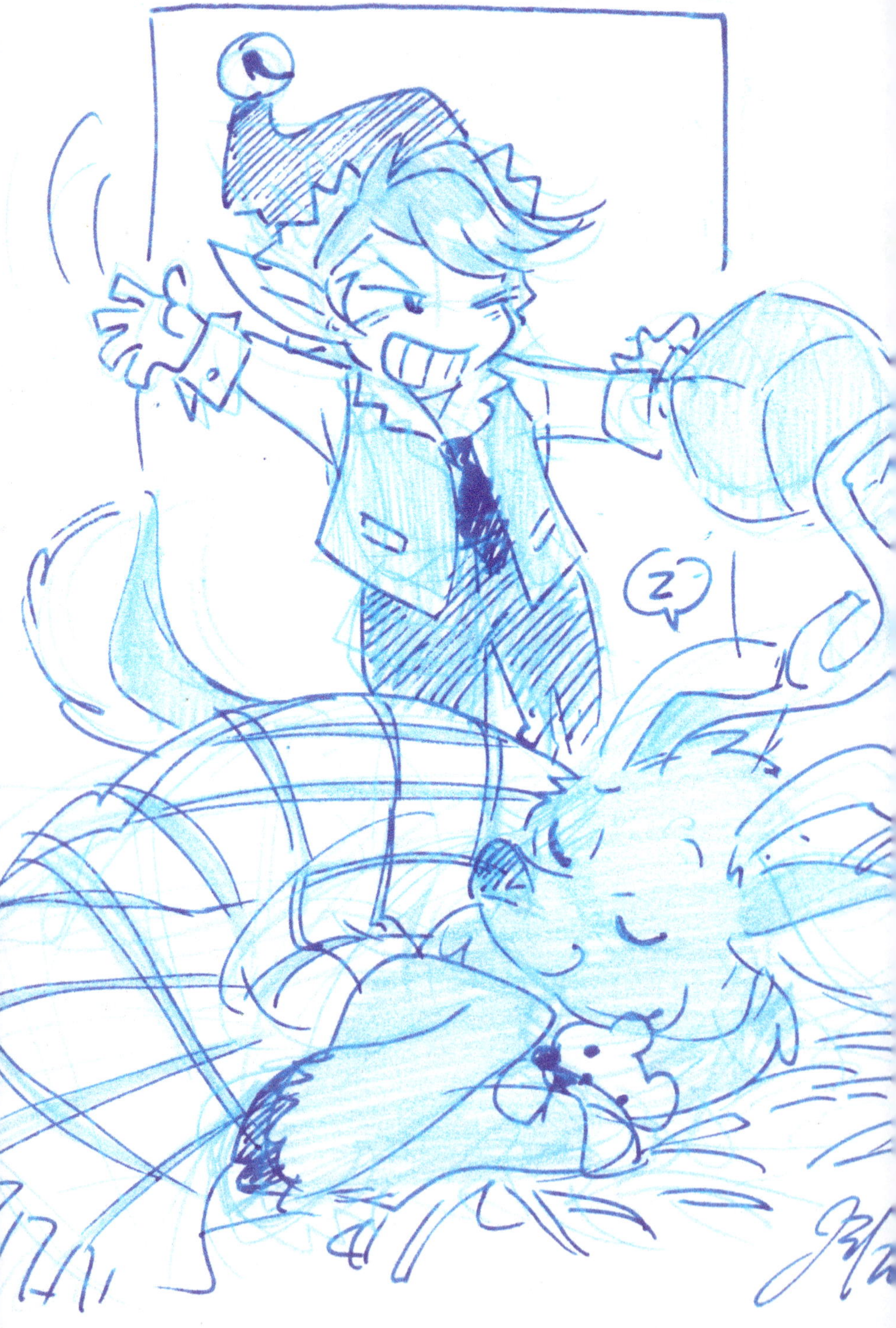
z

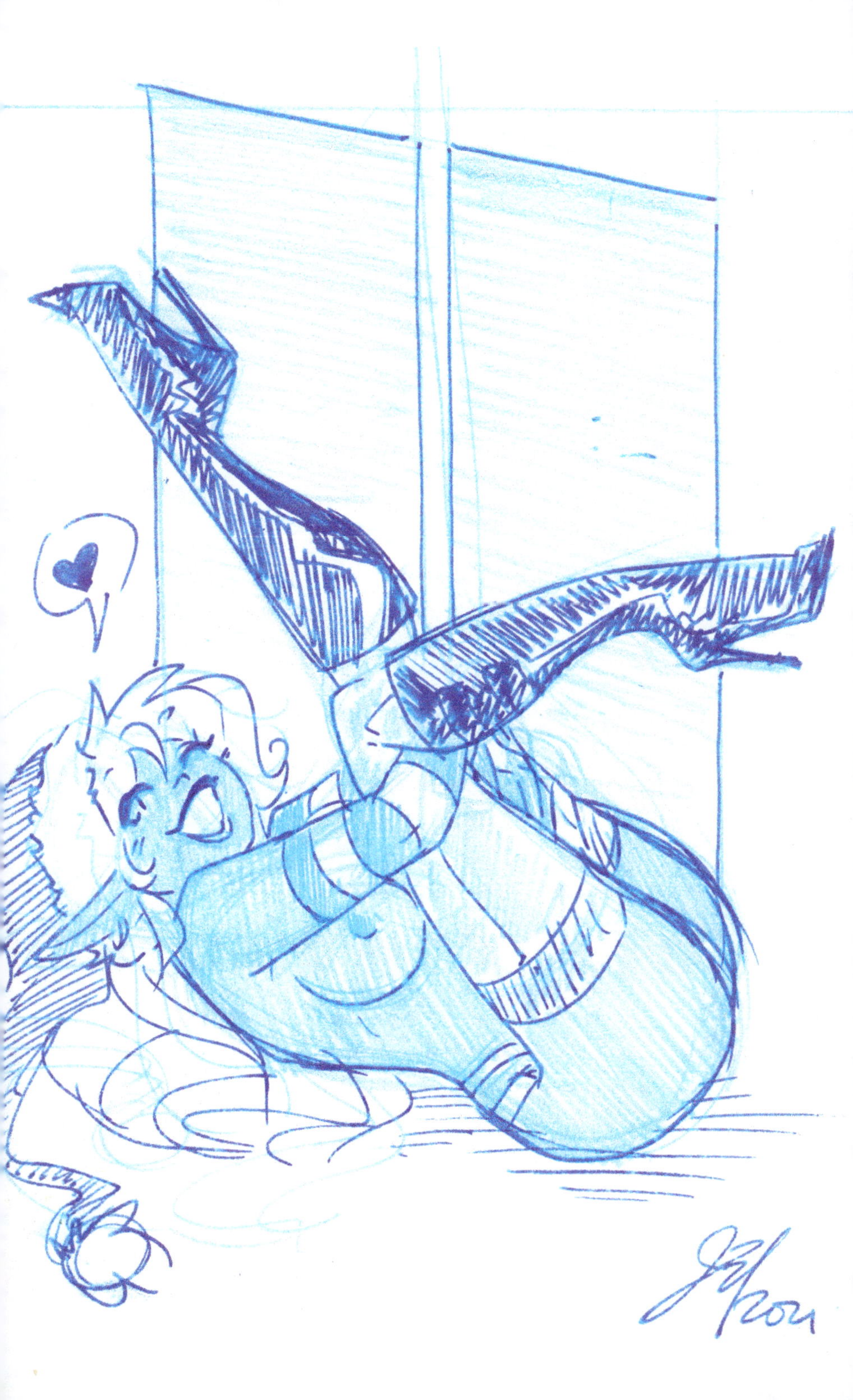

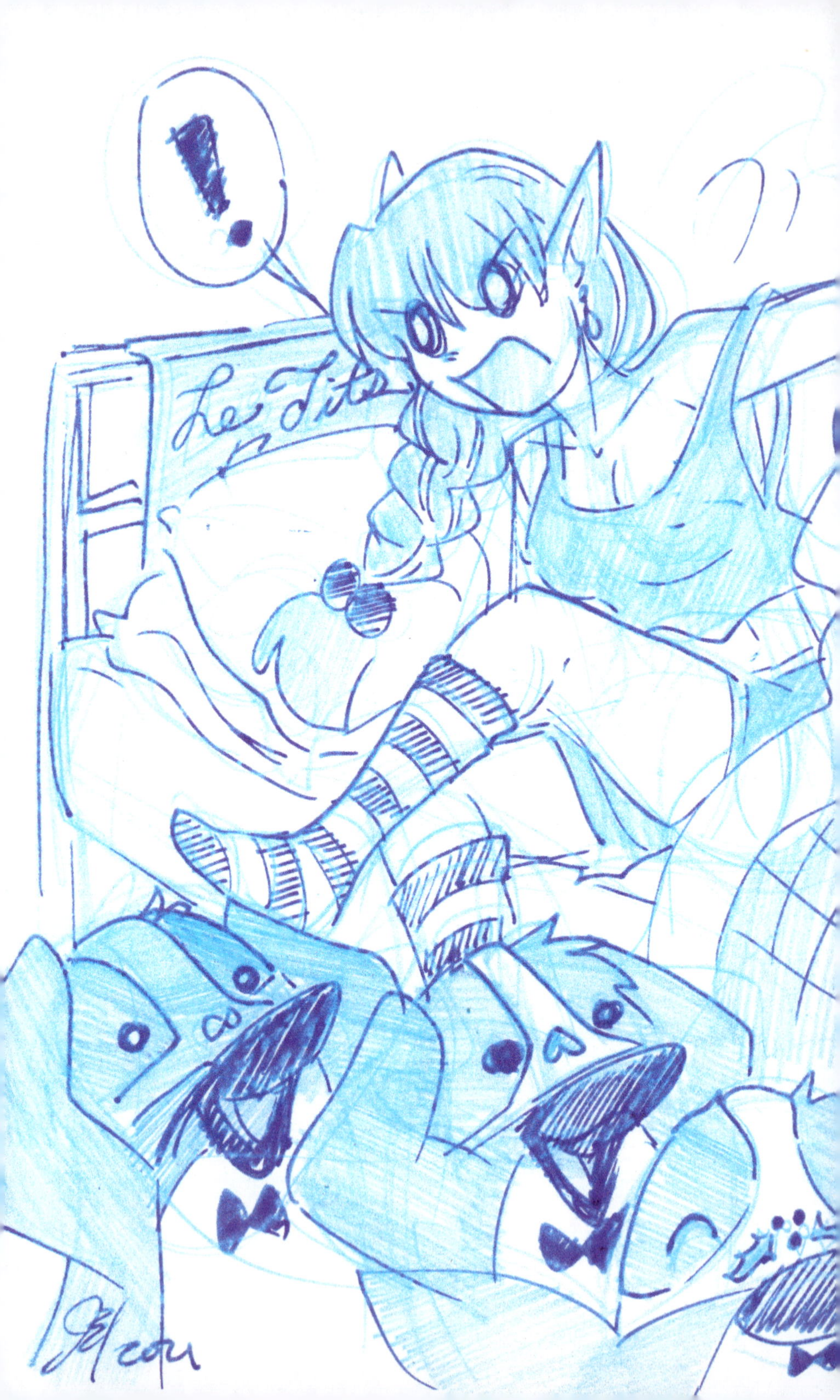
Le Tite

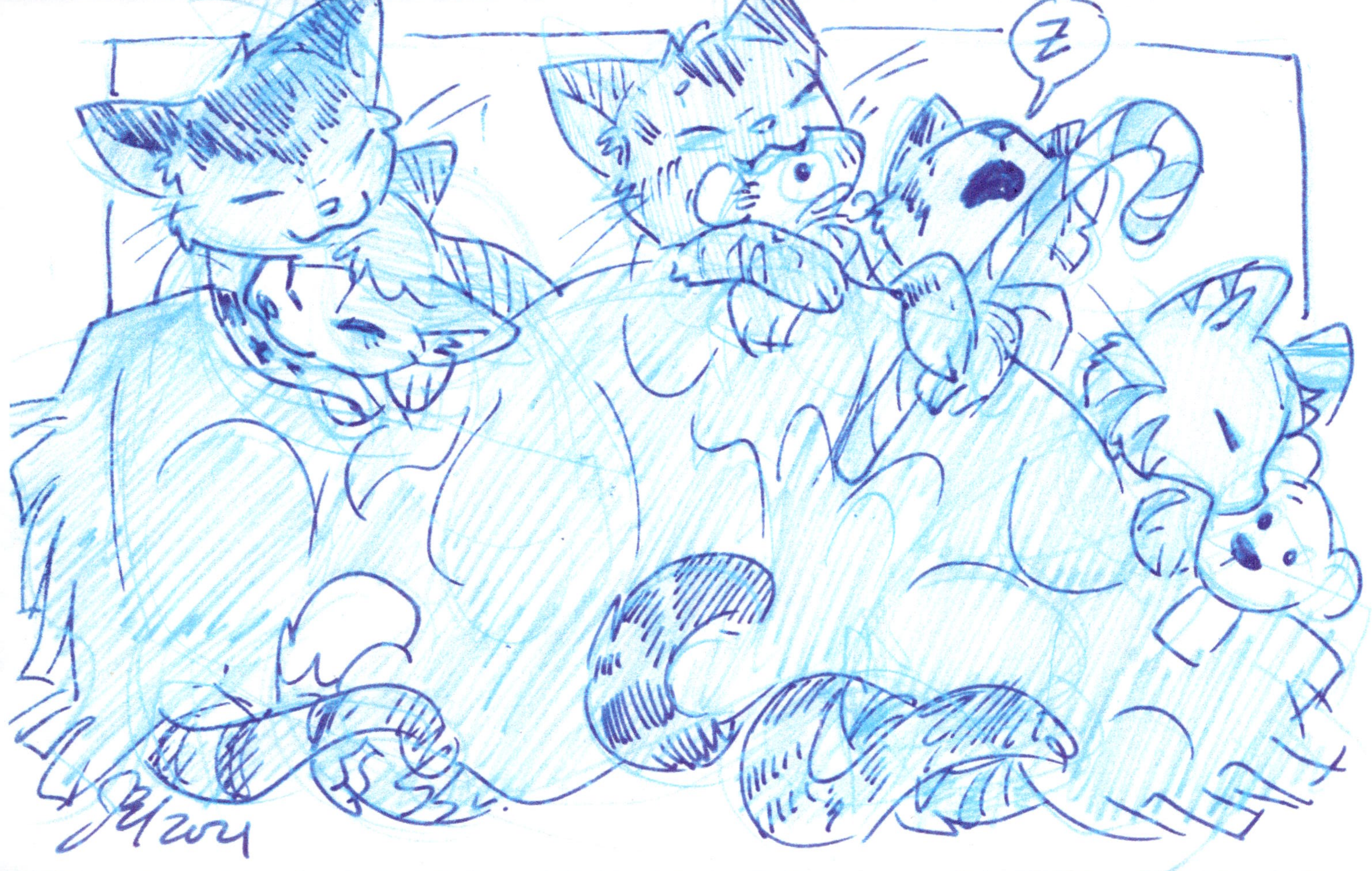
Z

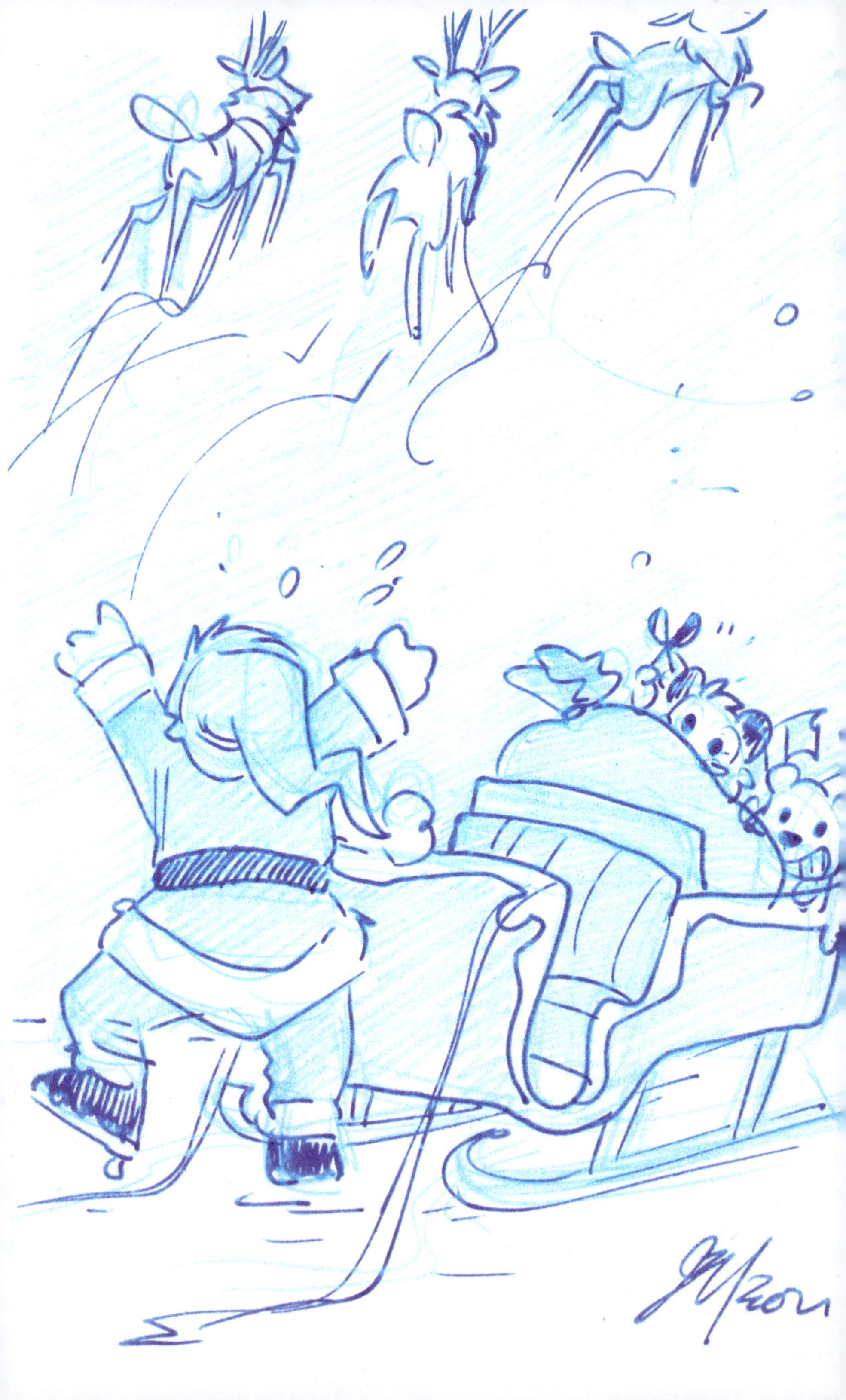

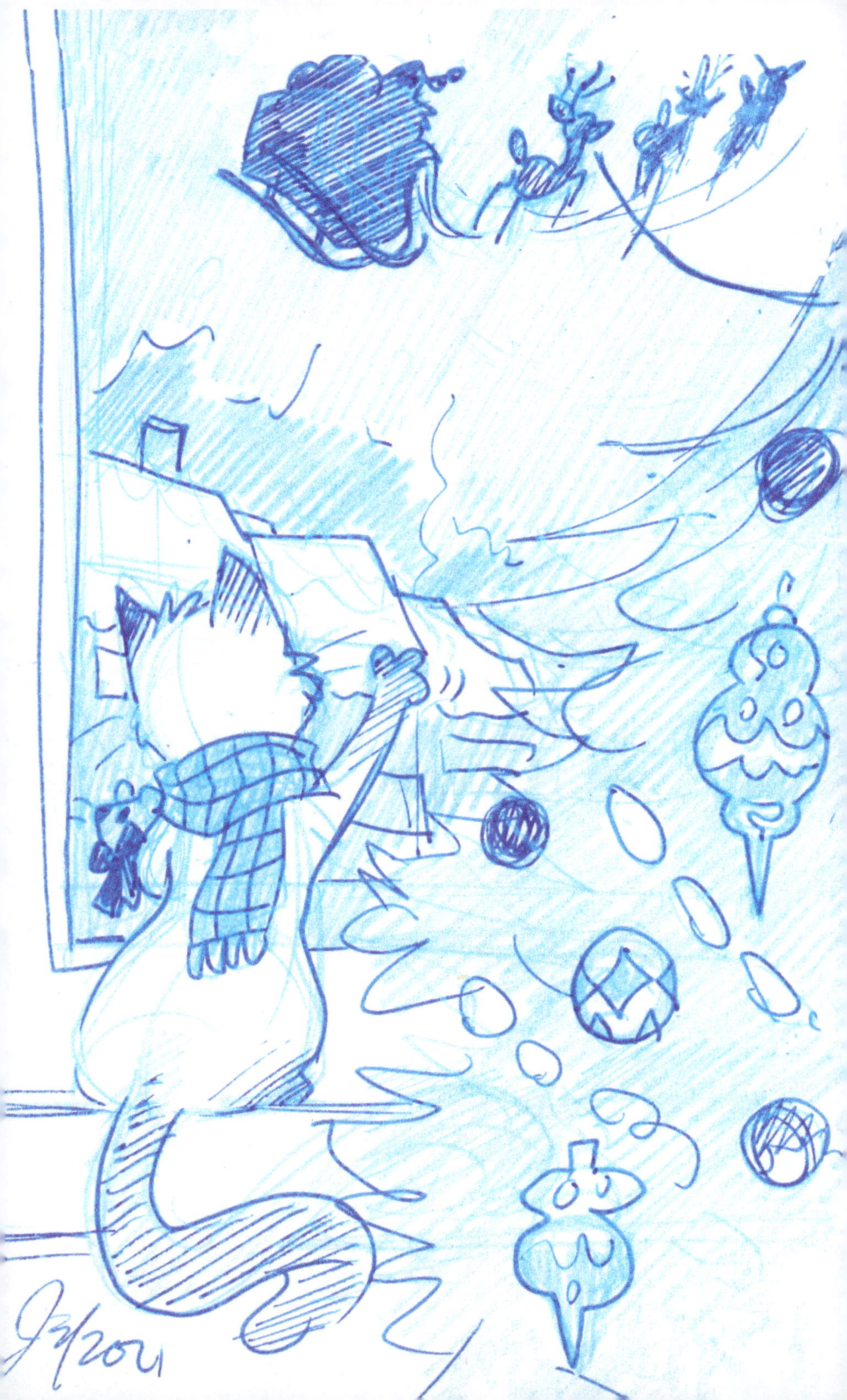

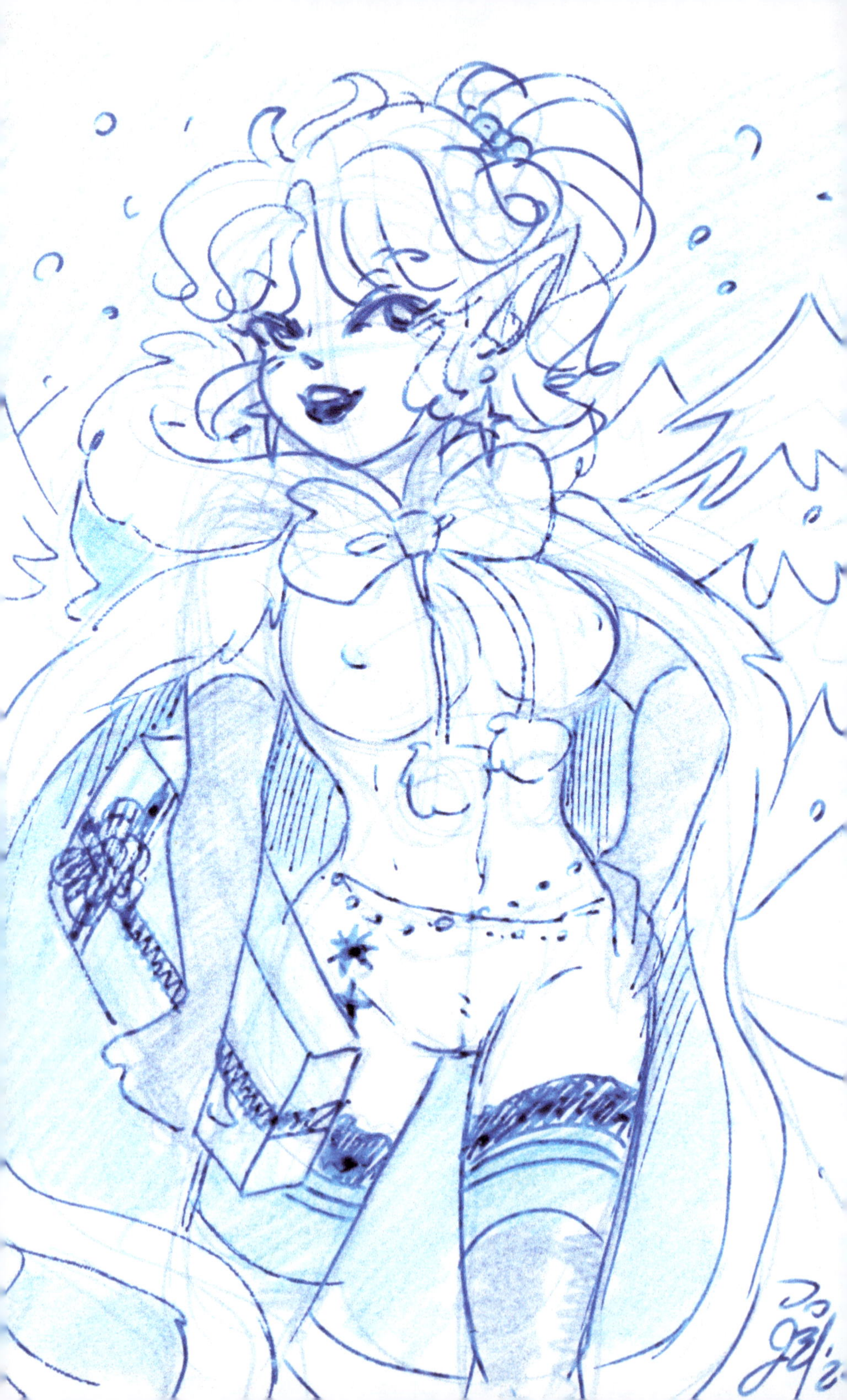

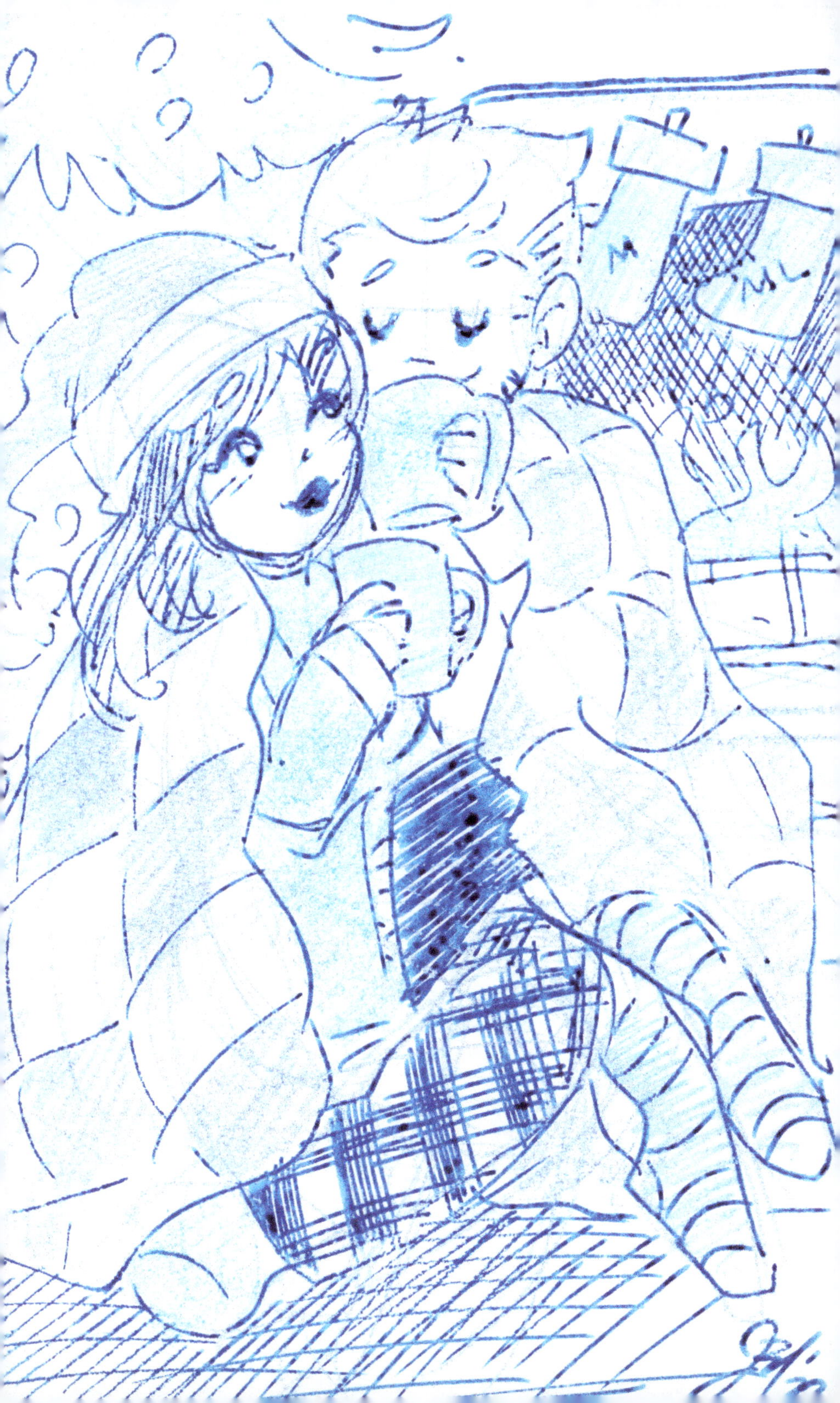

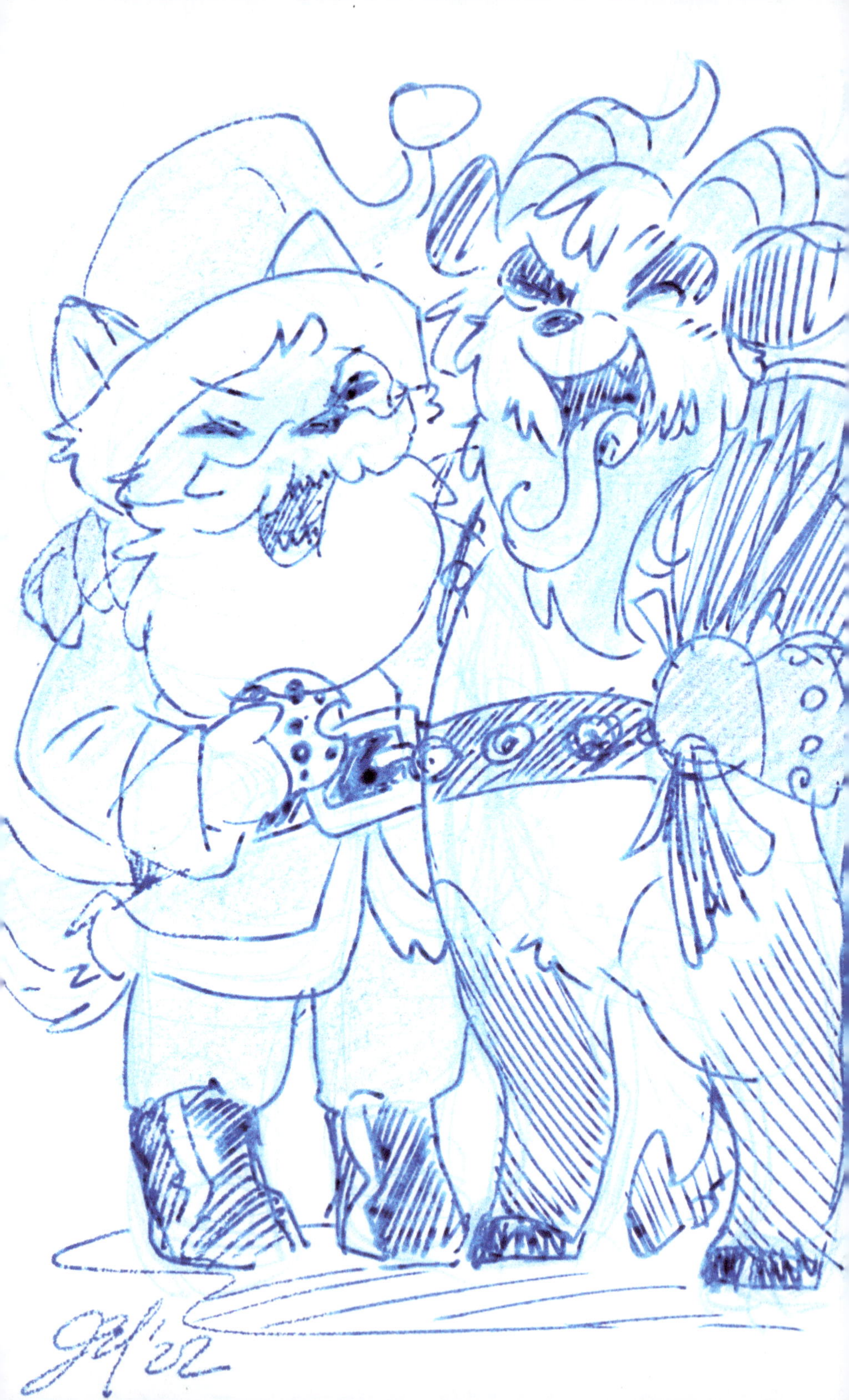

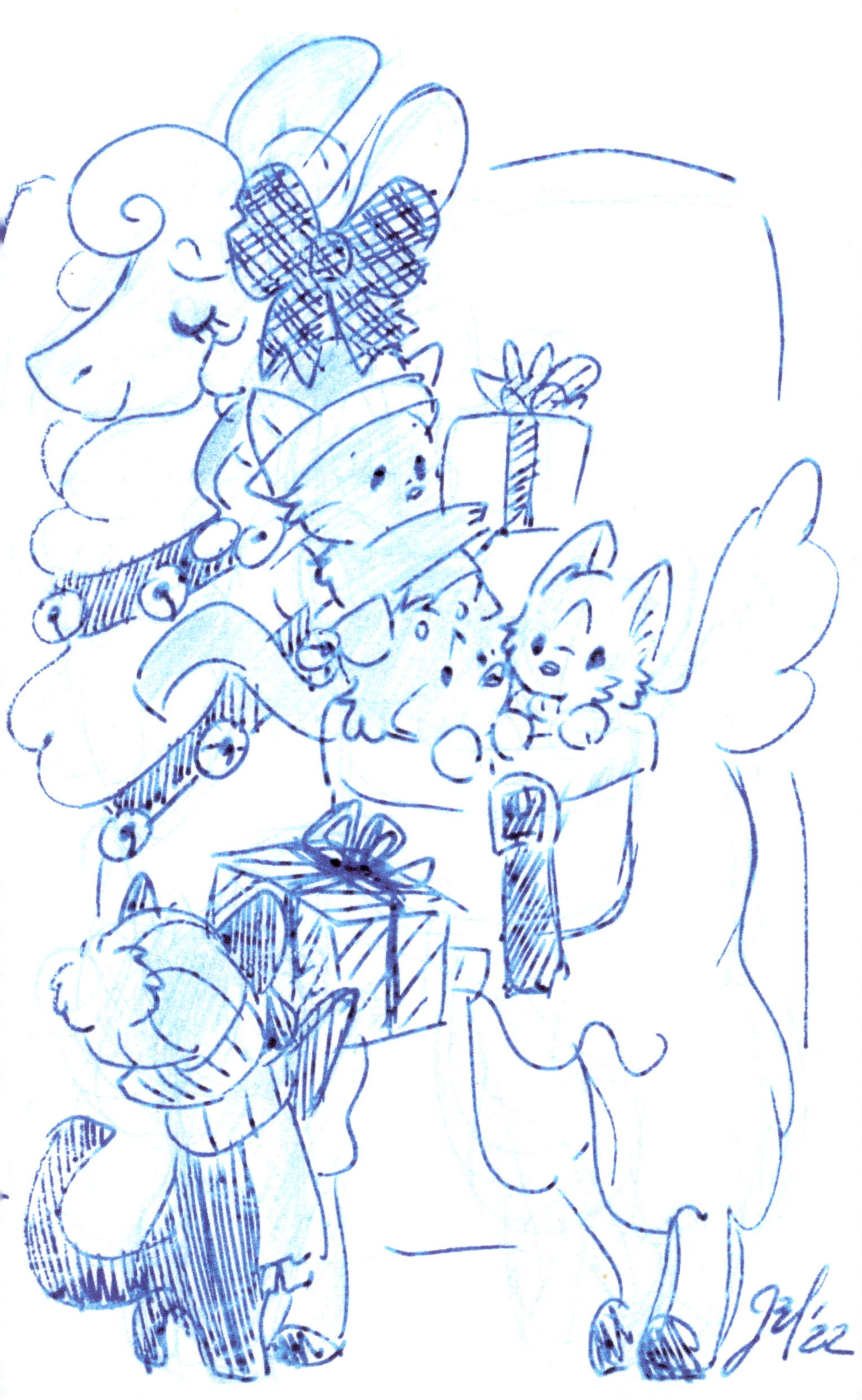

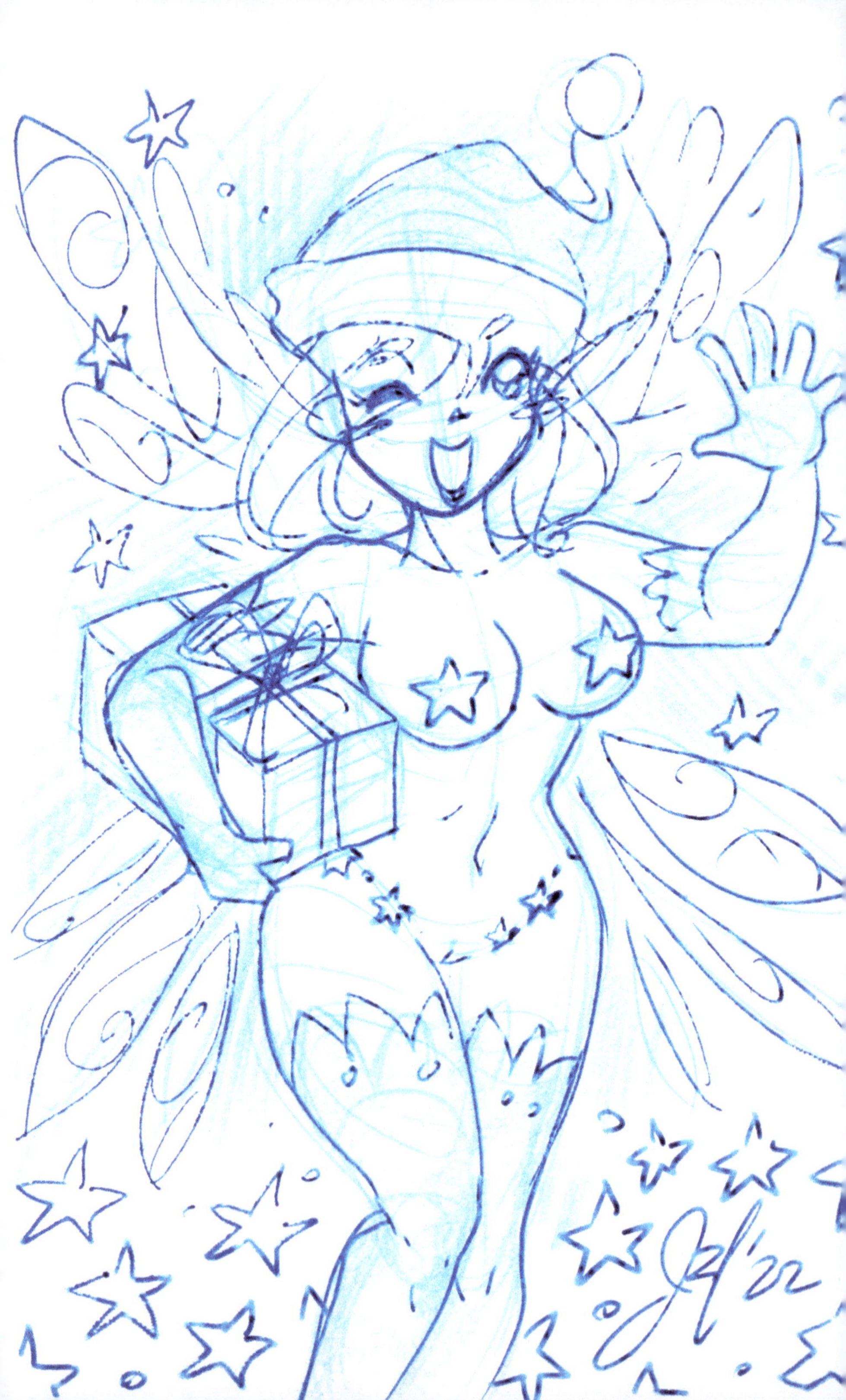

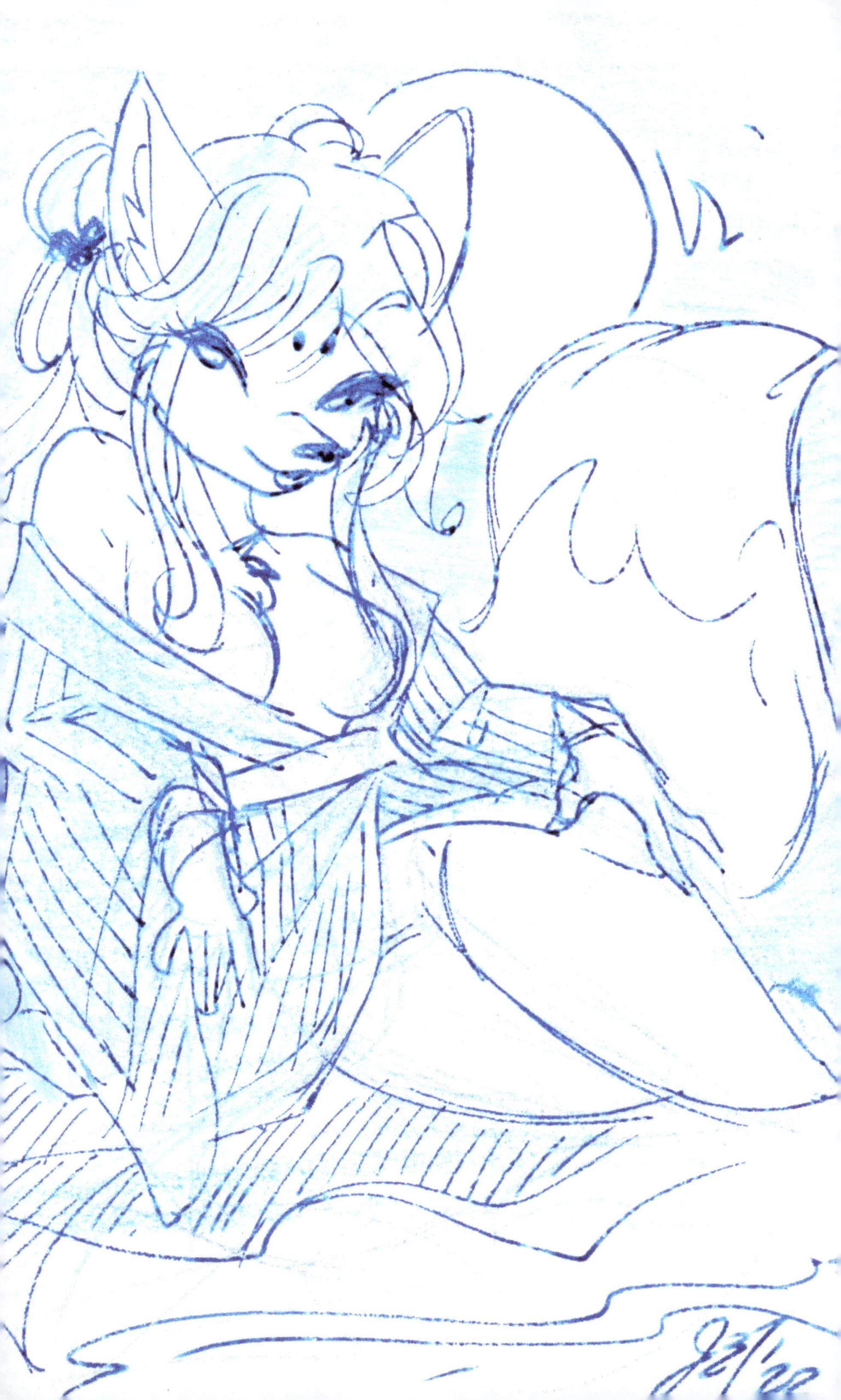

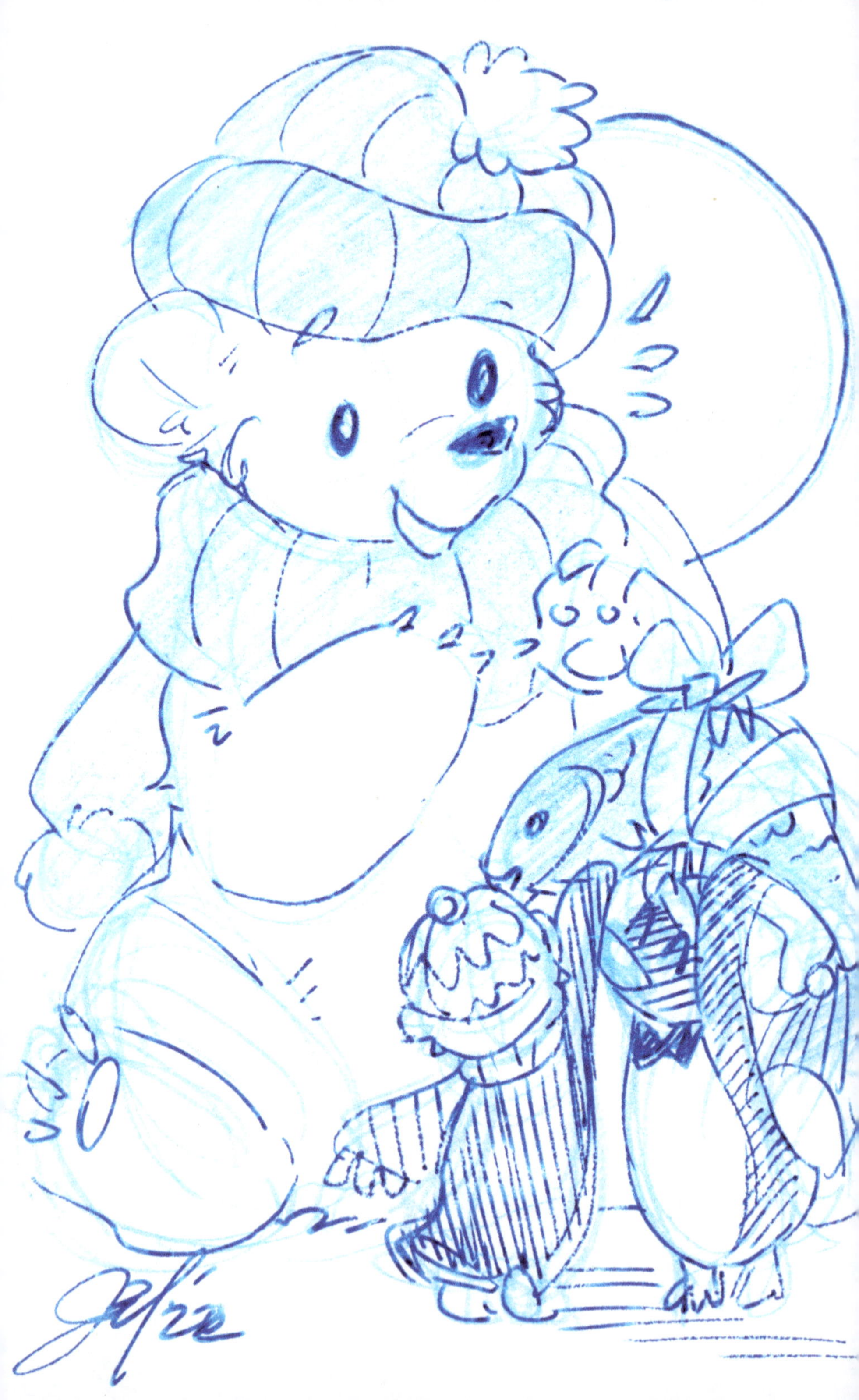

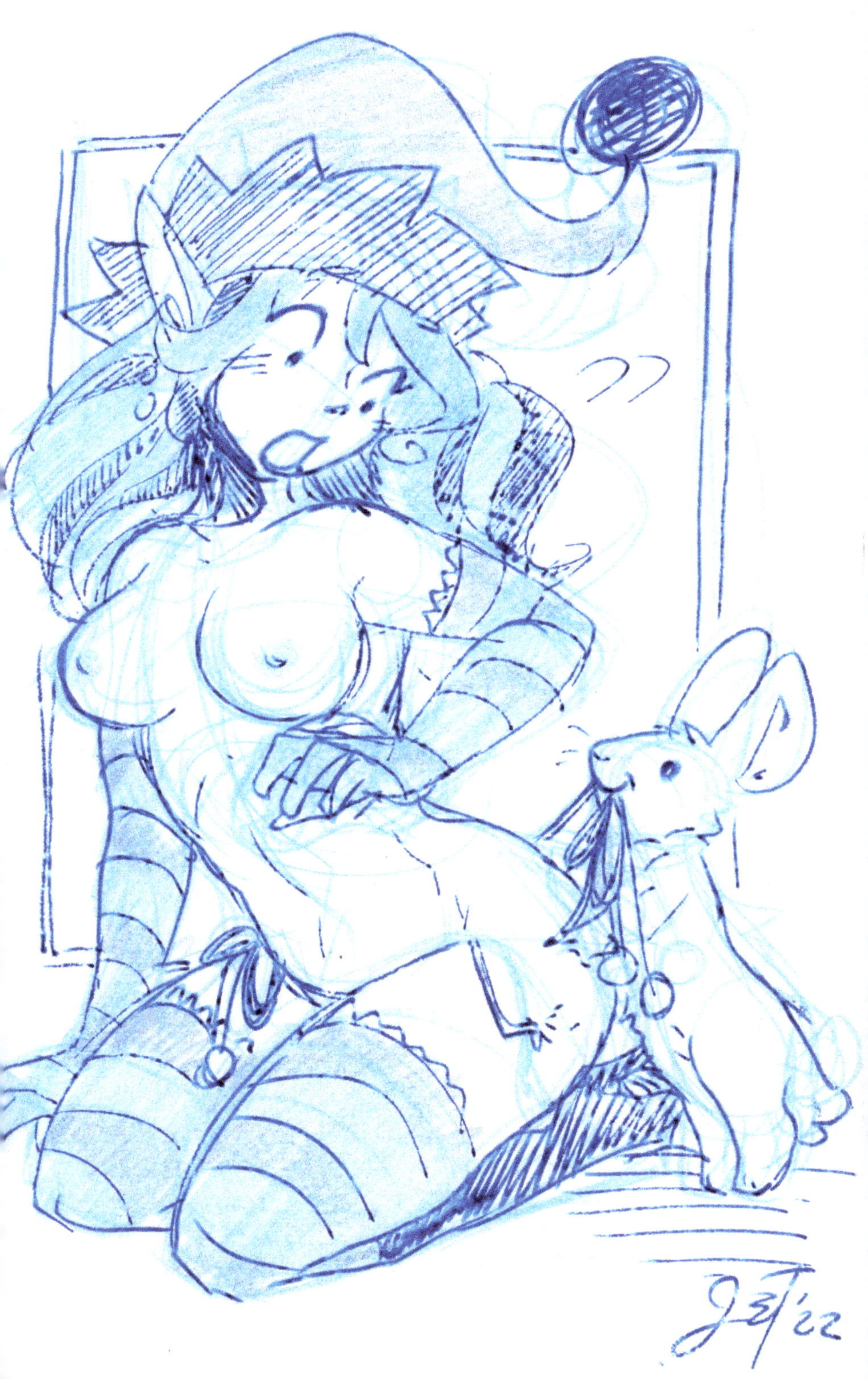

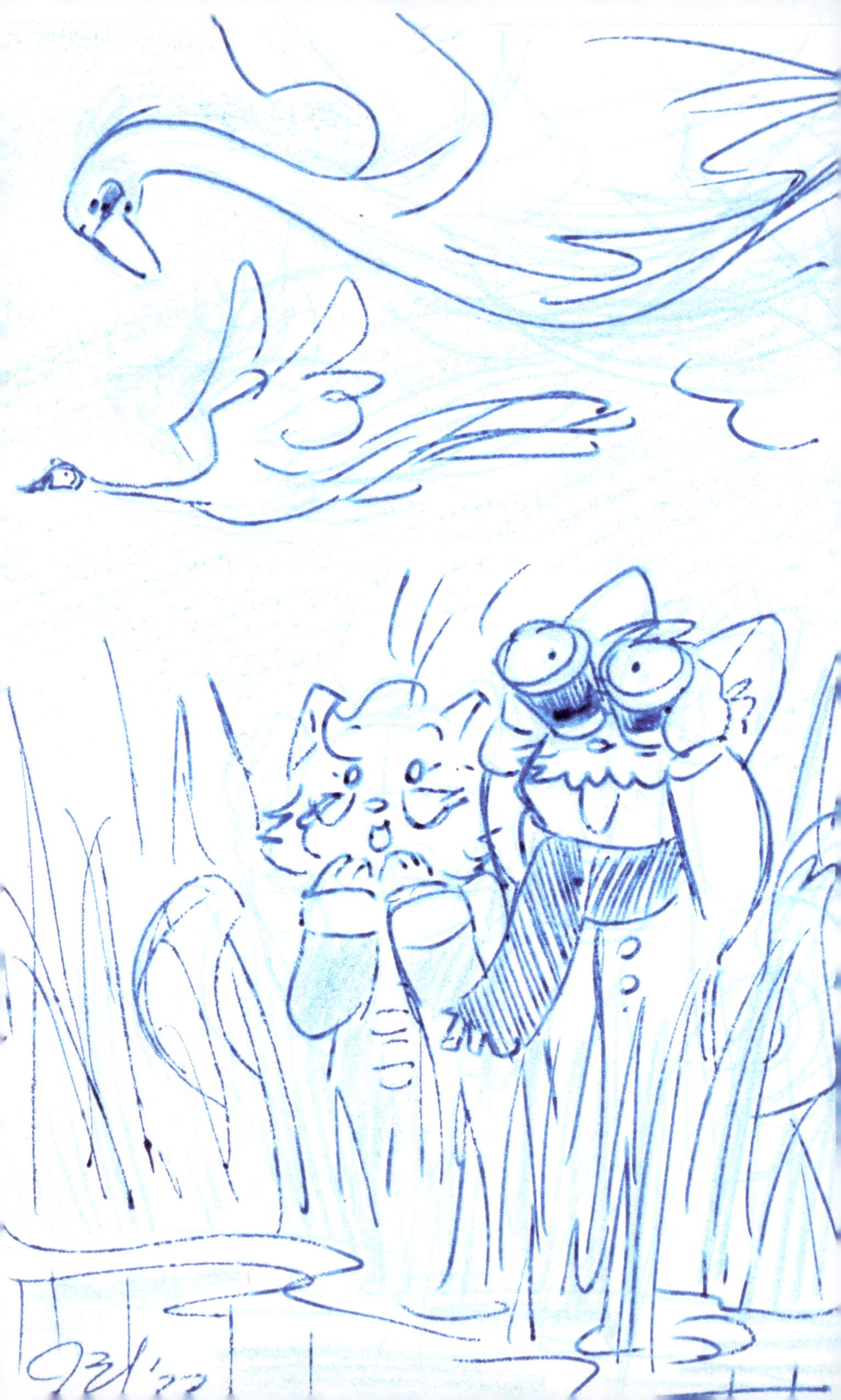

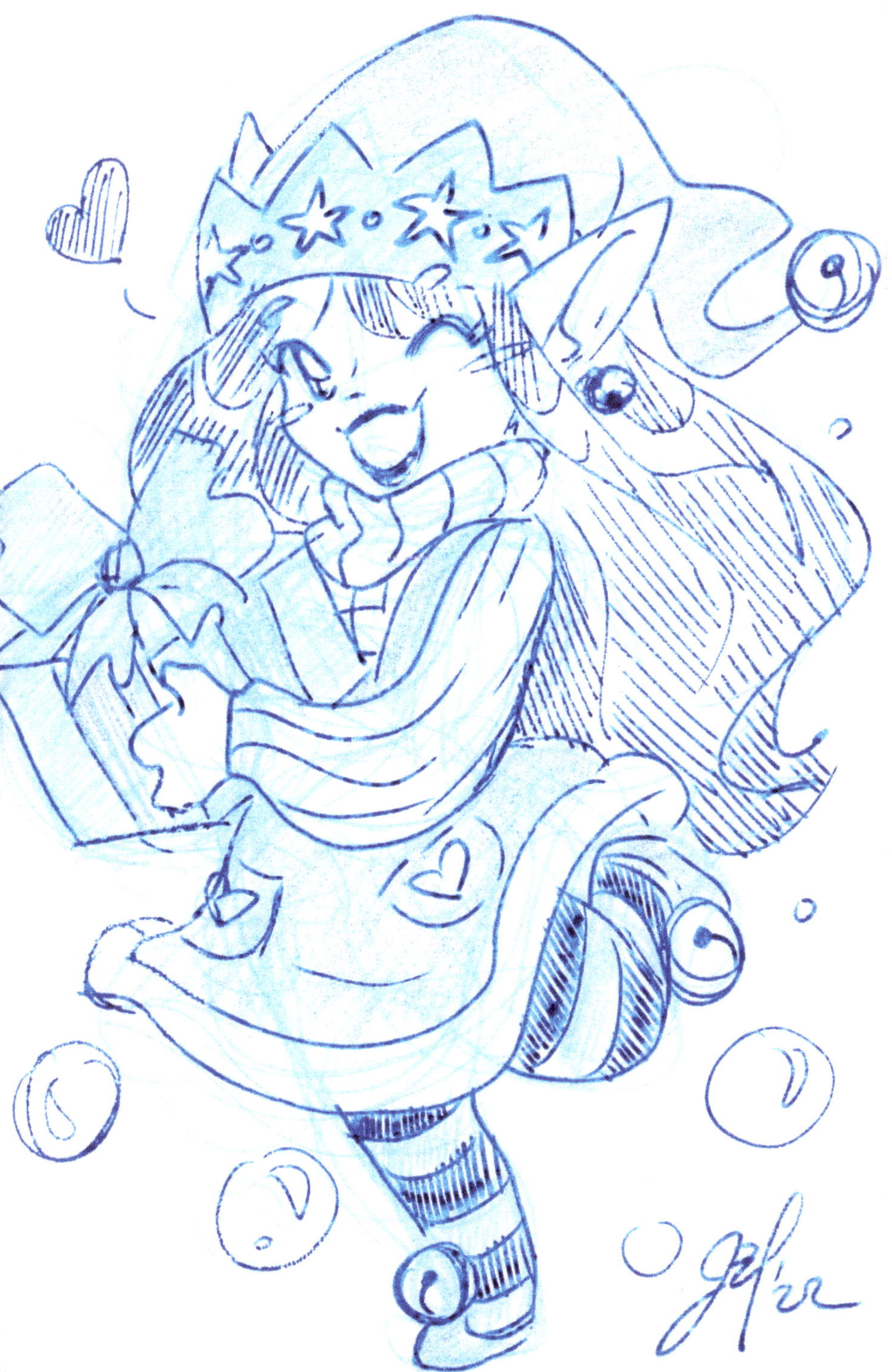

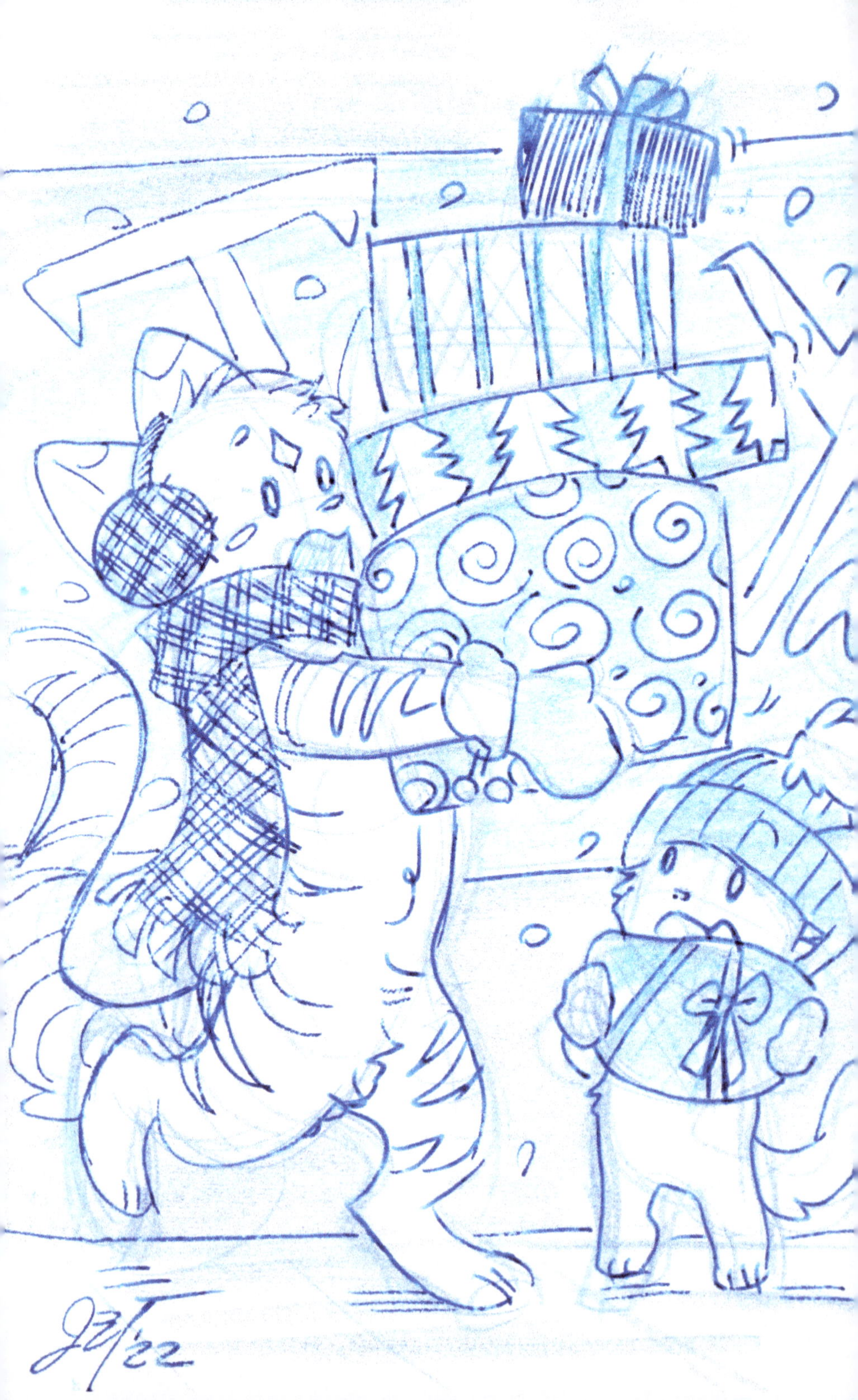

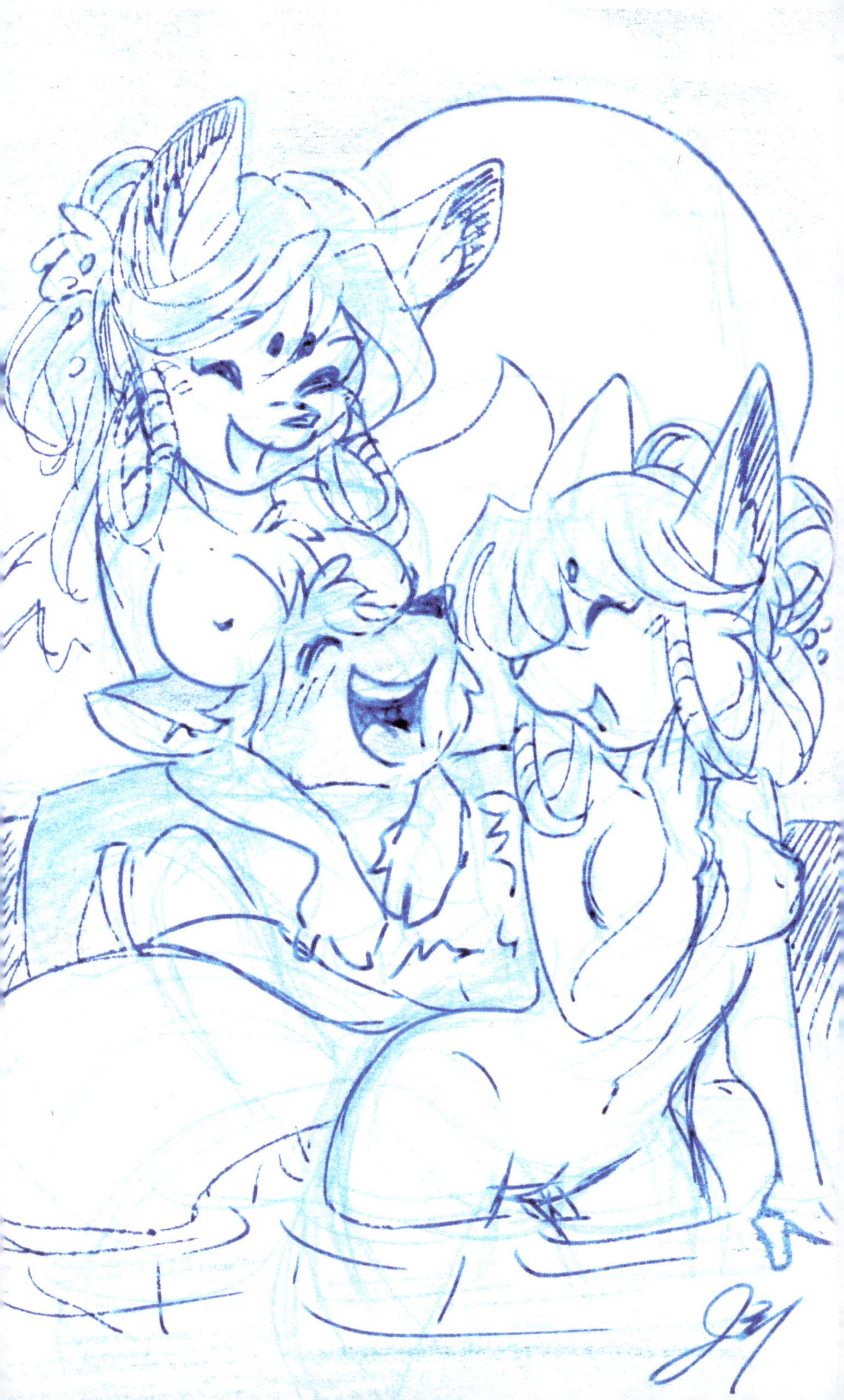

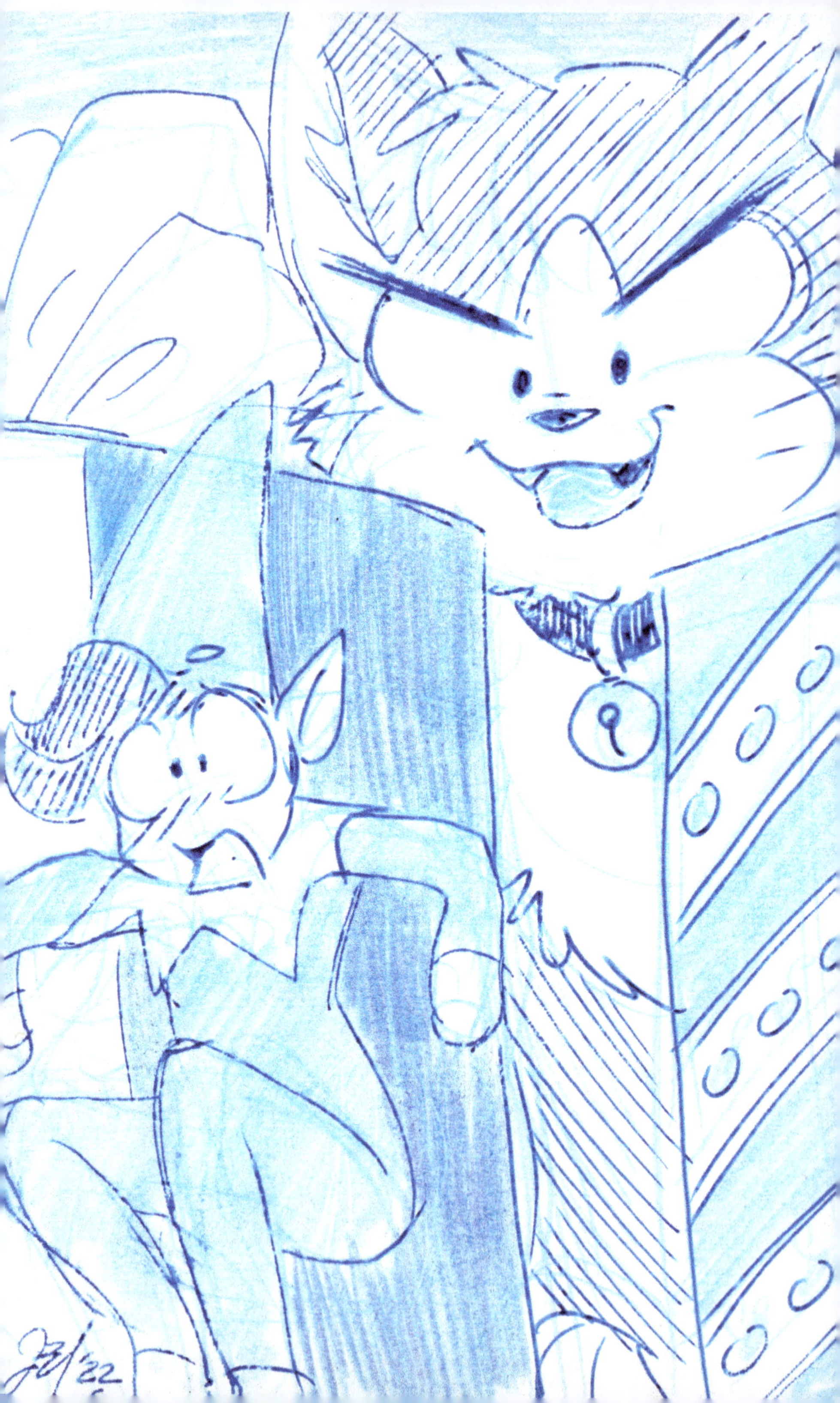

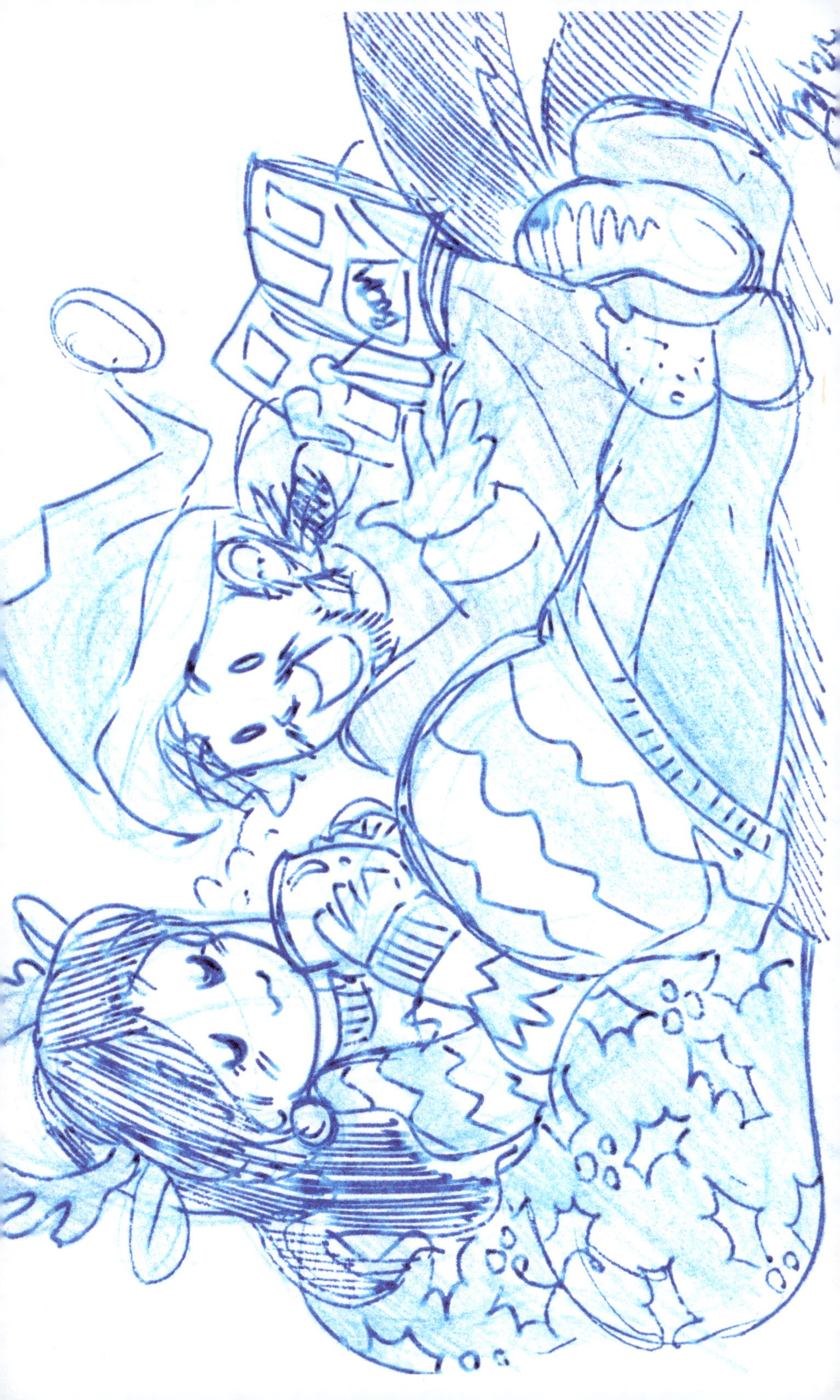

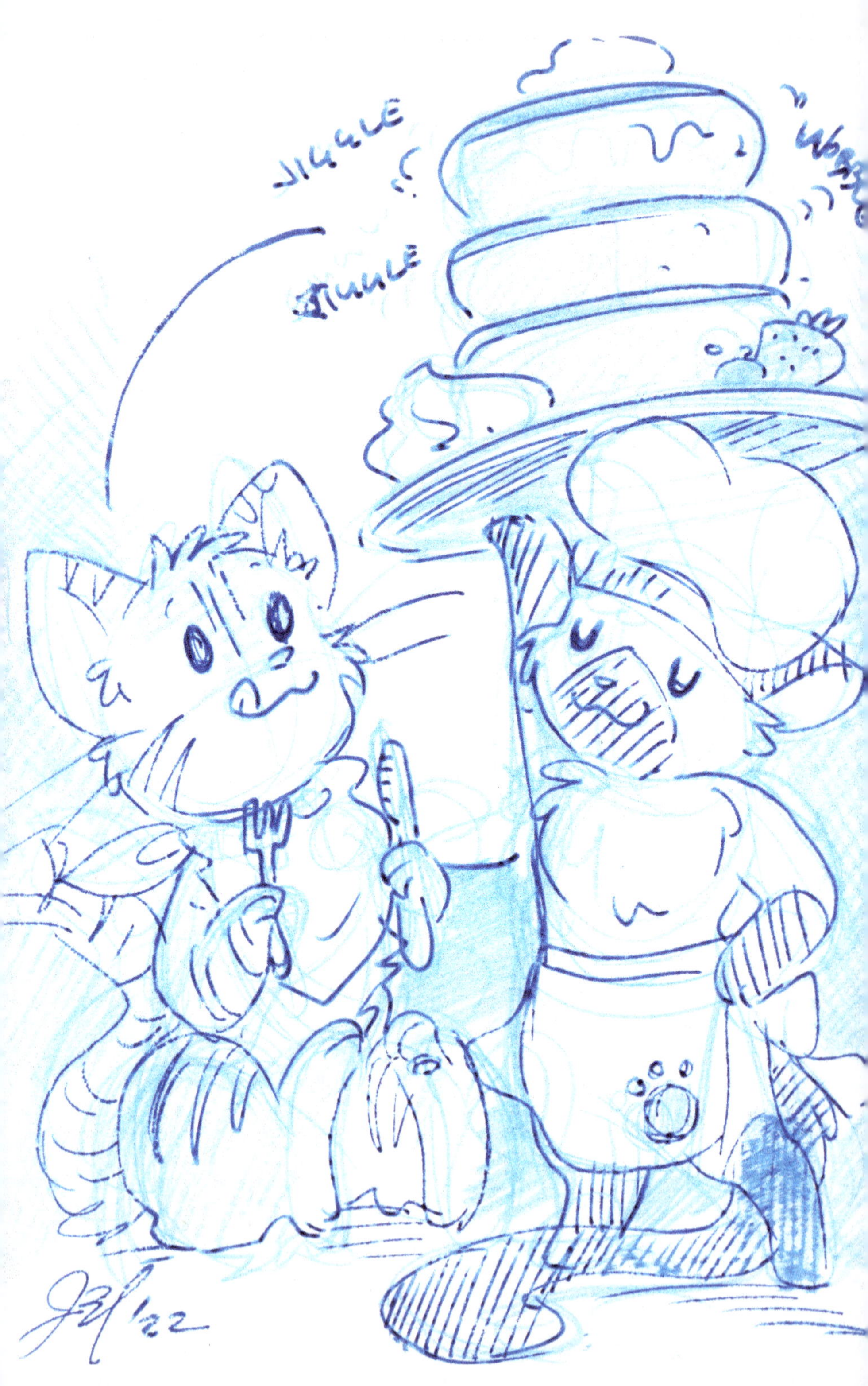

JIGGLE?
JIGGLE
WOBBLE

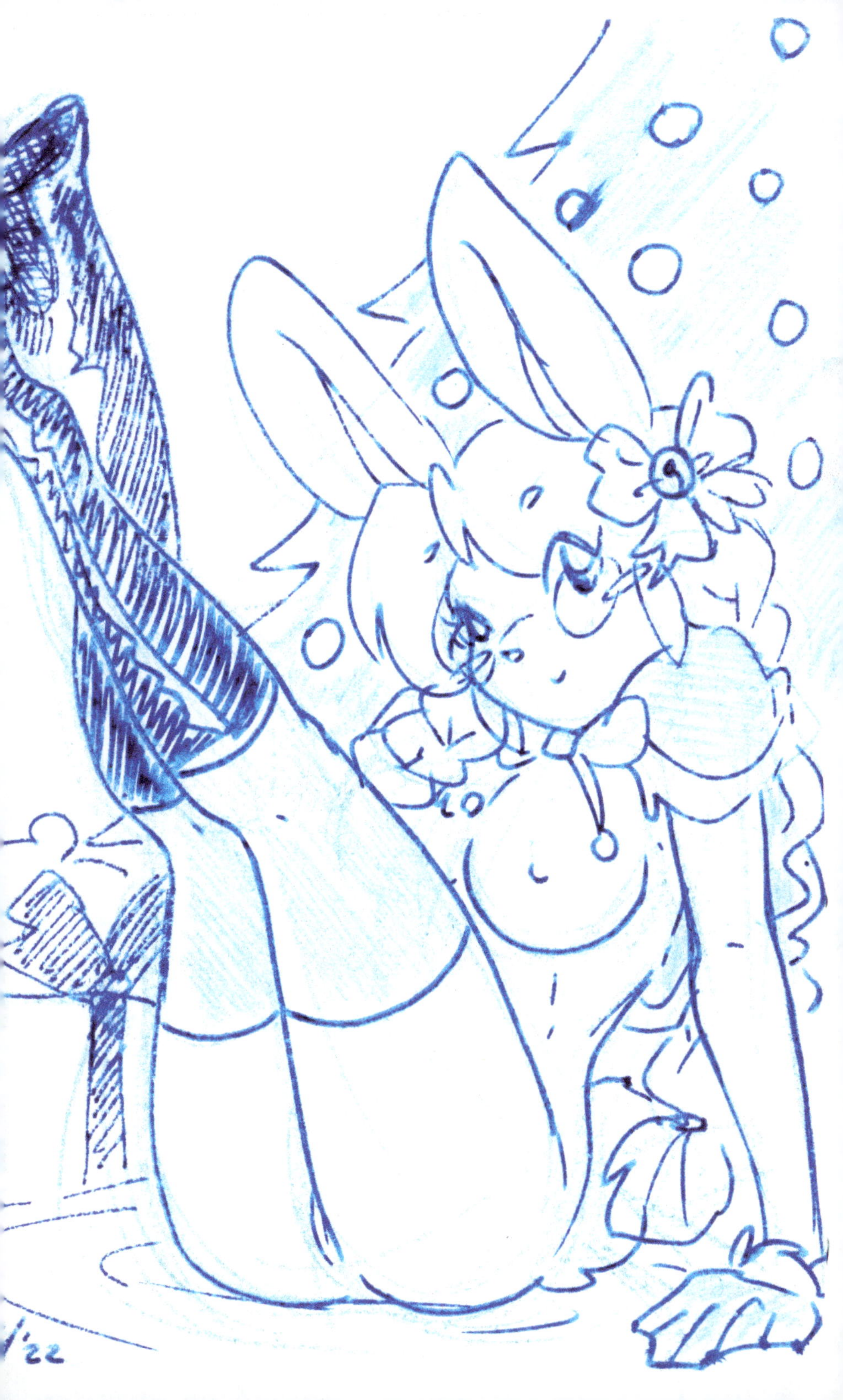

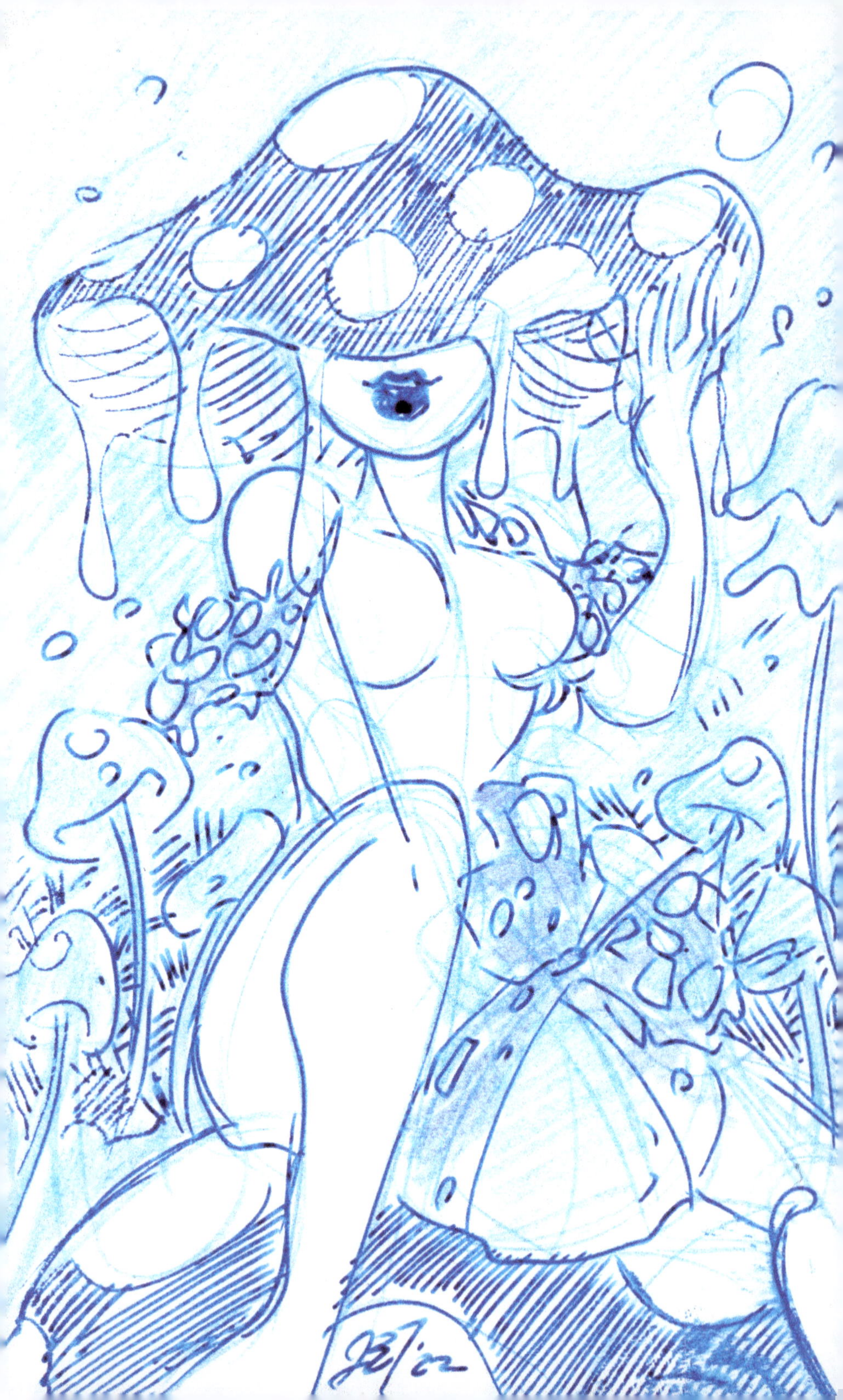

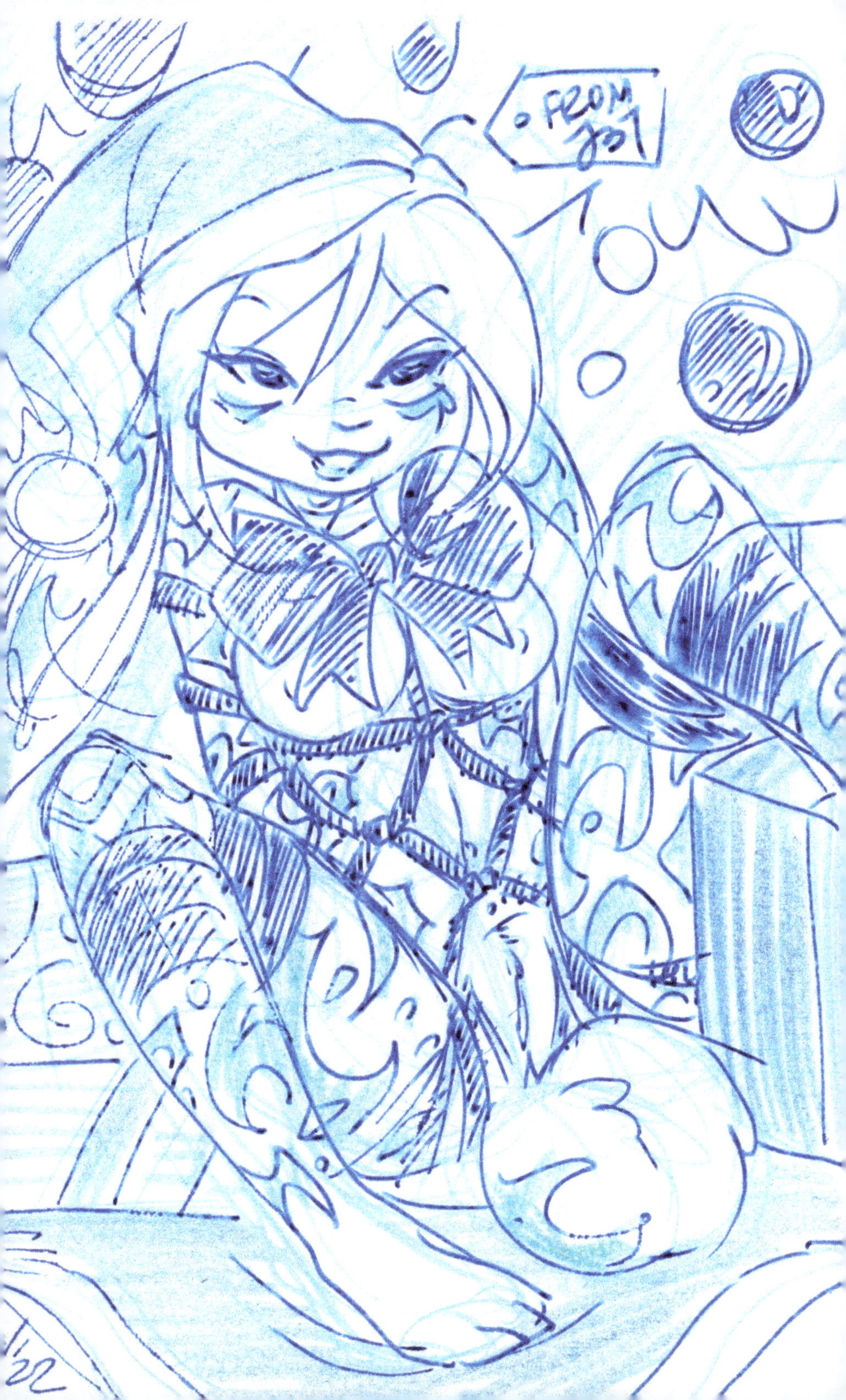

FROM
JO

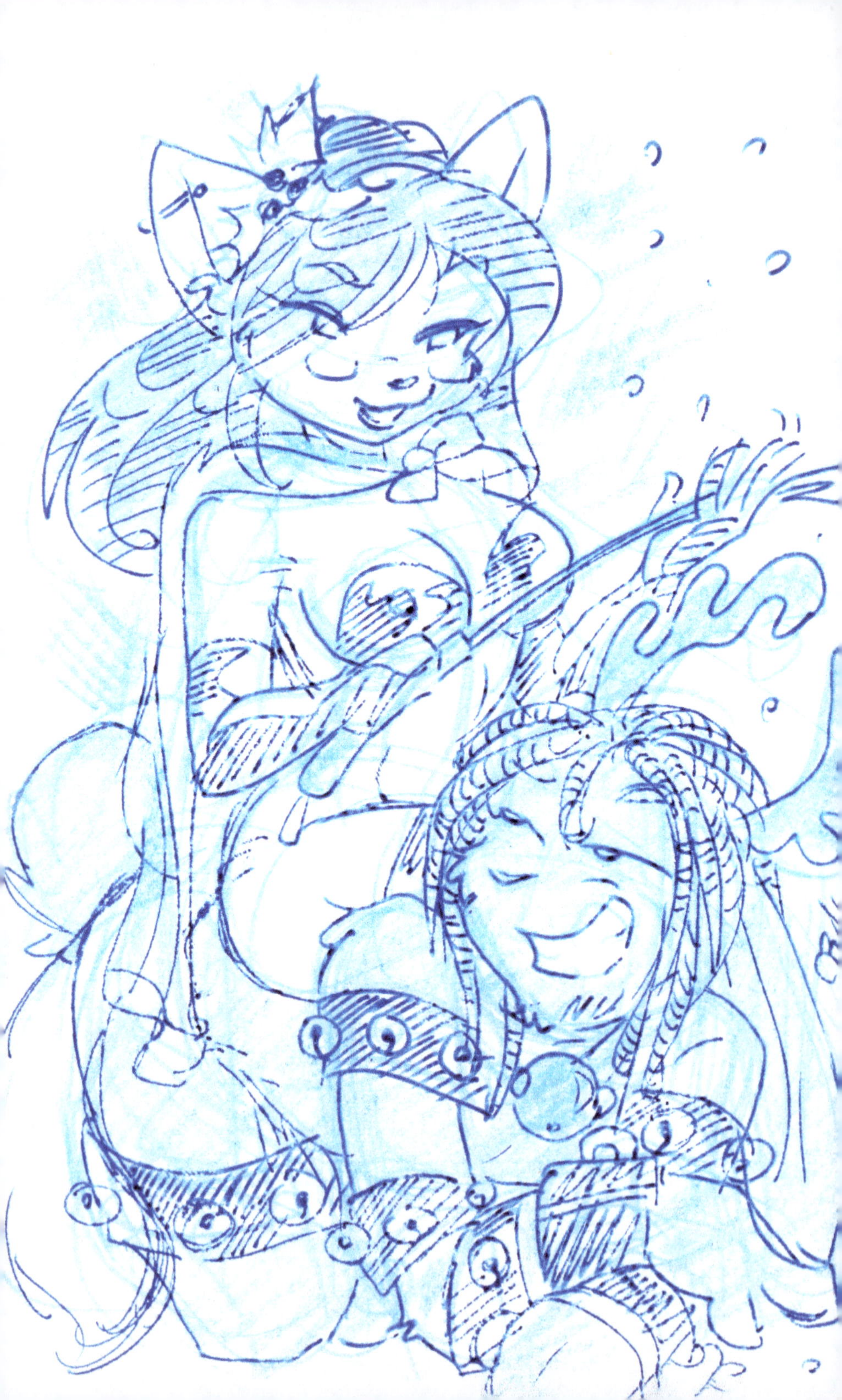

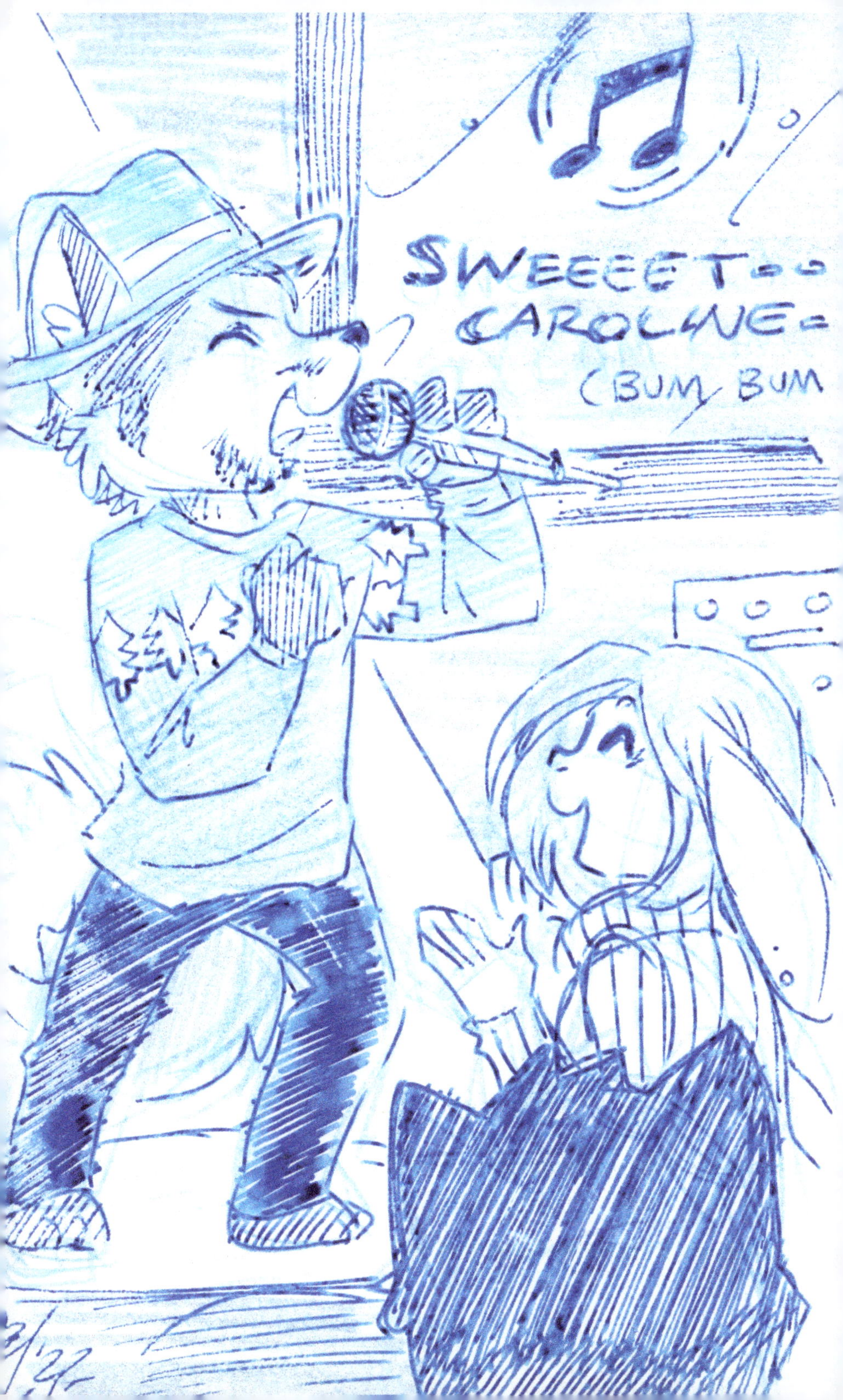

SWEEEET~~
CAROLINE~
(BUM BUM

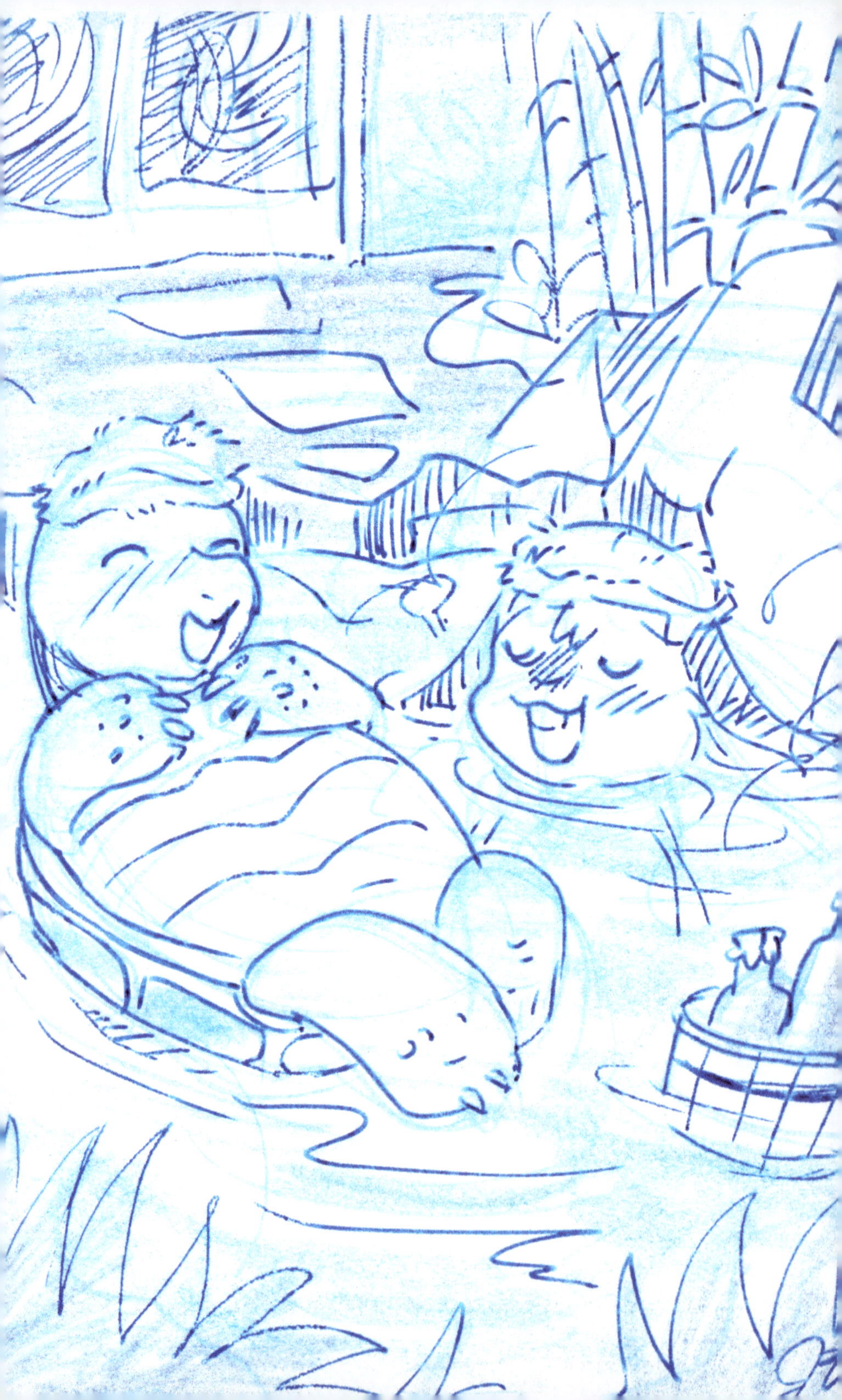

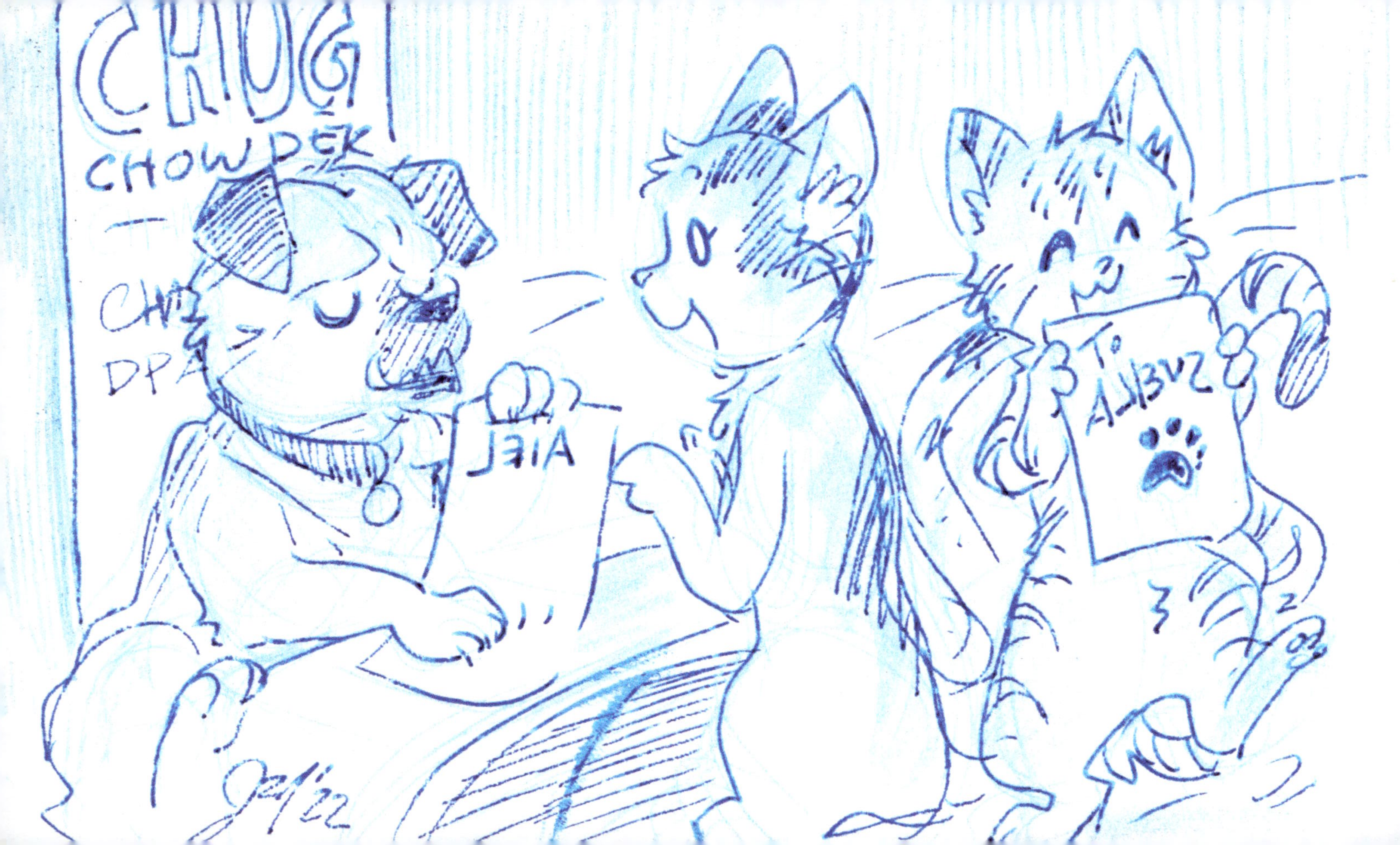

CHUG
CHOWDER
AIEL
To ALBUZ

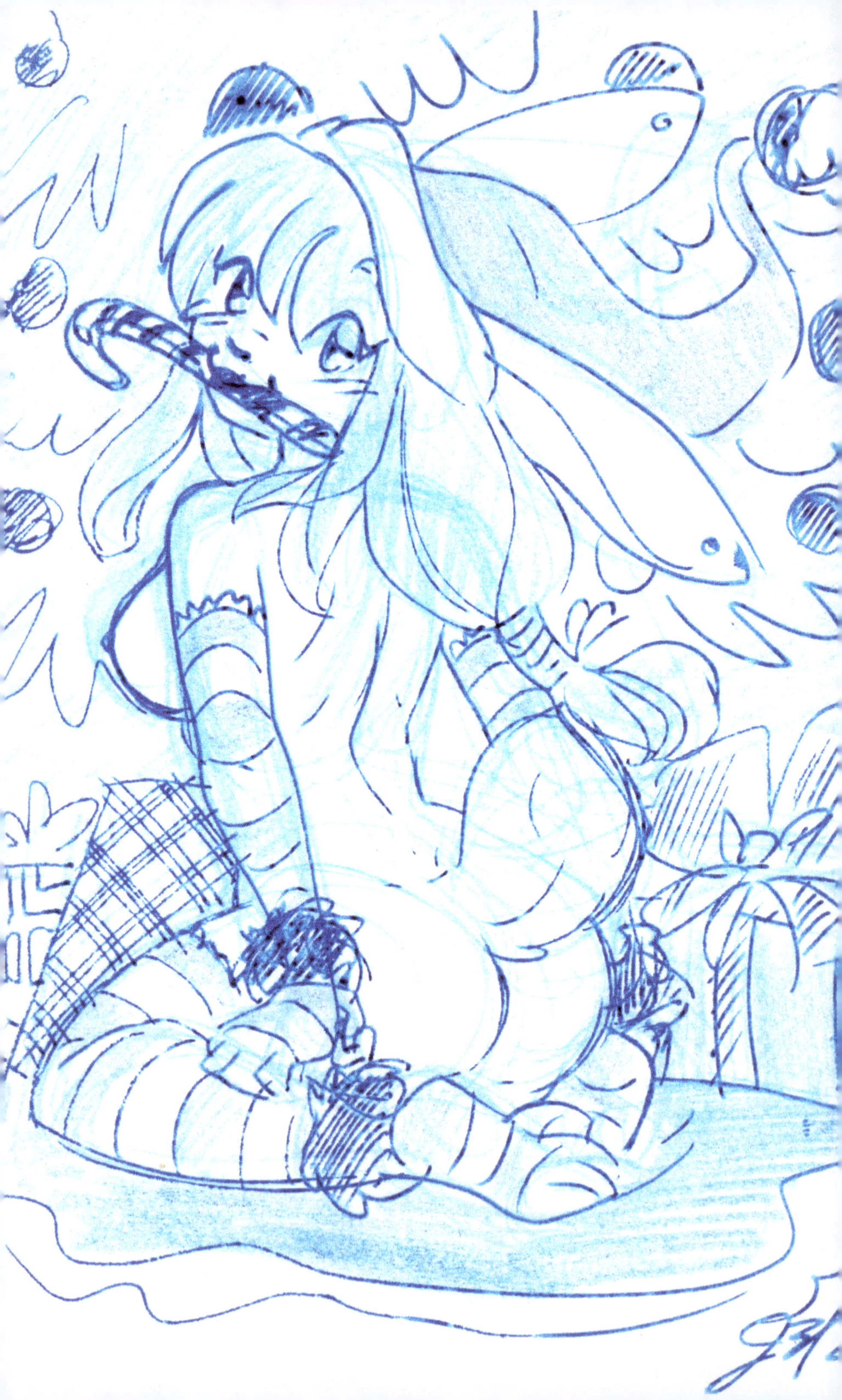

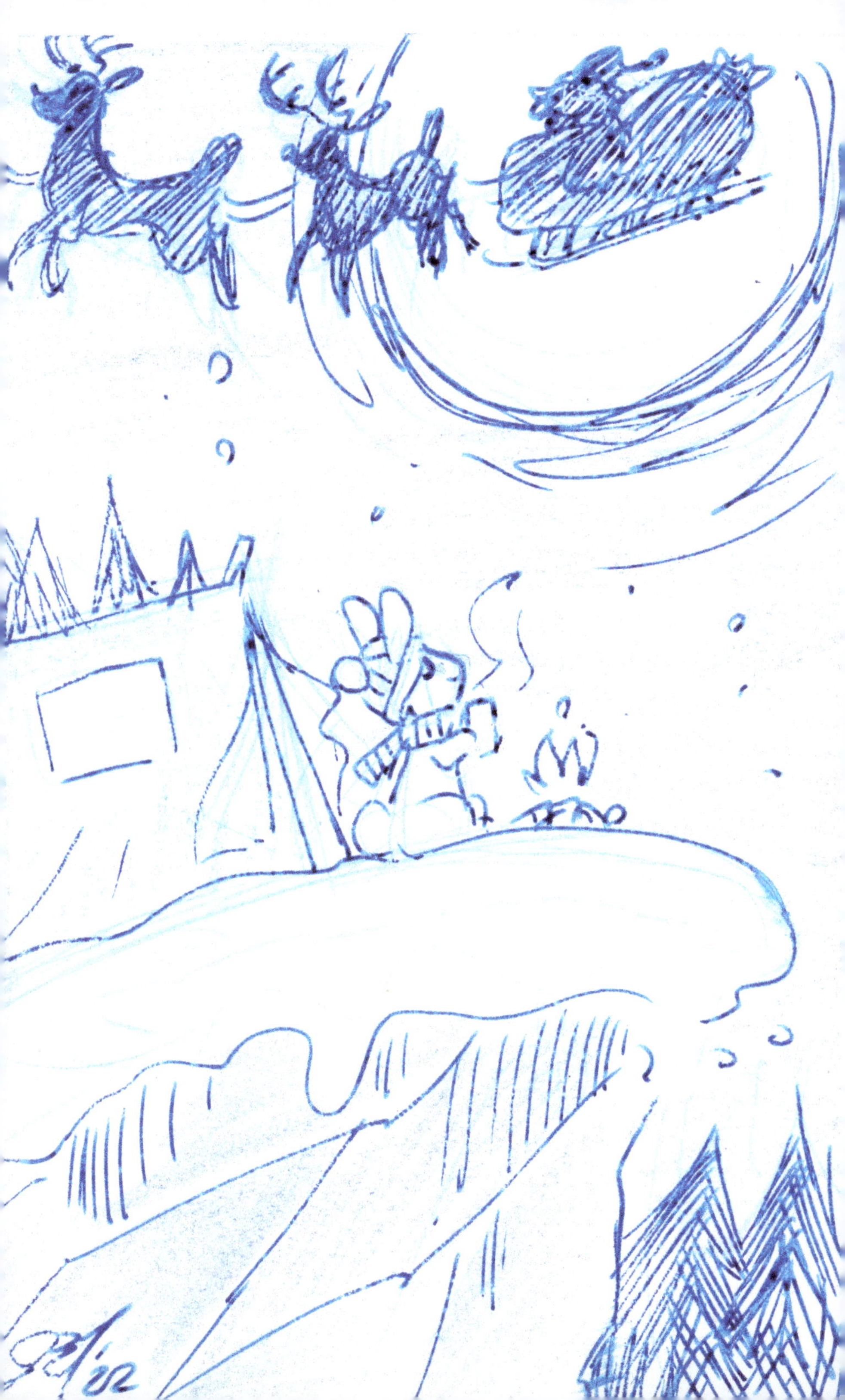

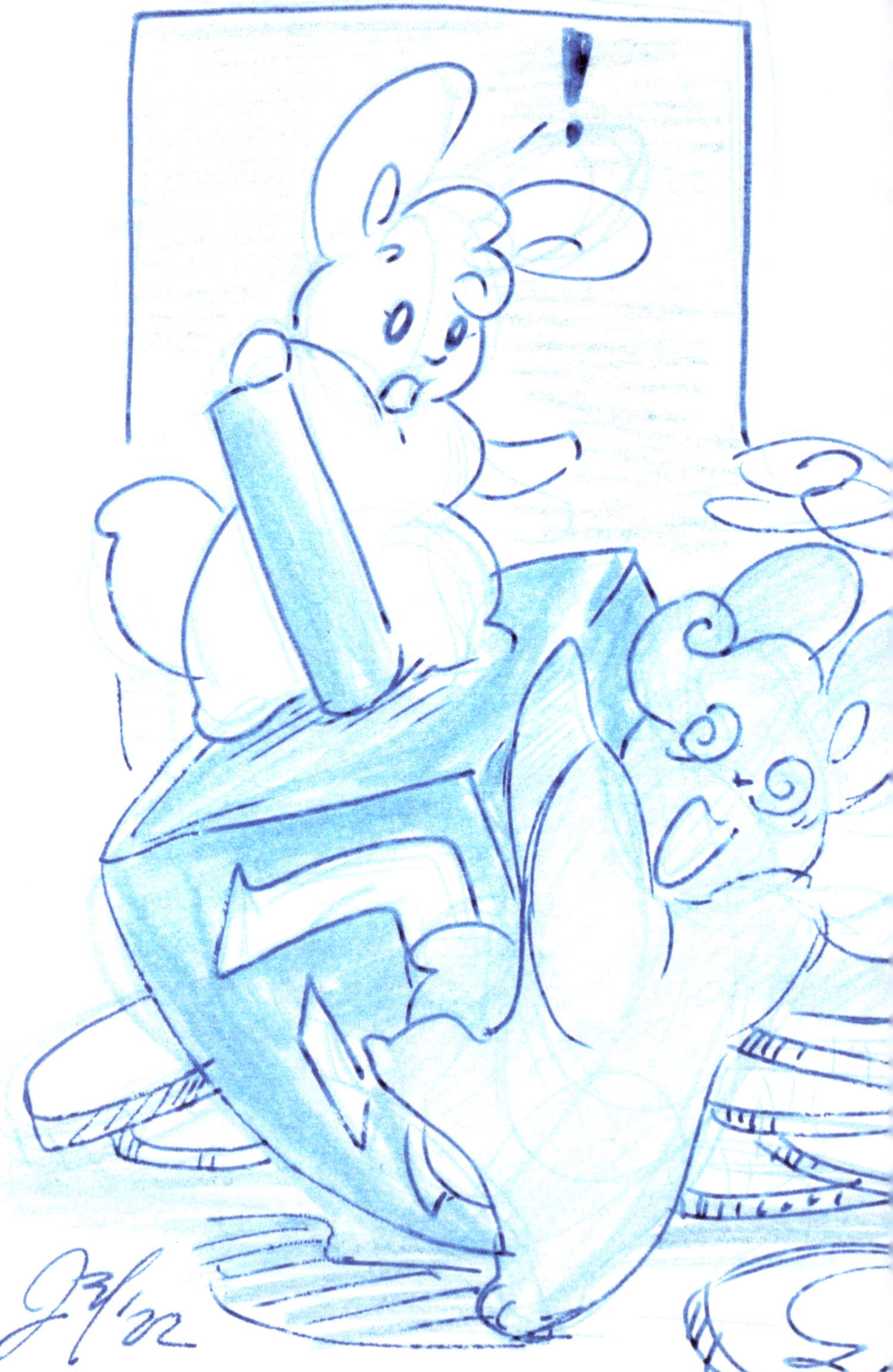

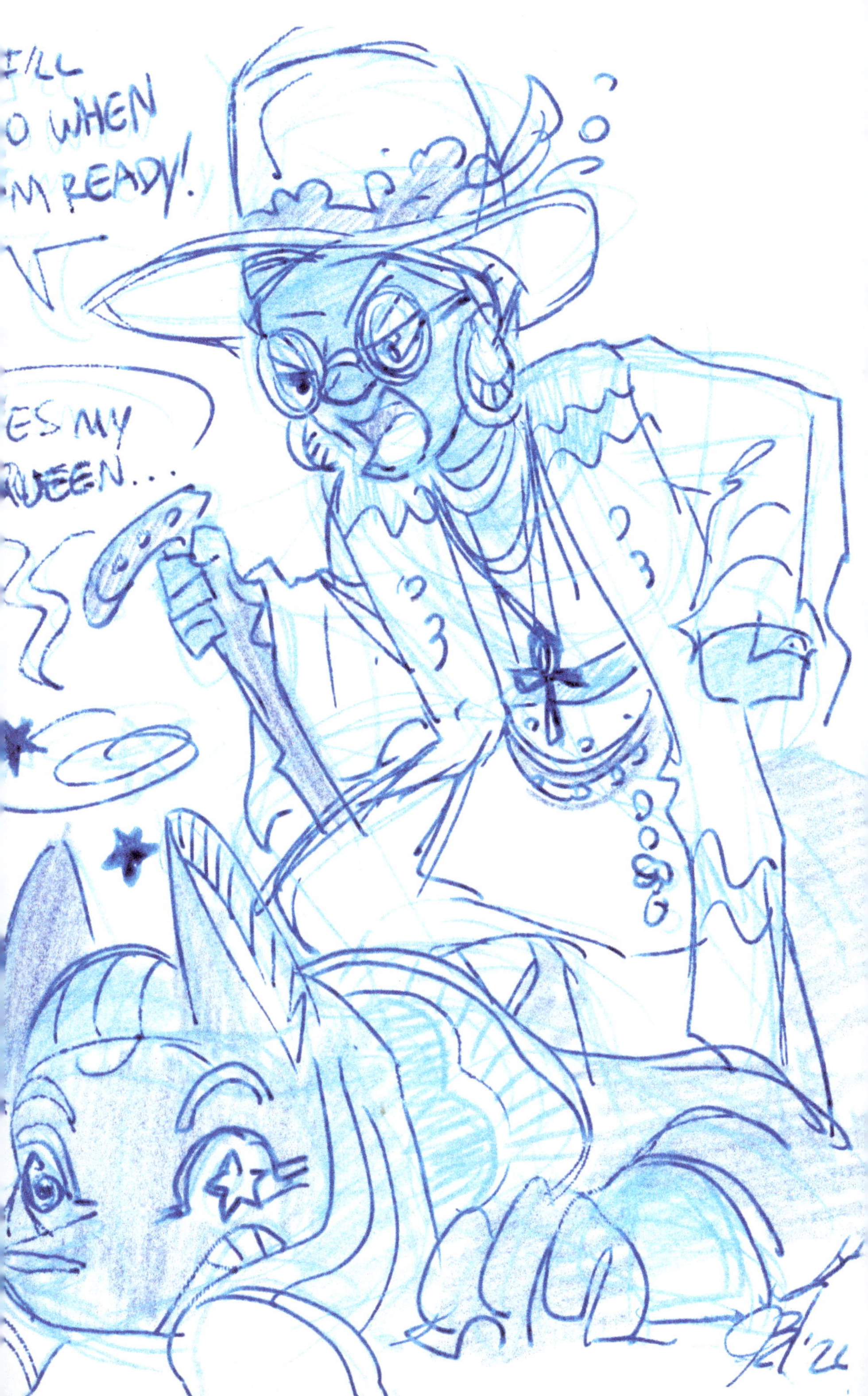
I'LL
O WHEN
M READY!

ES MY
UEEN...

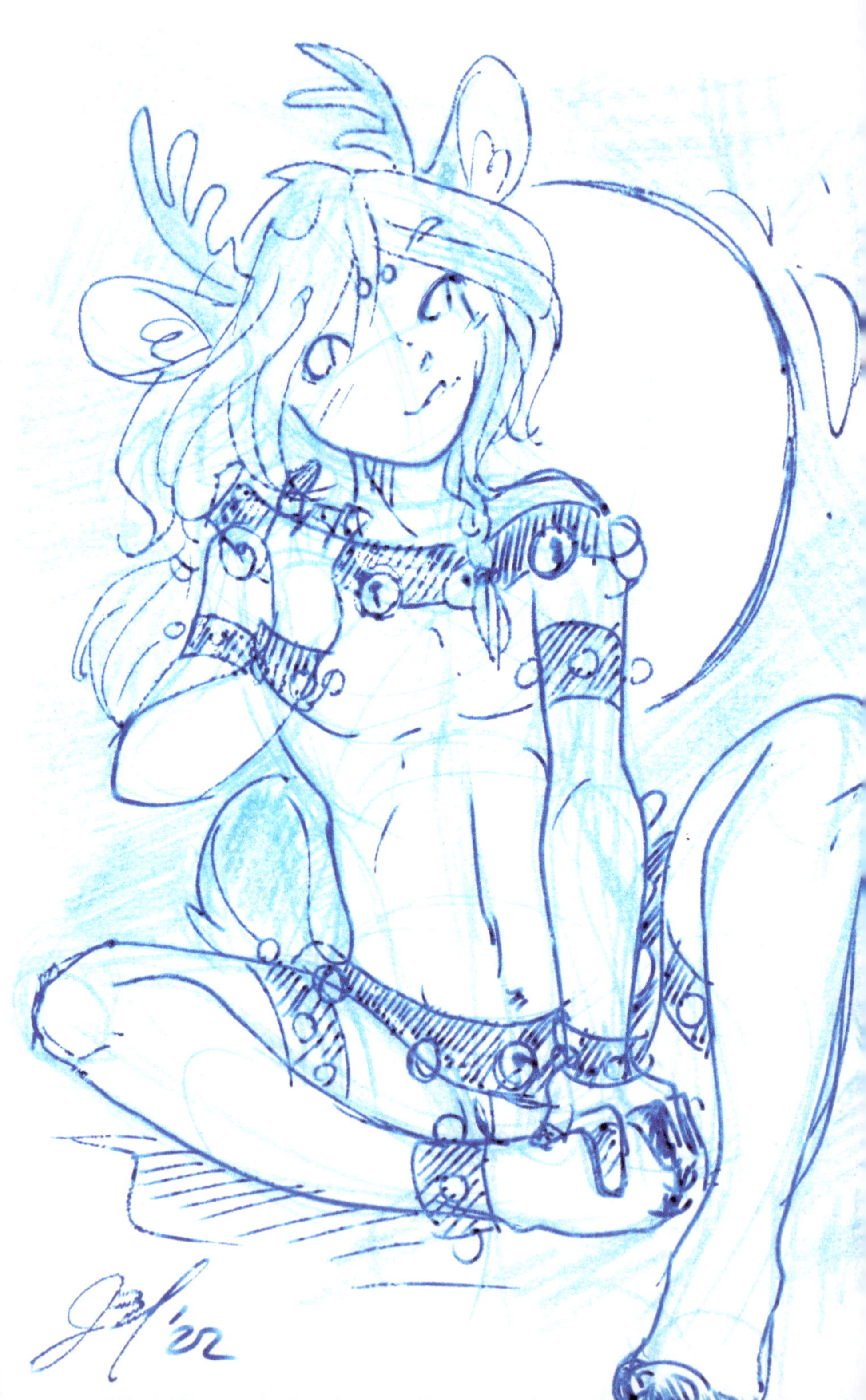

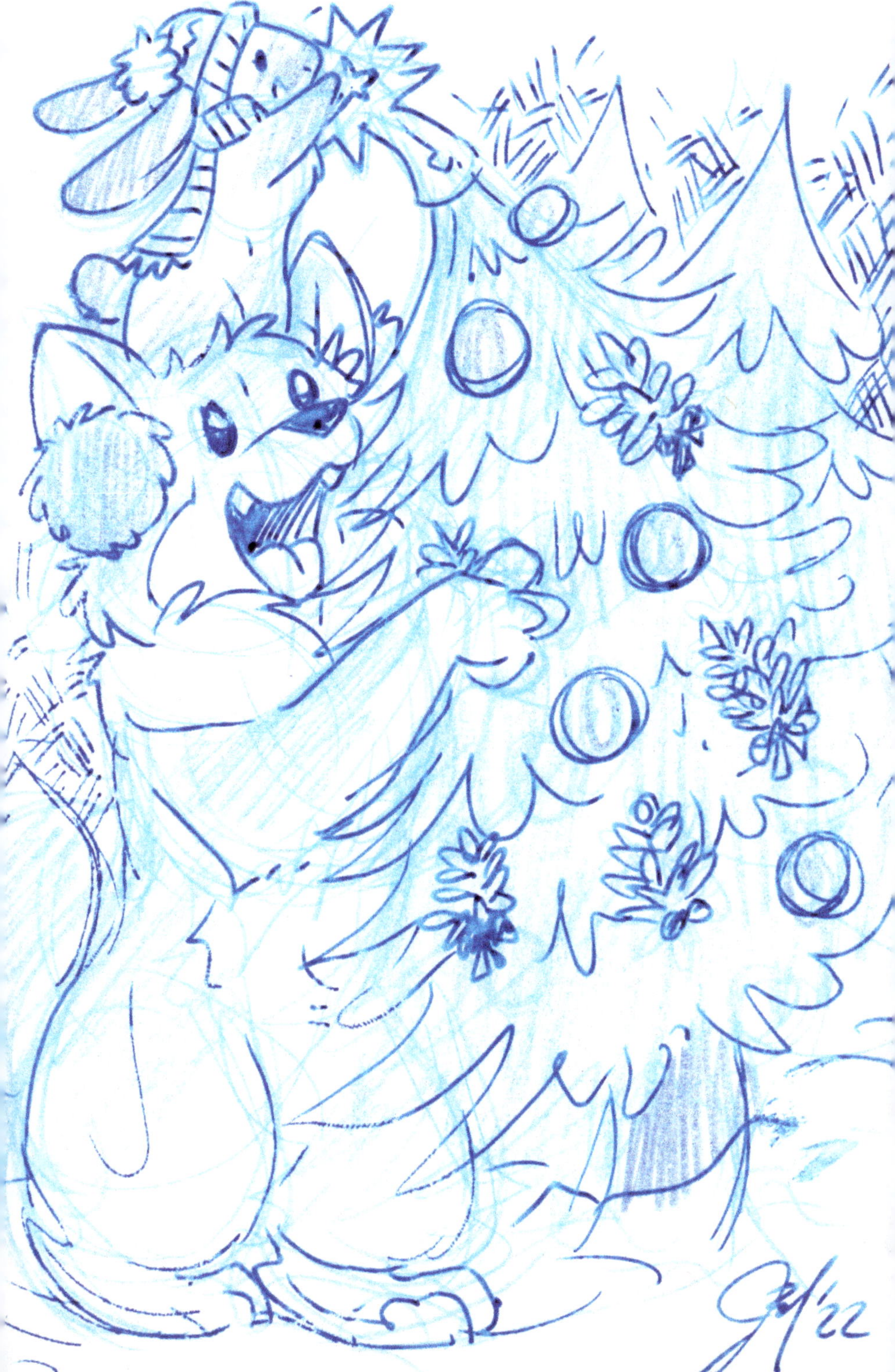

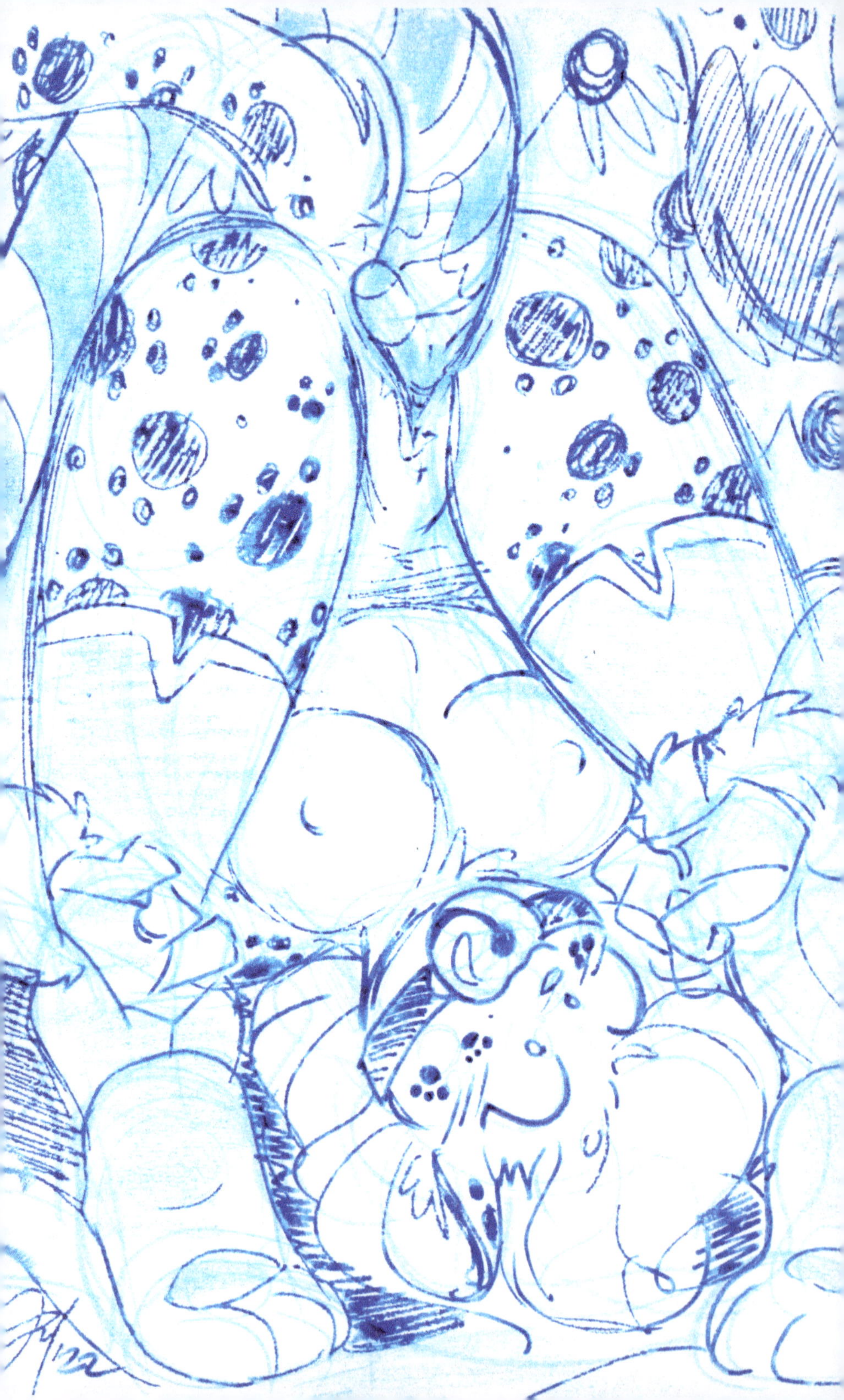

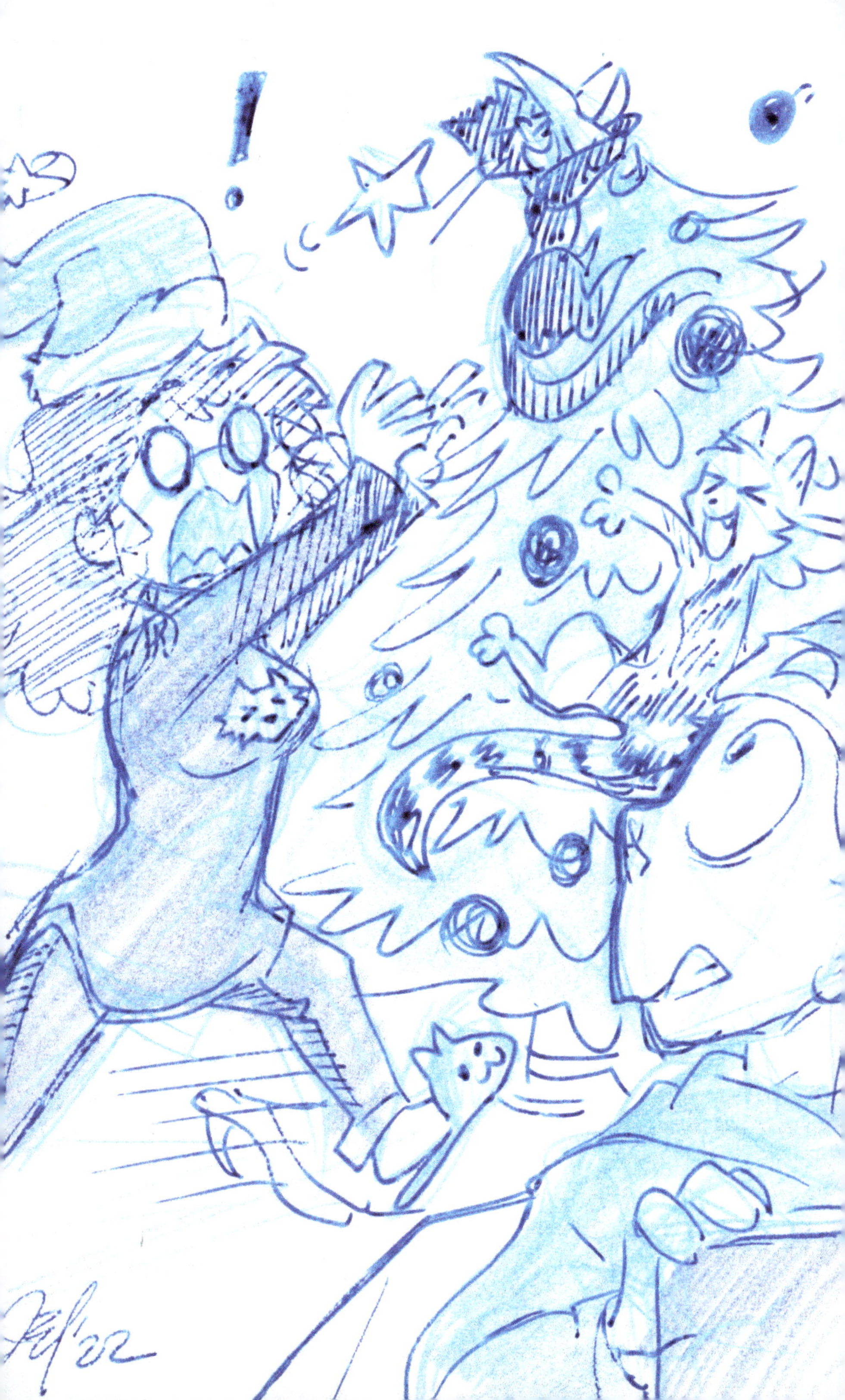

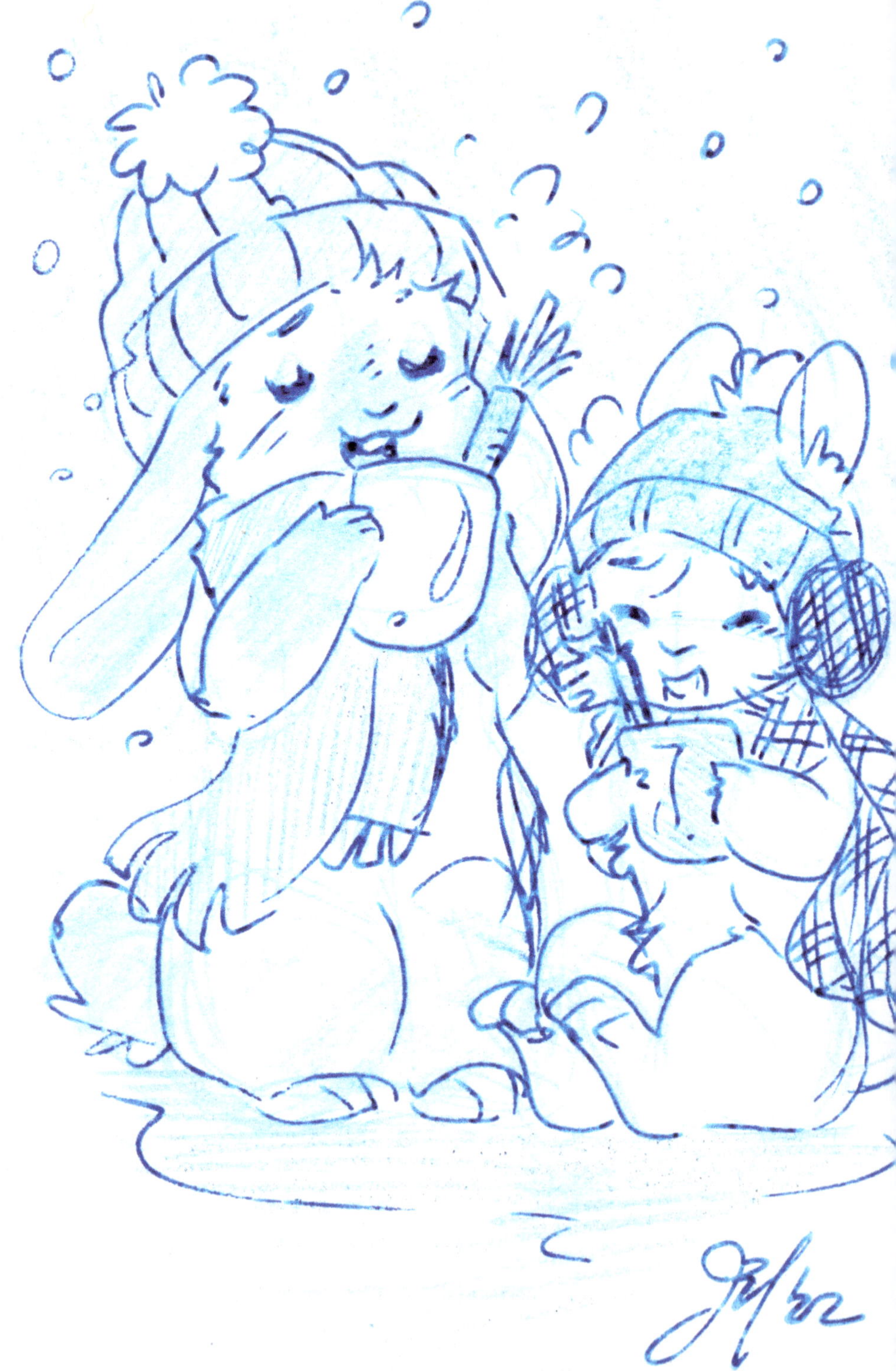

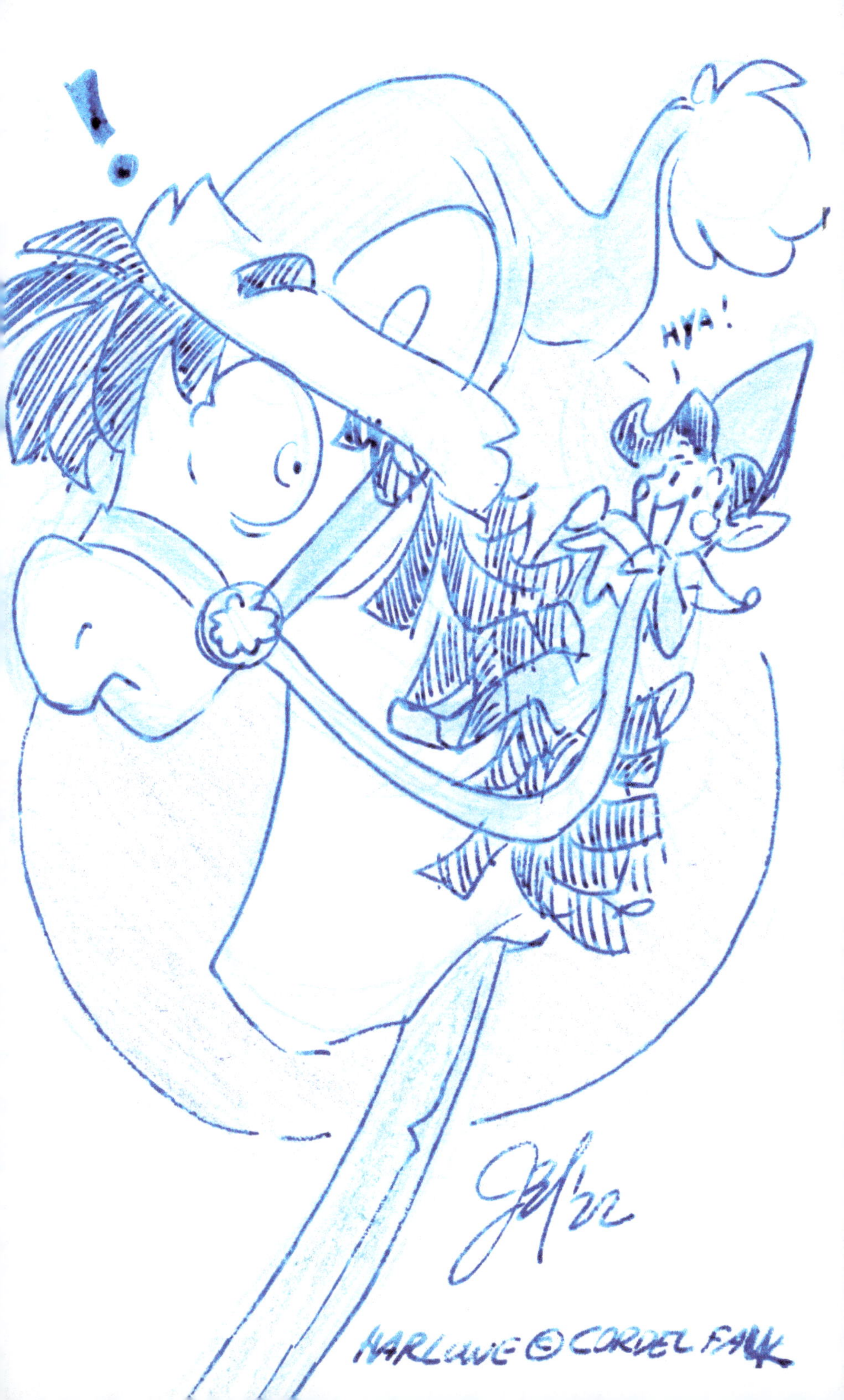
!
HYA!
MARLANE © CORDEL FALK

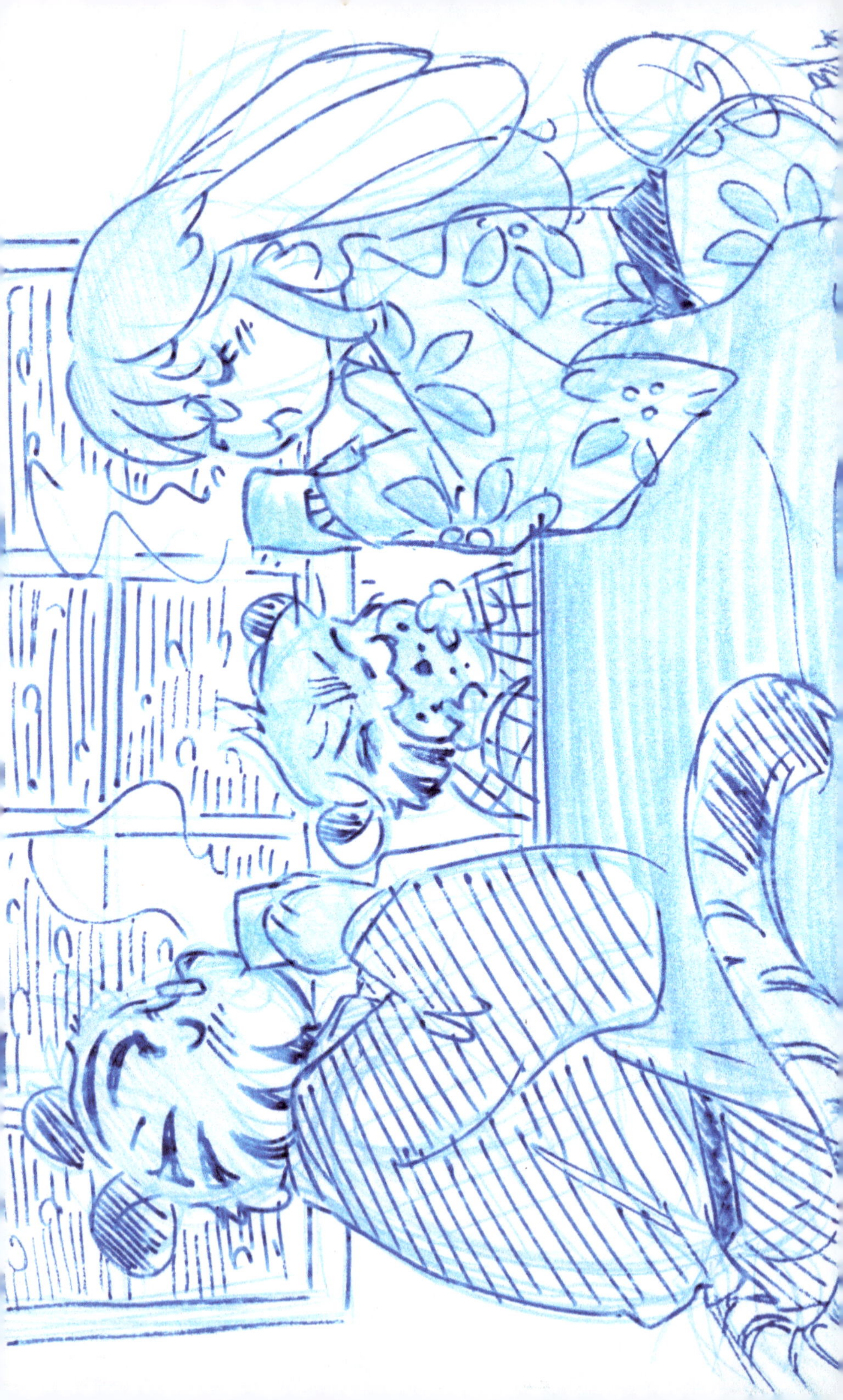

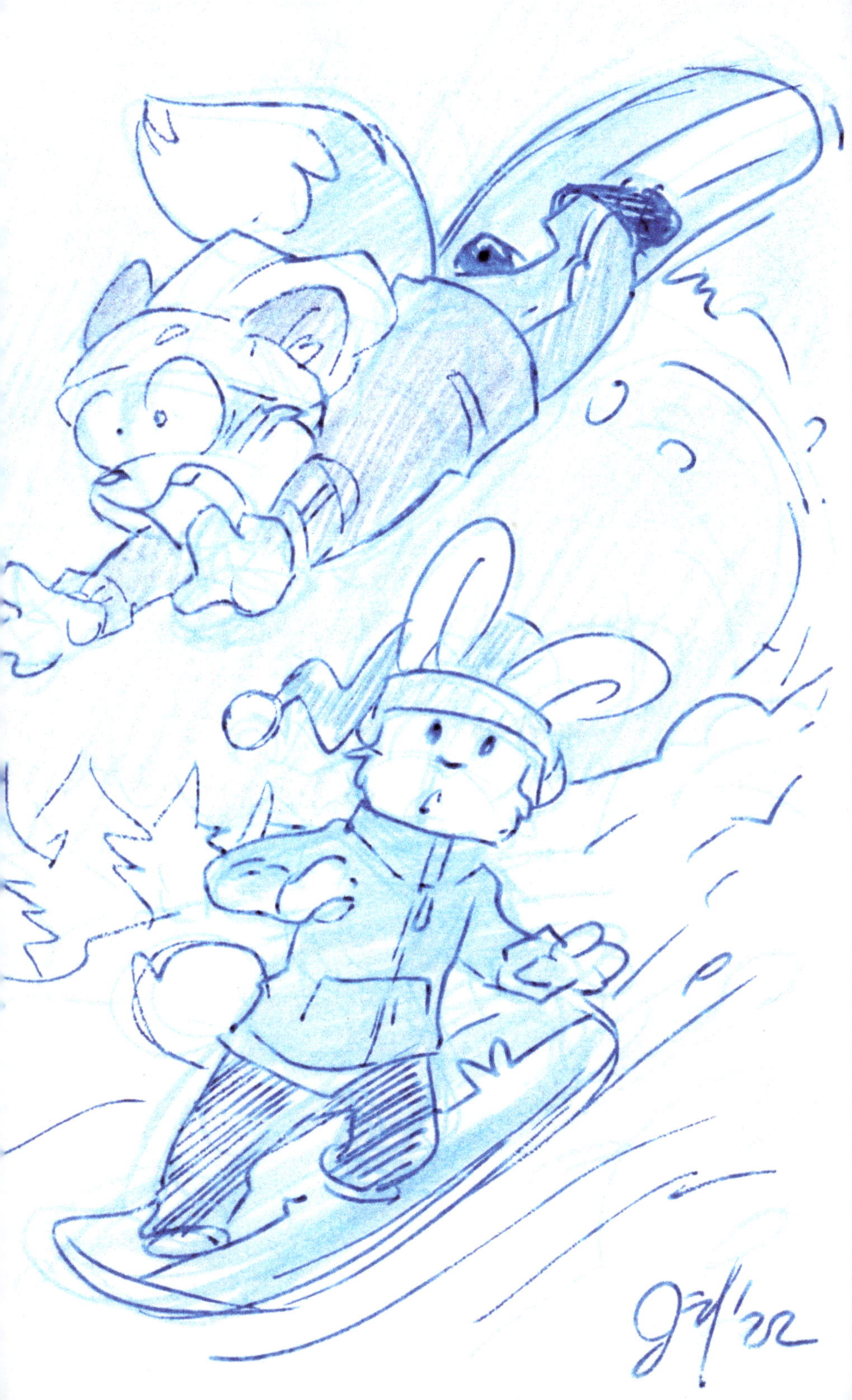

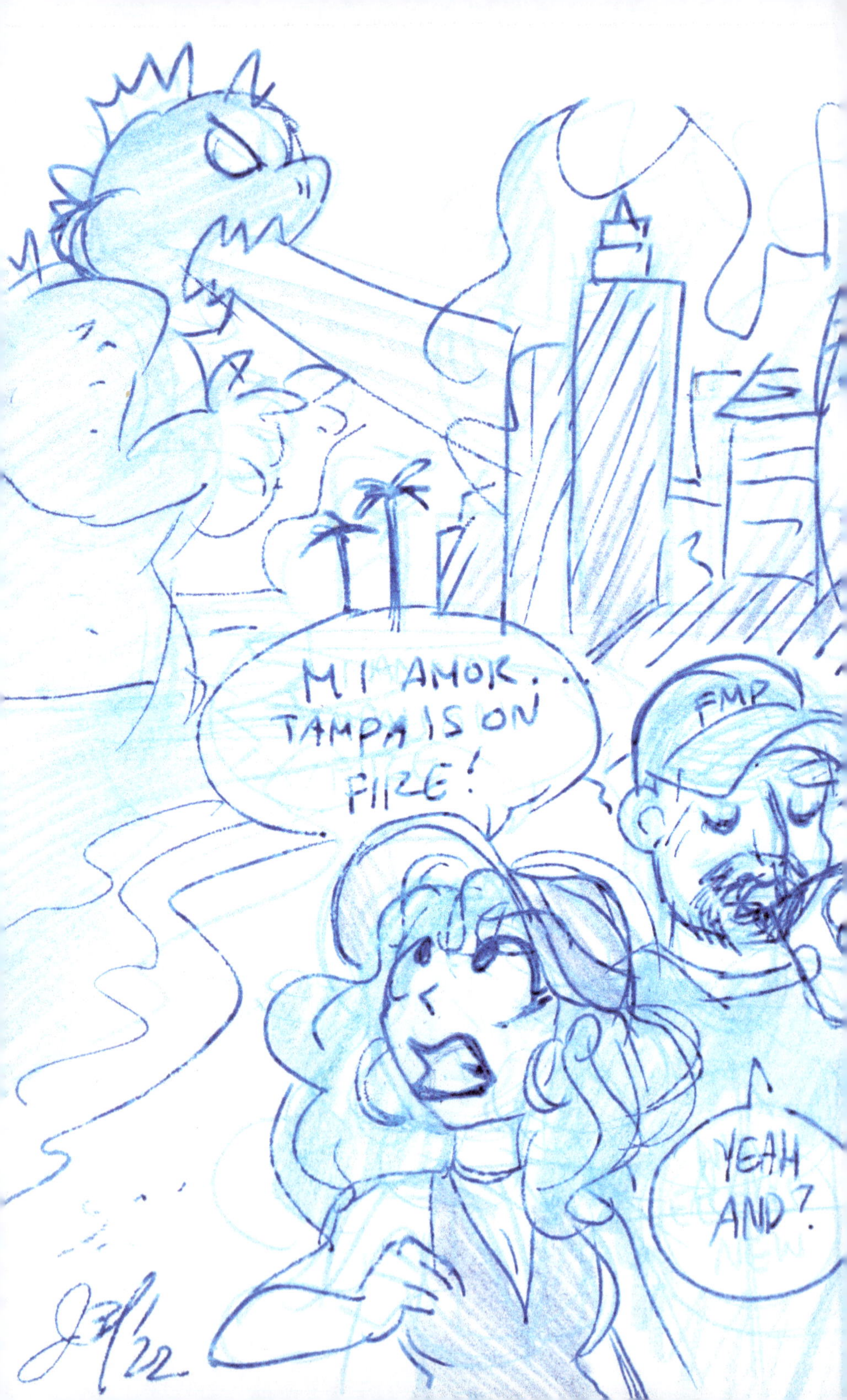

MI AMOR... TAMPA IS ON FIRE!
FMP
YEAH AND?

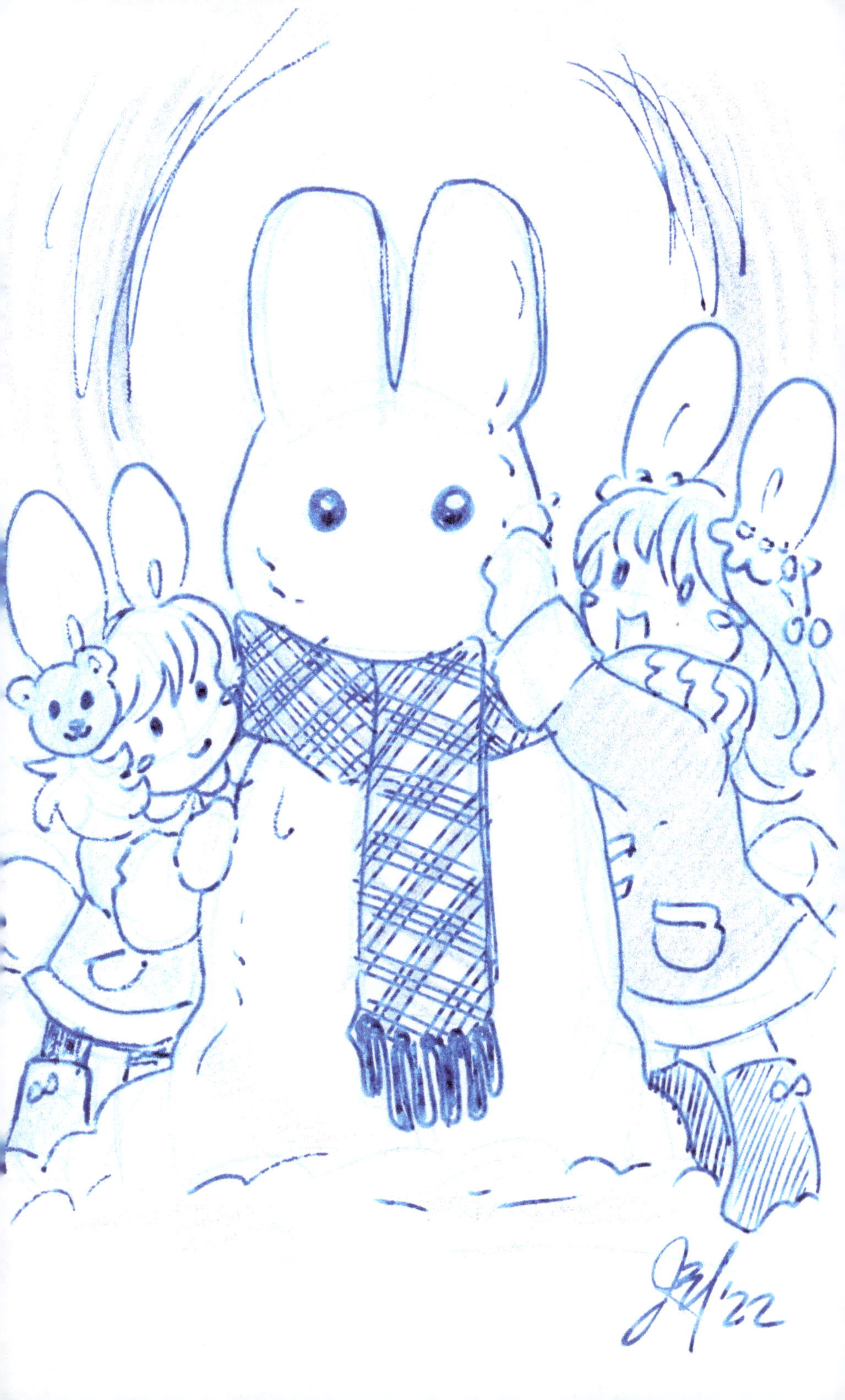

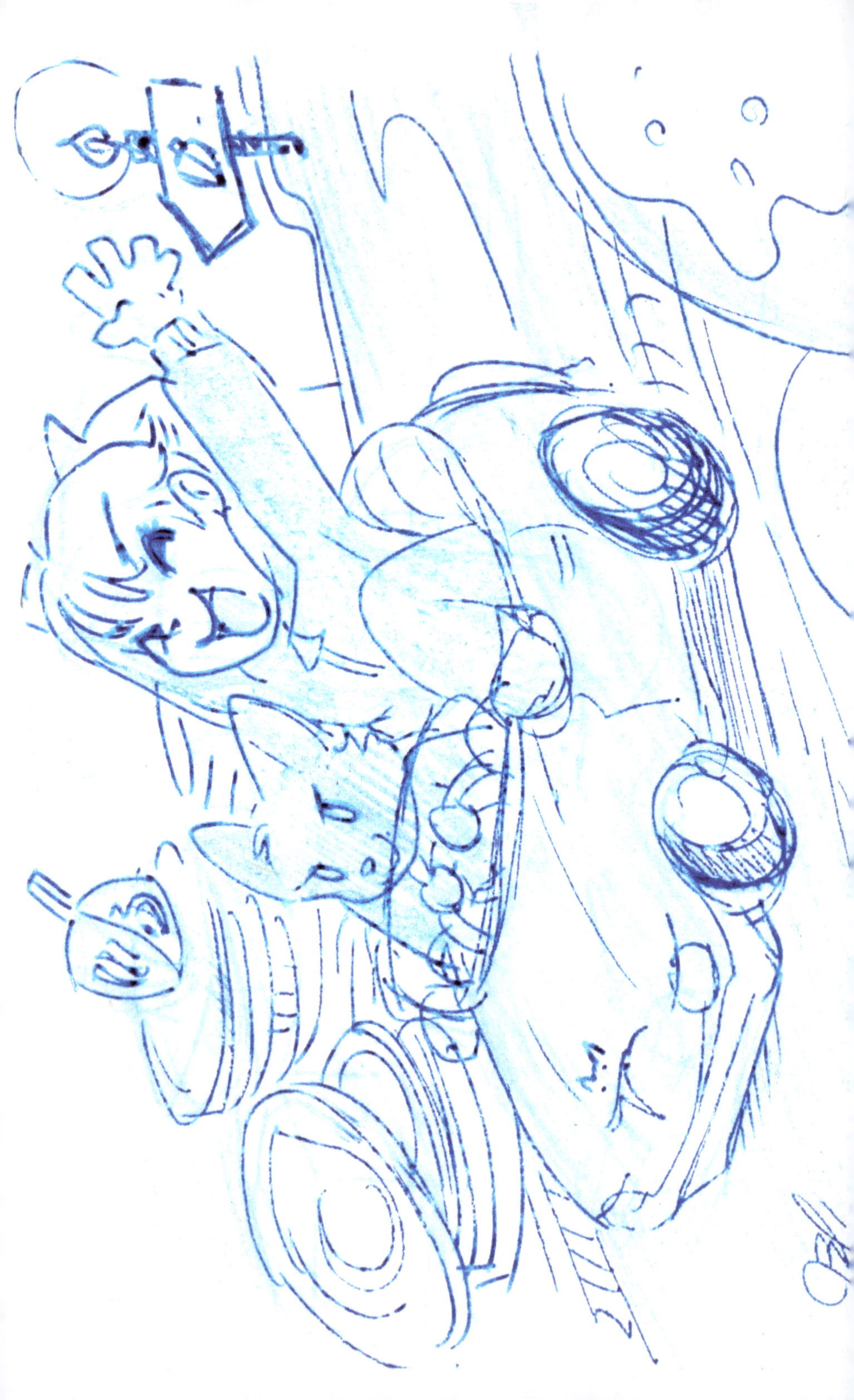

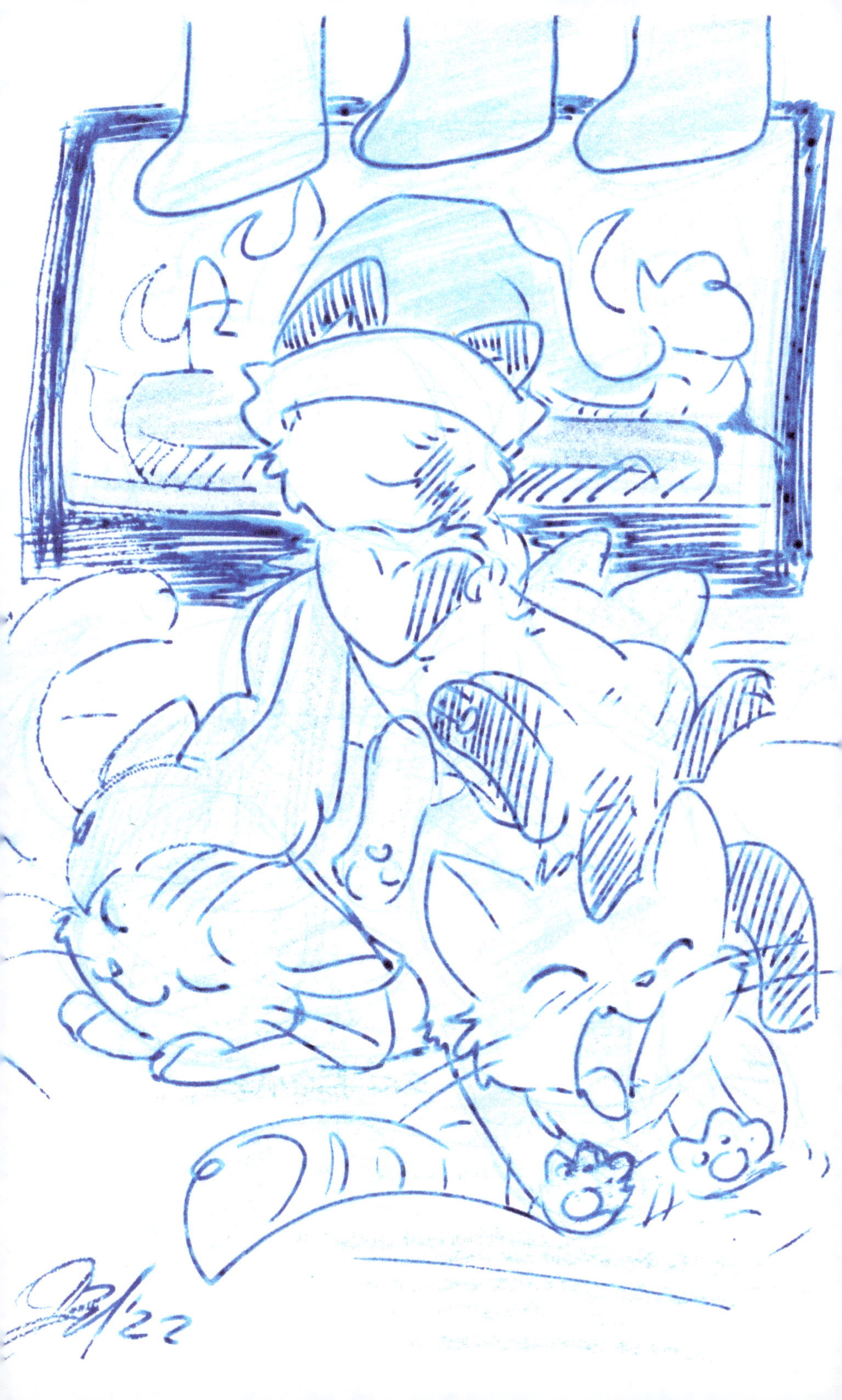

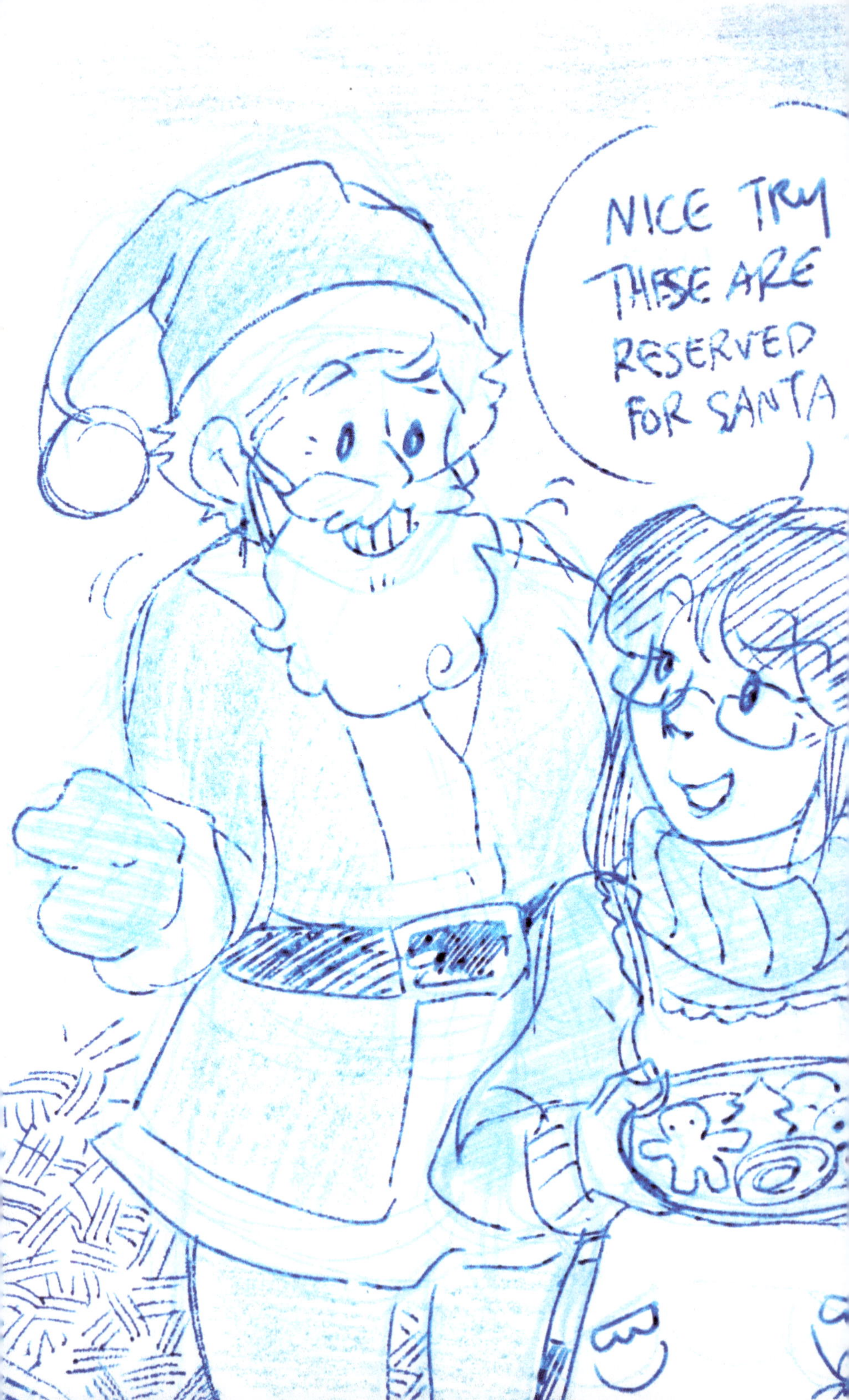

NICE TRY
THESE ARE
RESERVED
FOR SANTA

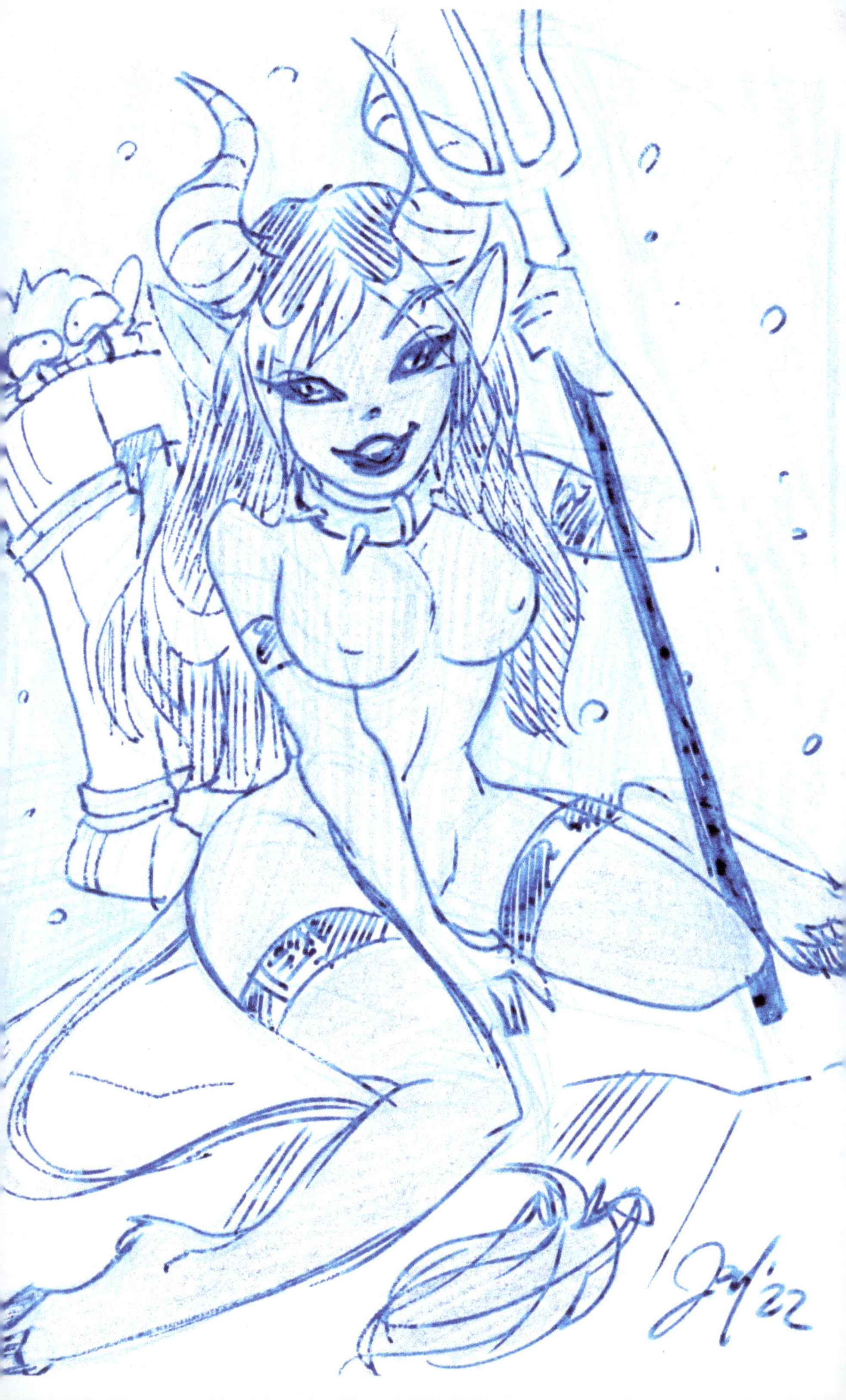

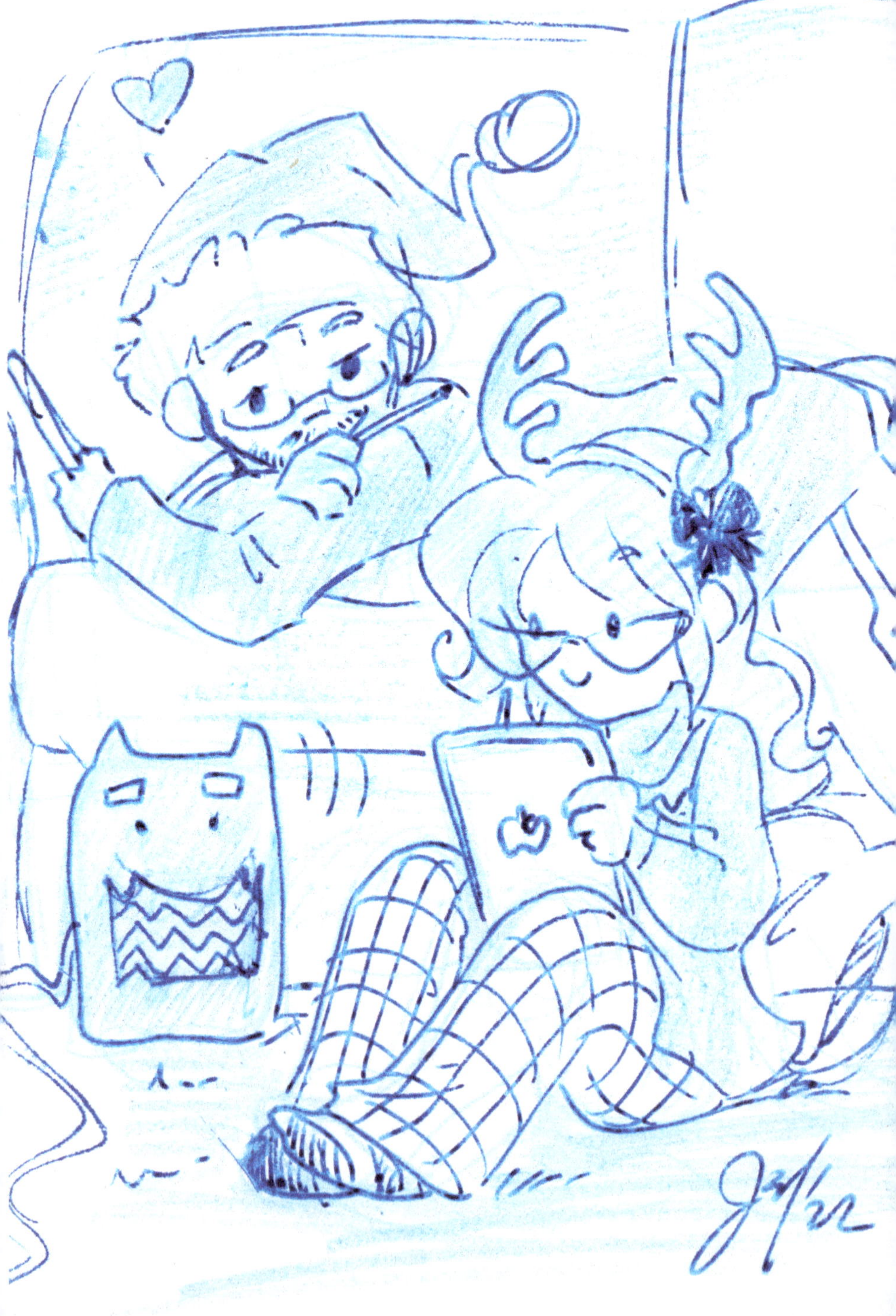

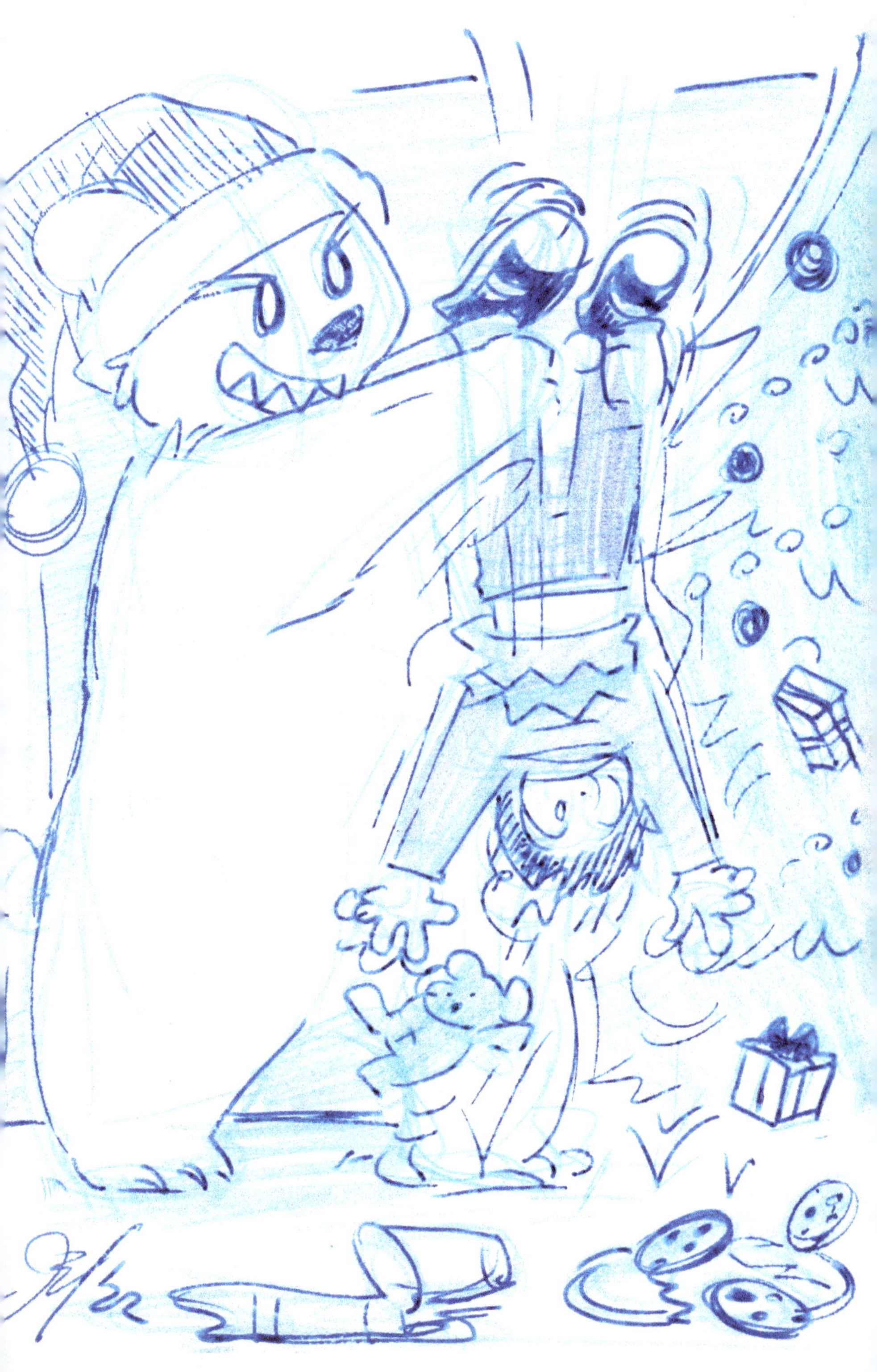

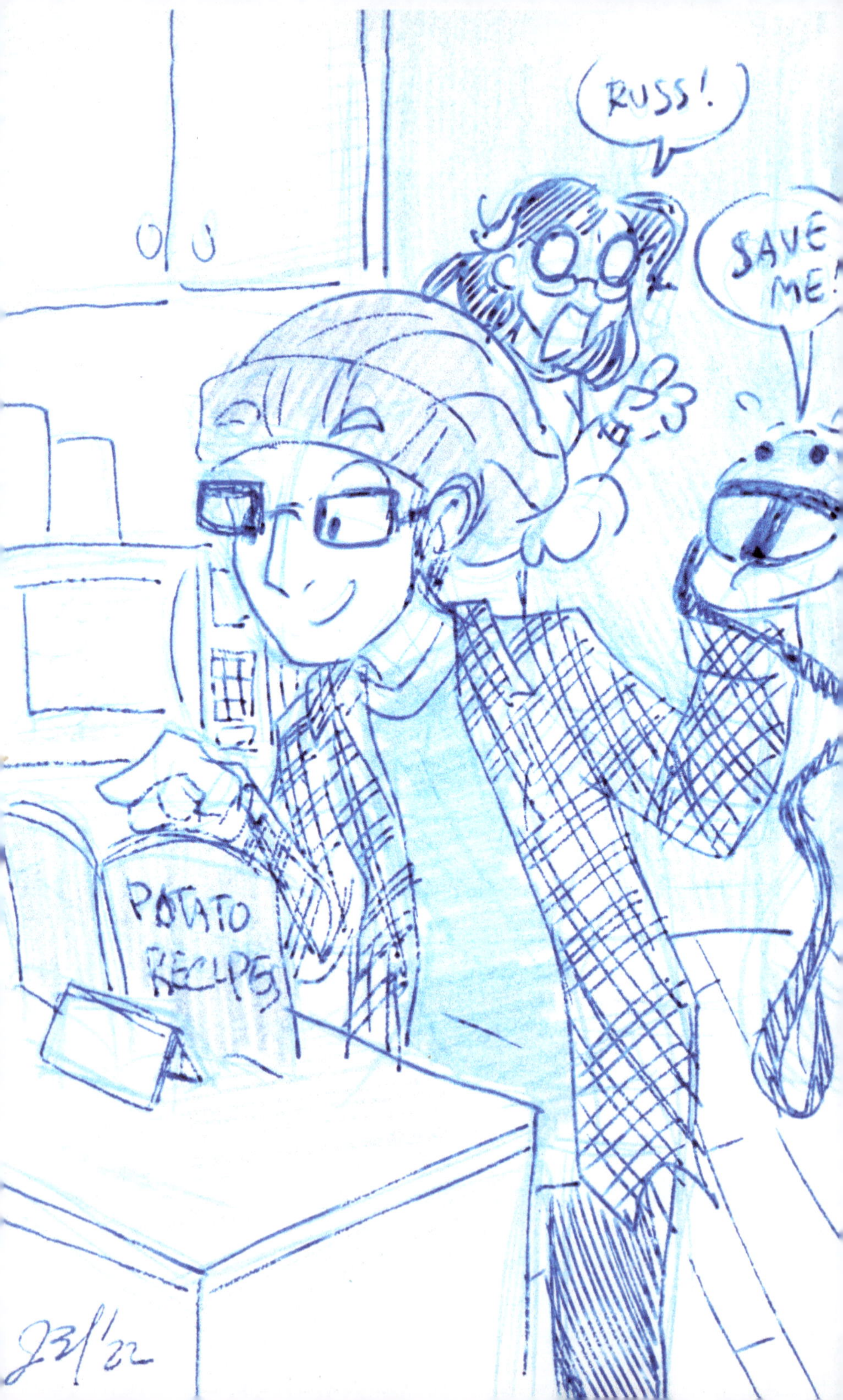

RUSS!
SAVE ME!
POTATO RECIPES

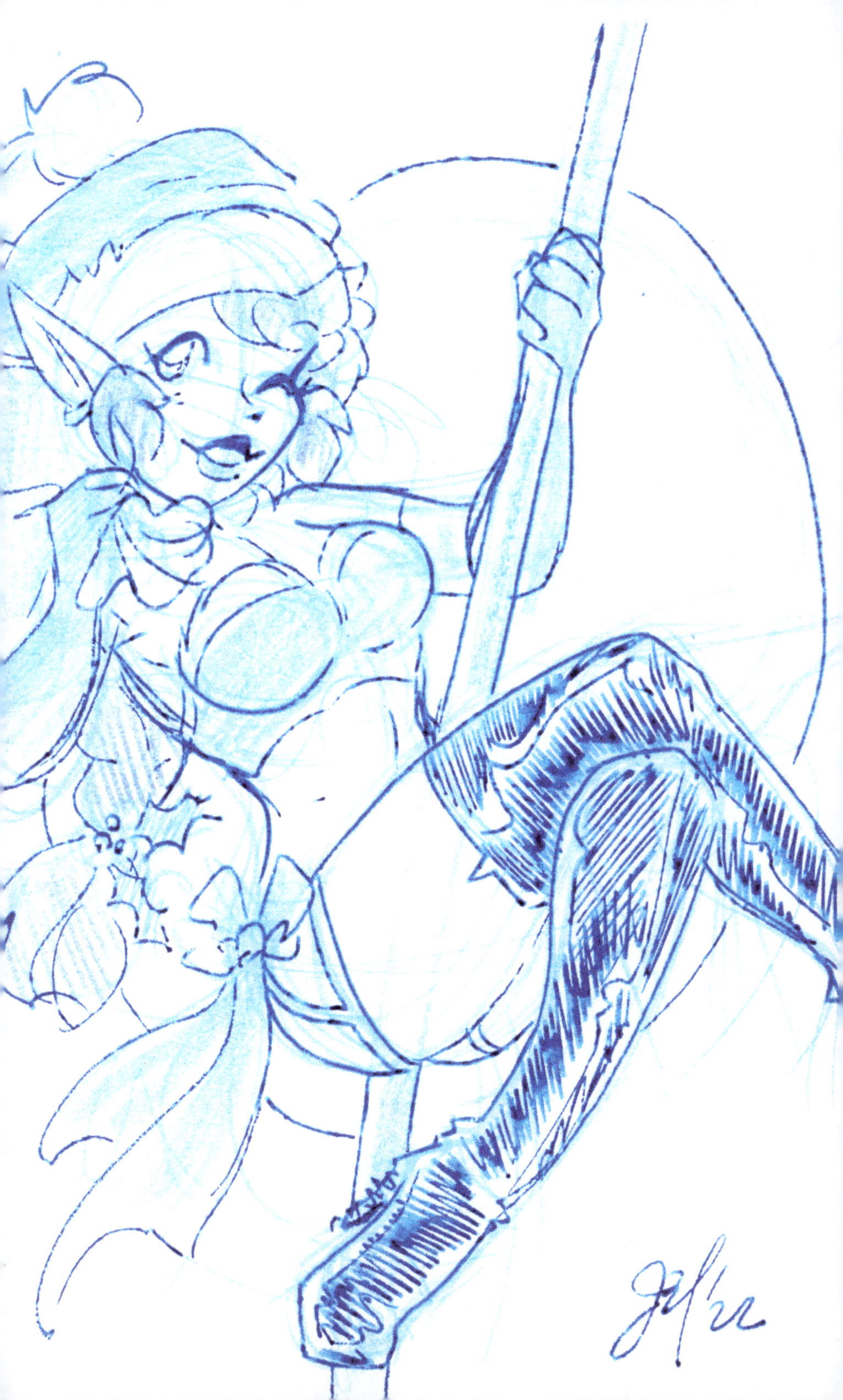

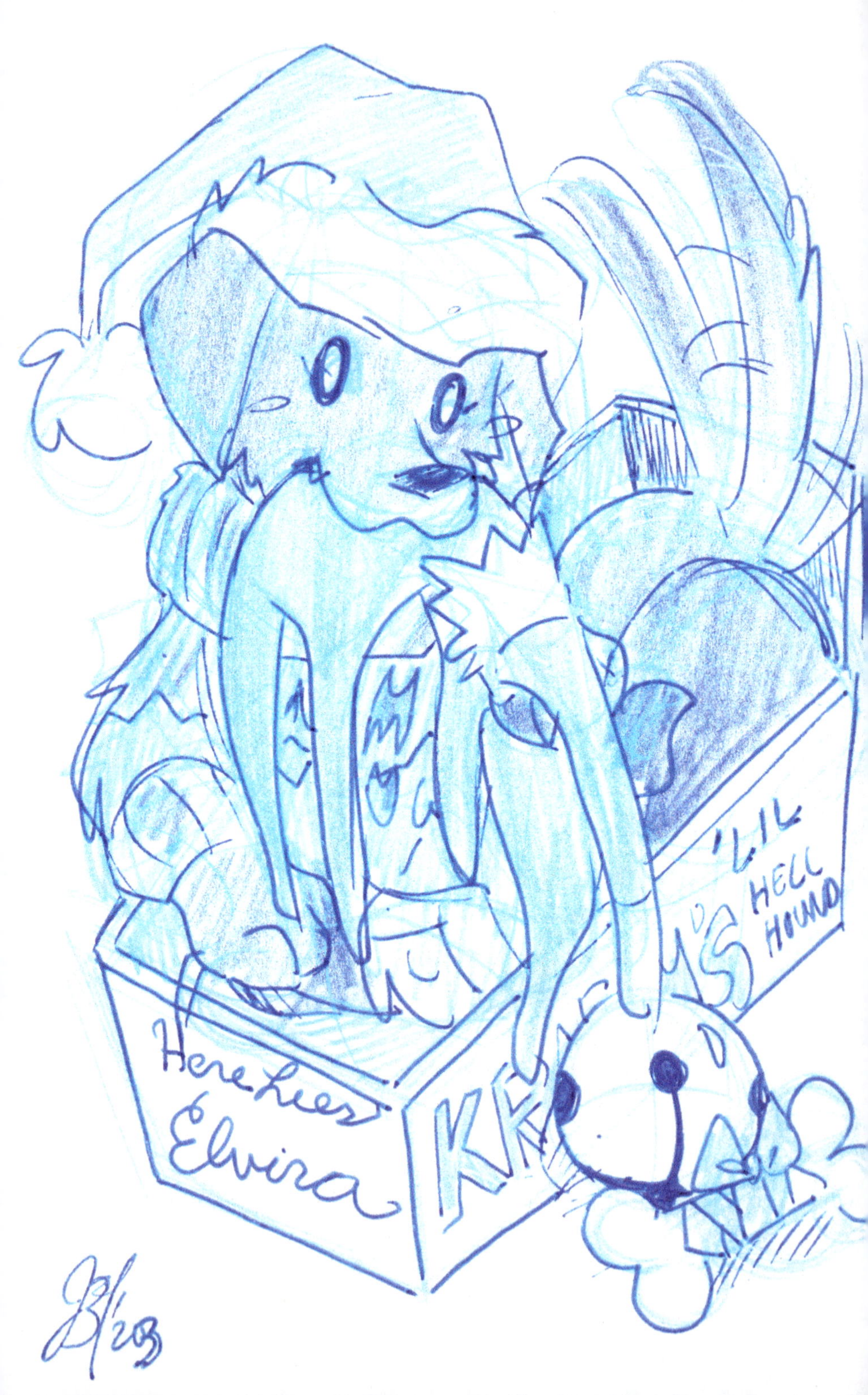

Here lies
Elvira
'LIL HELL HOUND
KRAMPUS

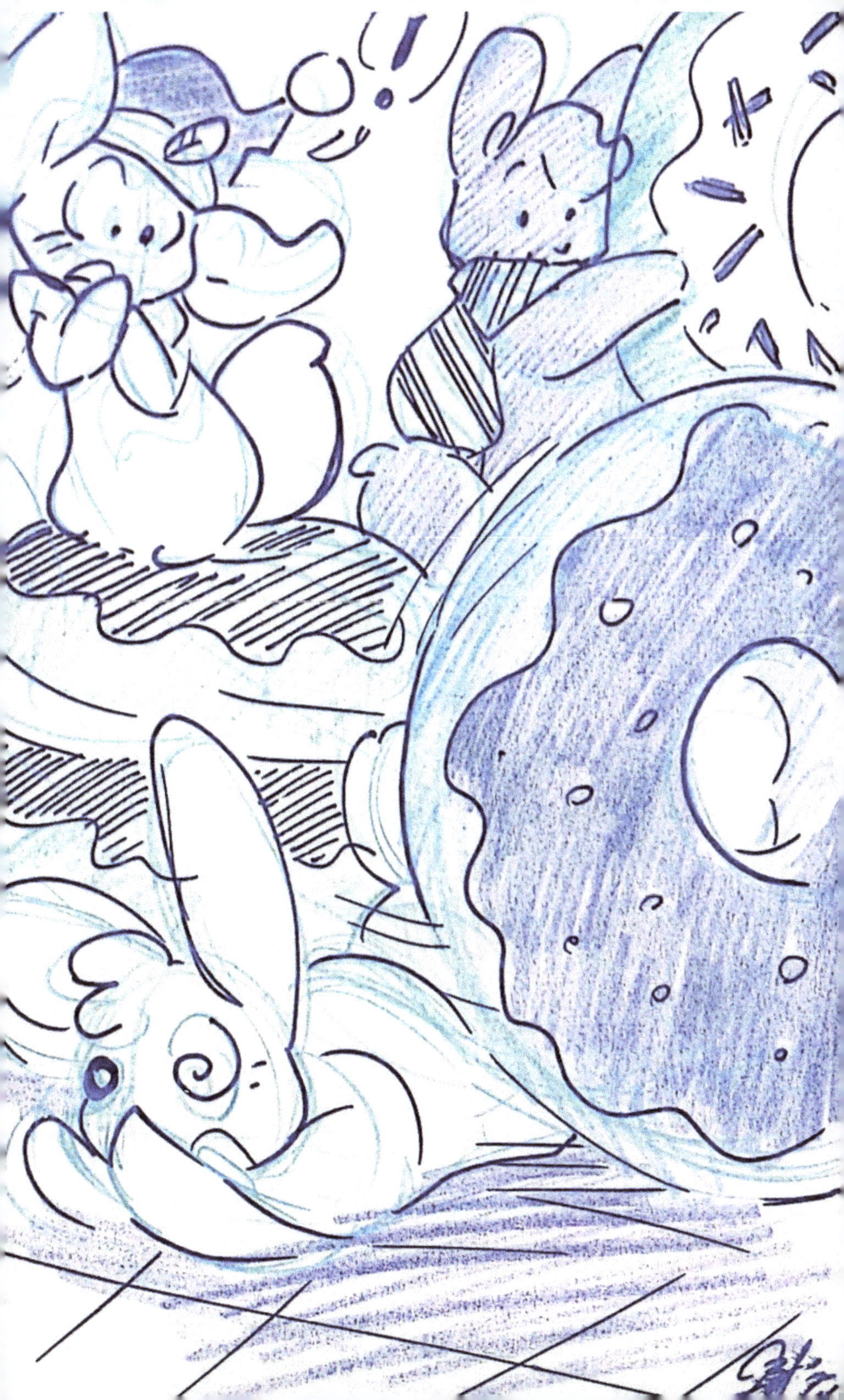

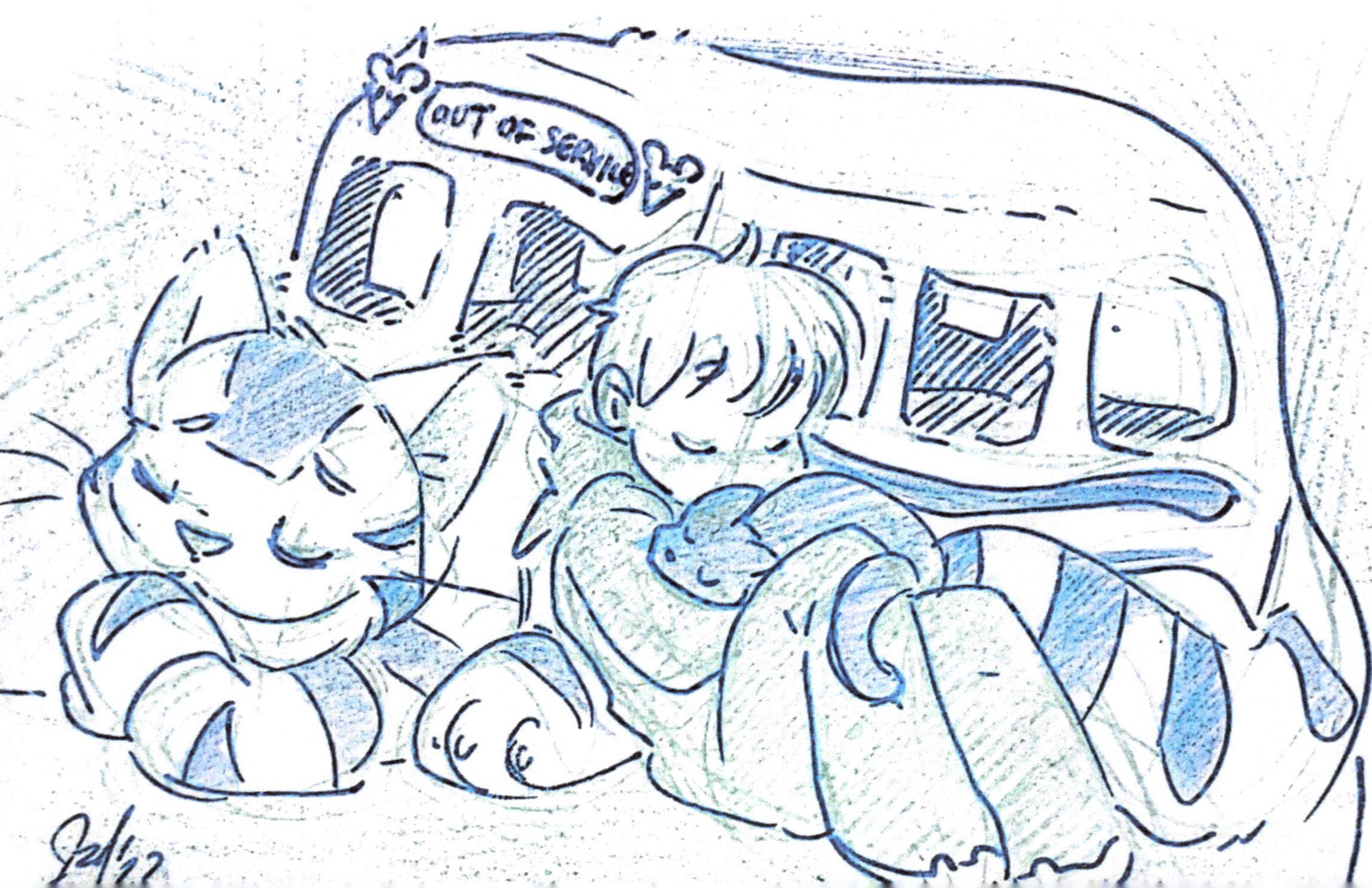

OUT OF SERVICE

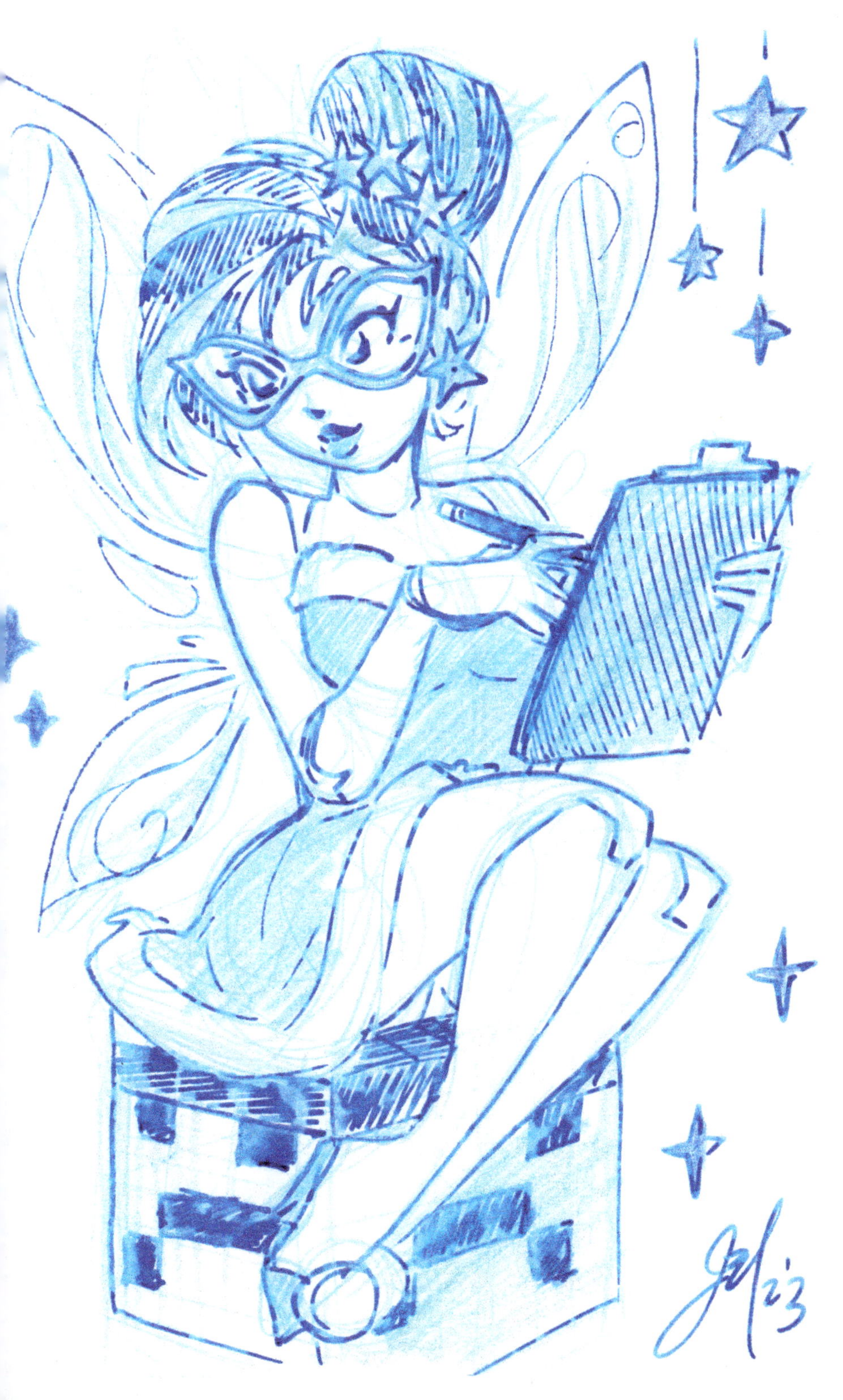

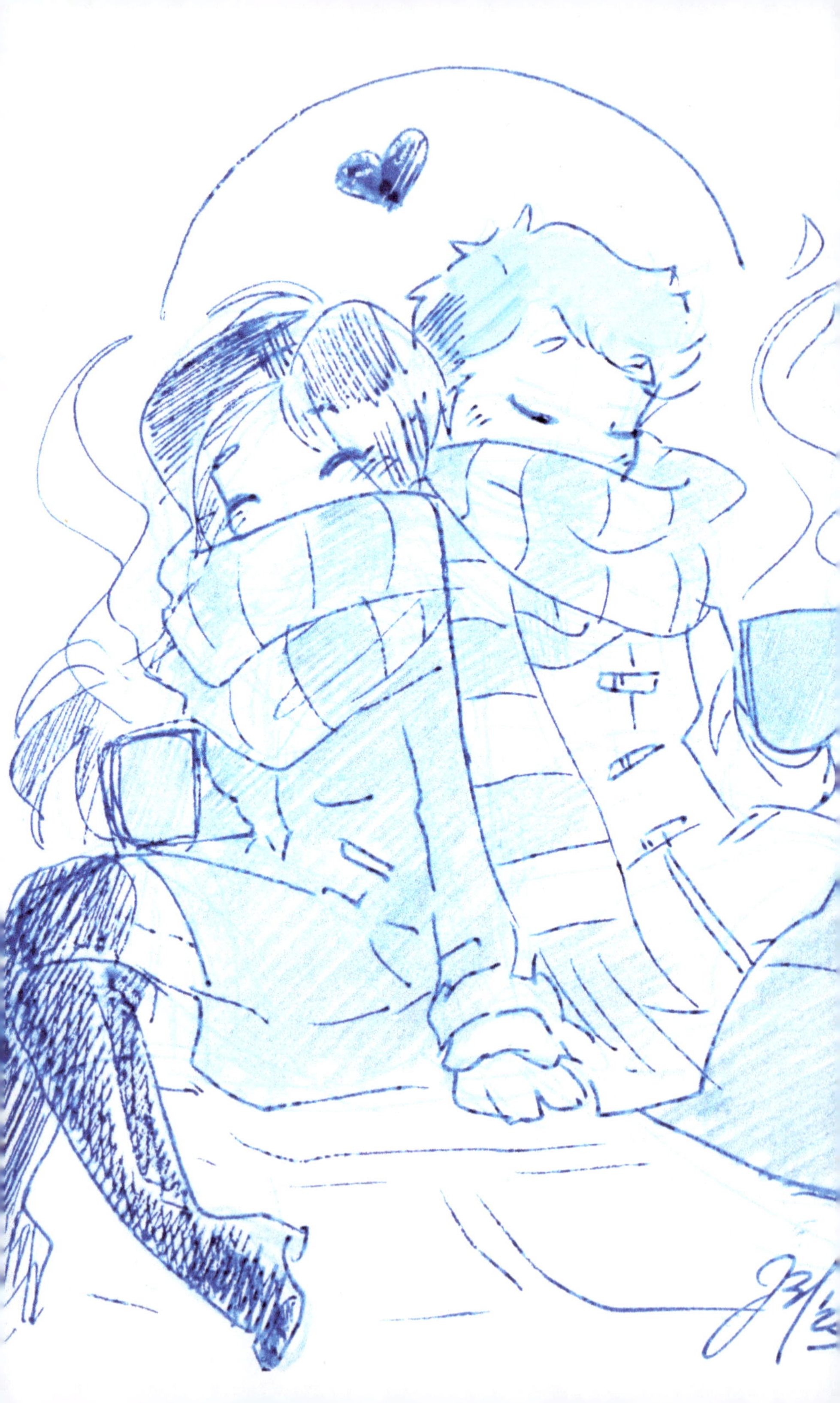

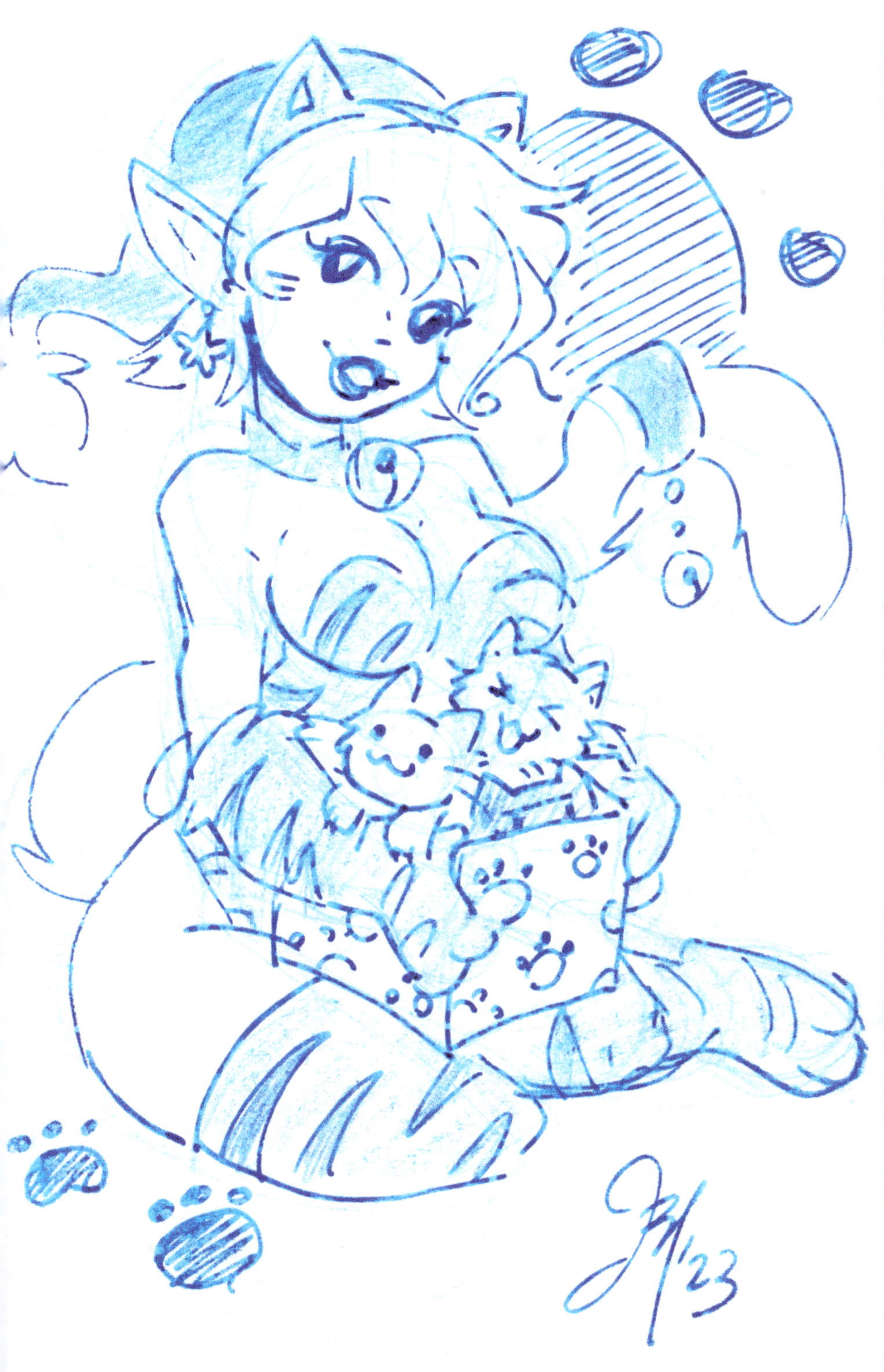

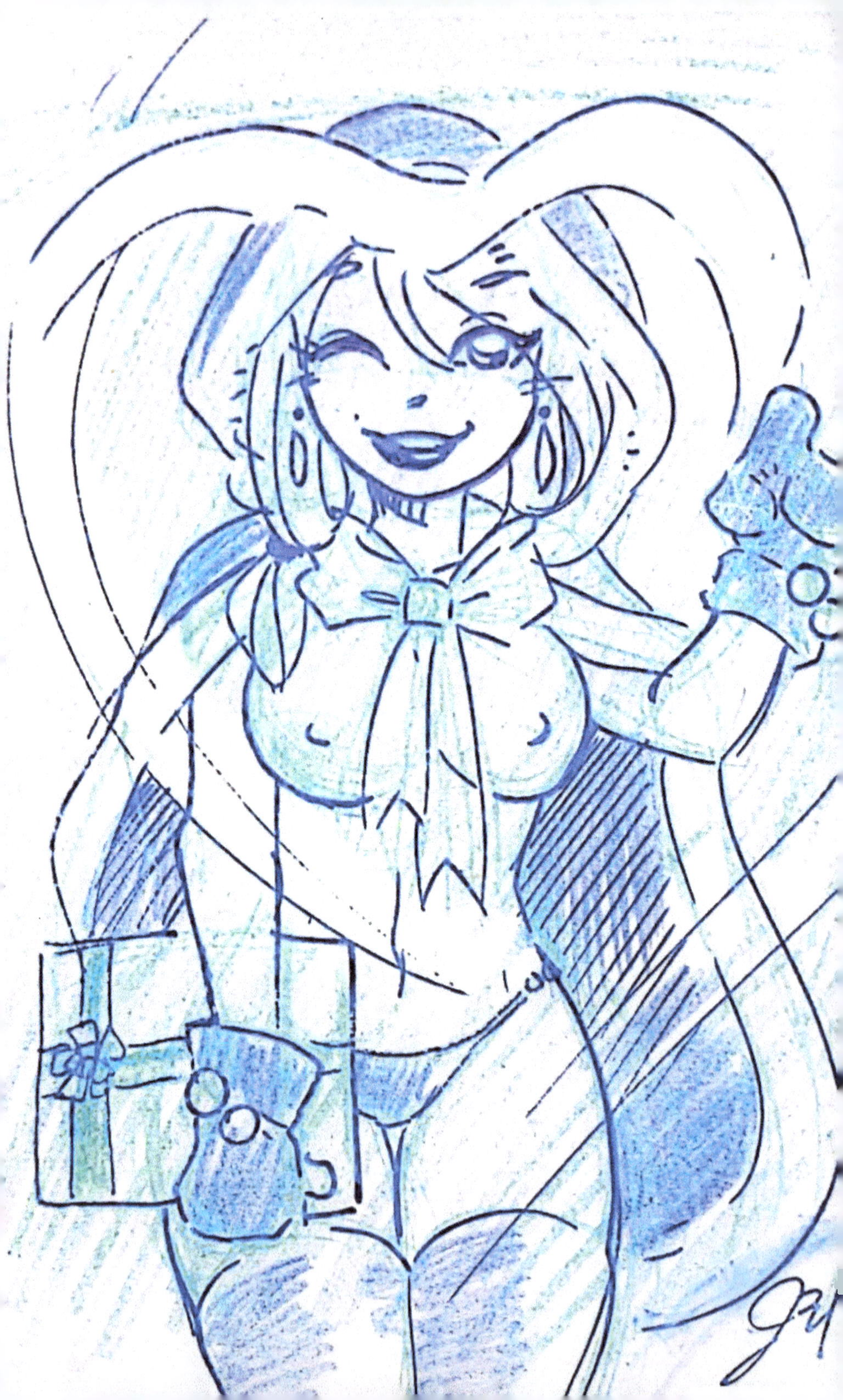

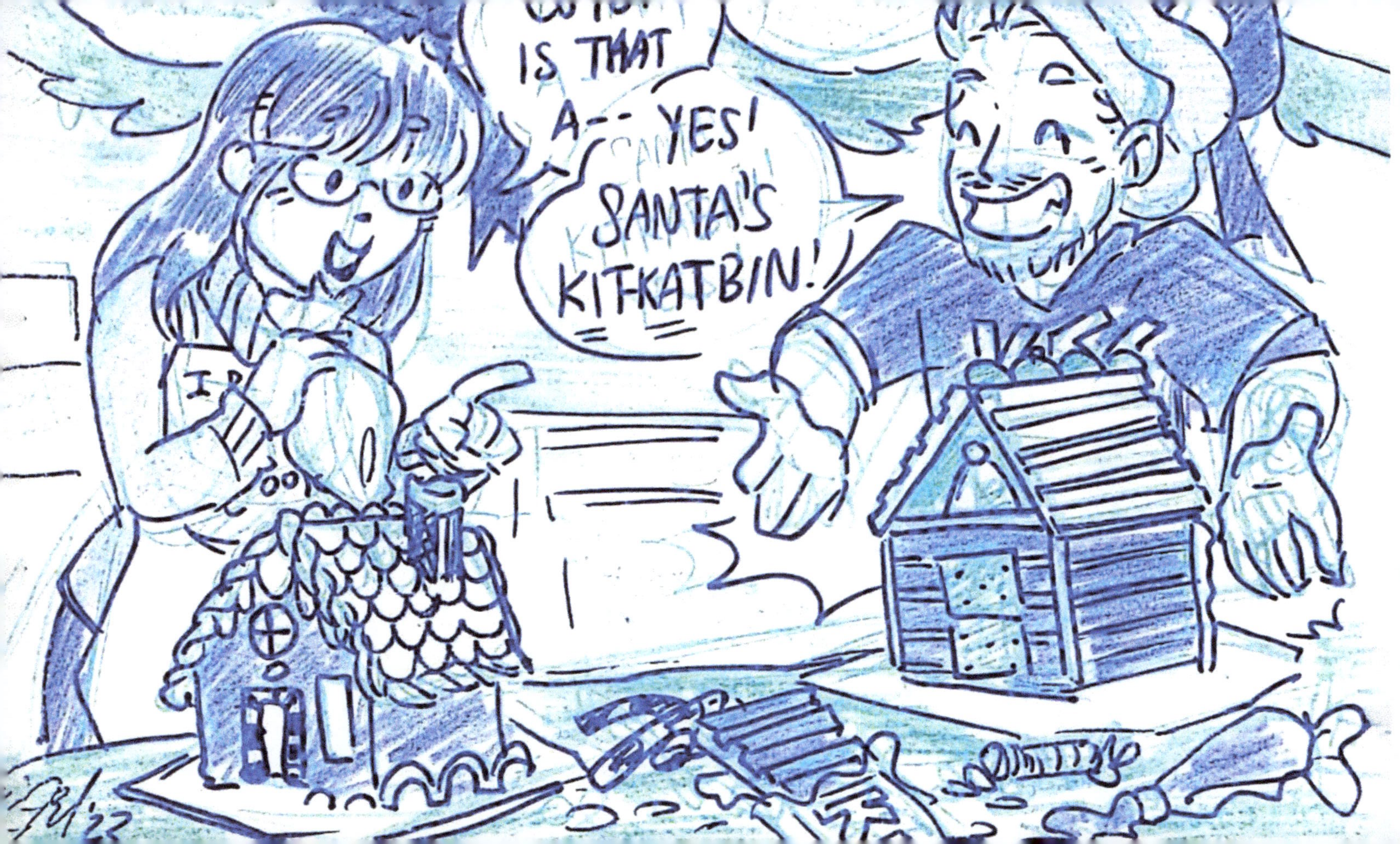
WHAT IS THAT A-- YES!
SANTA'S KITKATBIN!

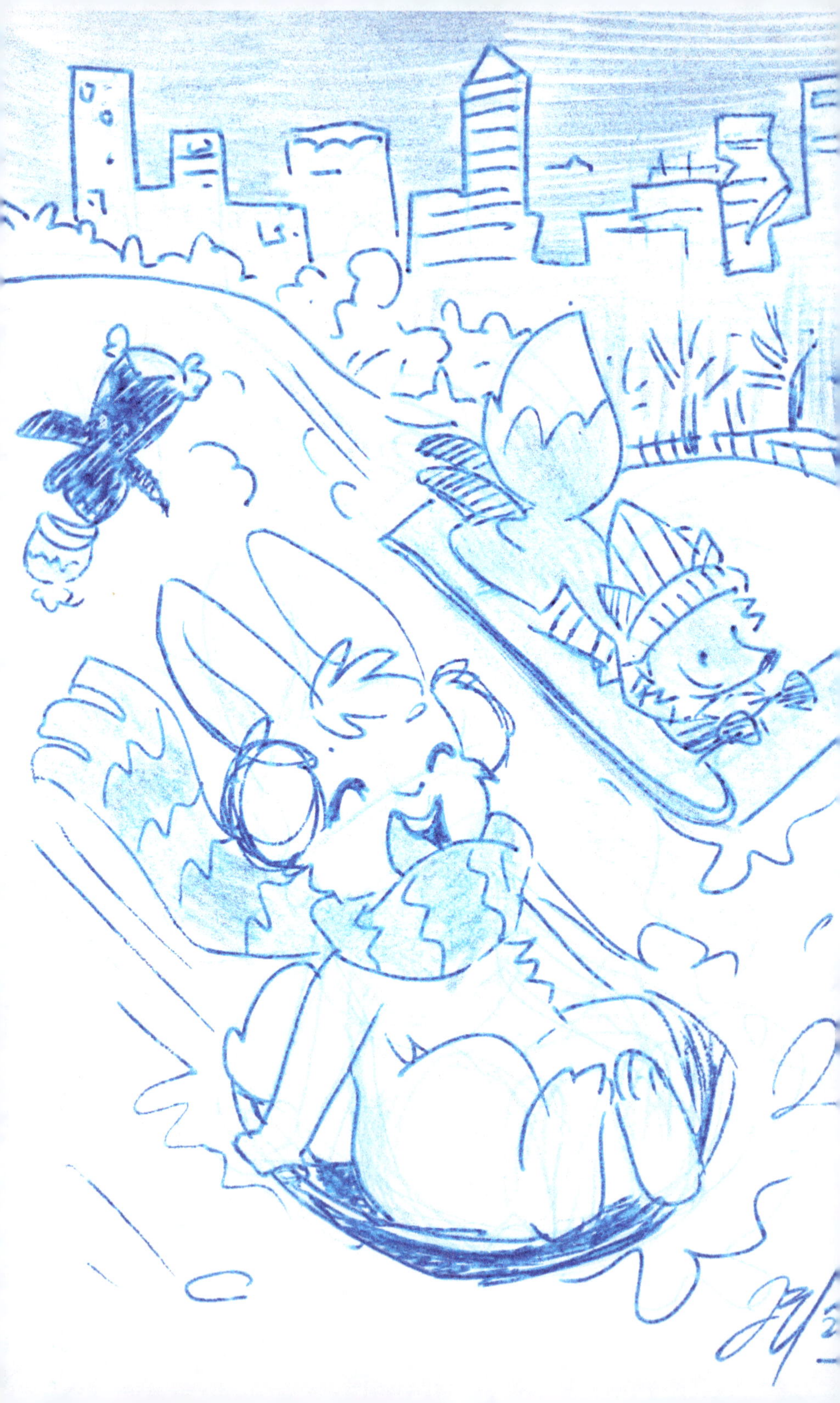

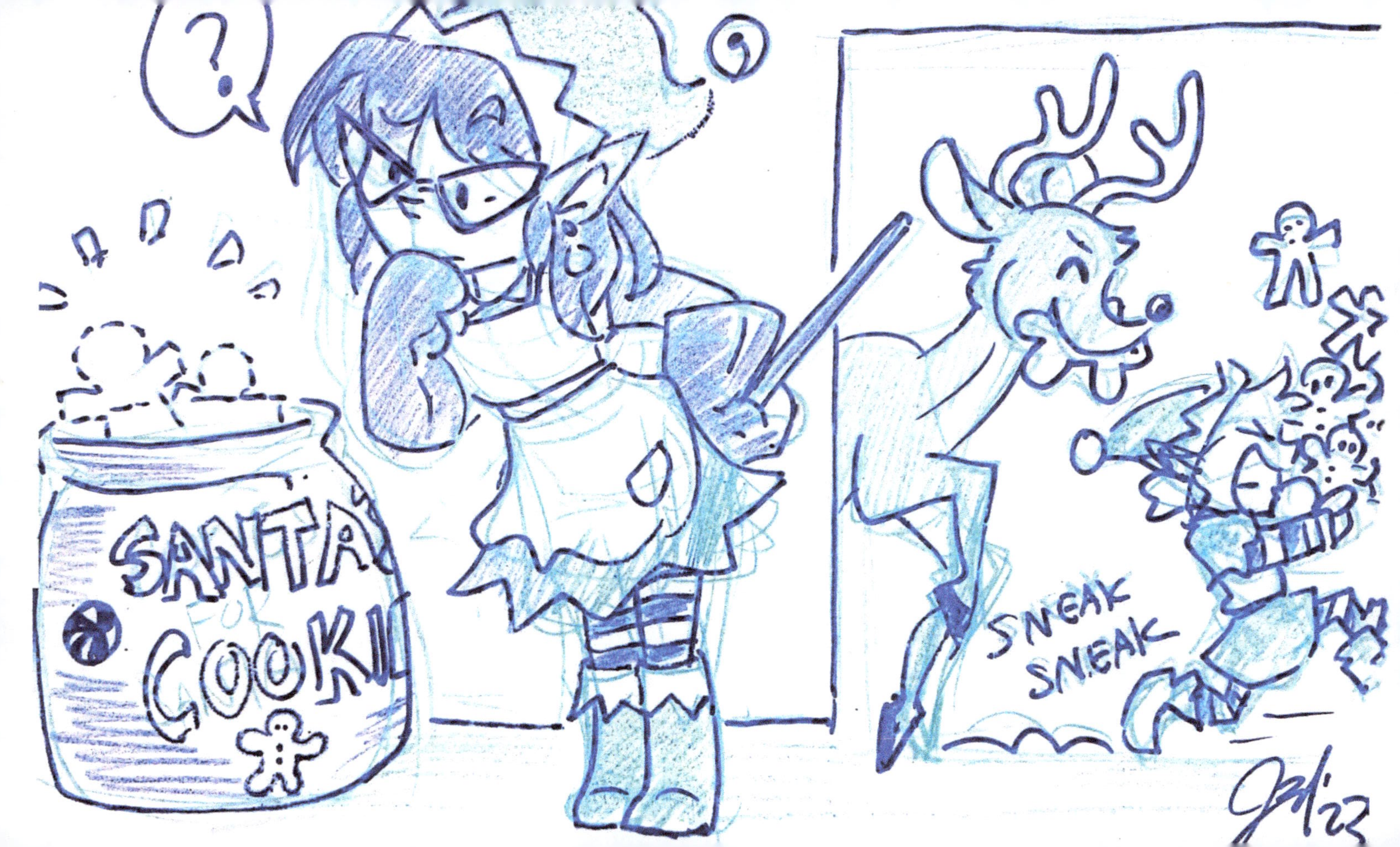

SANTA COOKII
SNEAK SNEAK

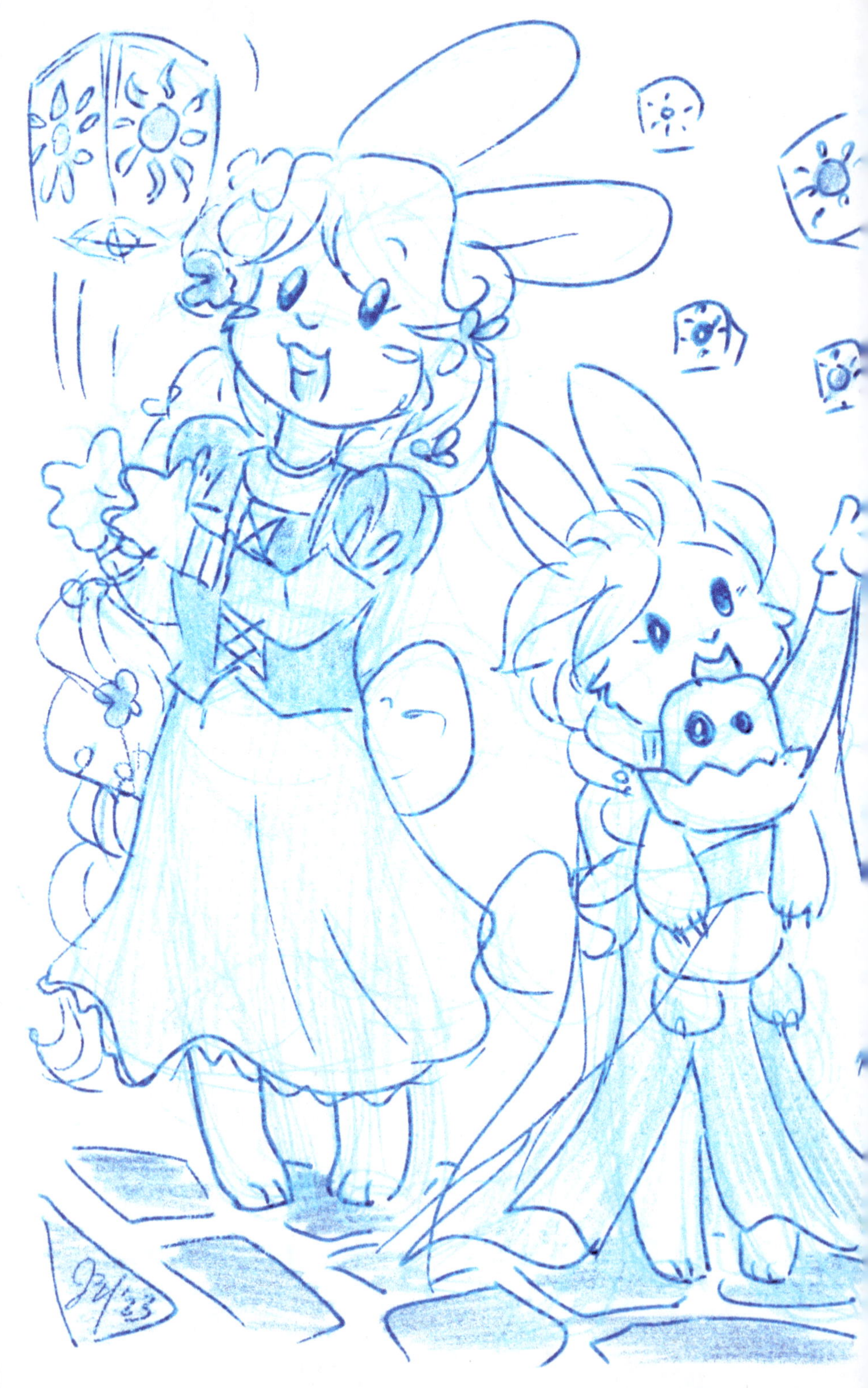

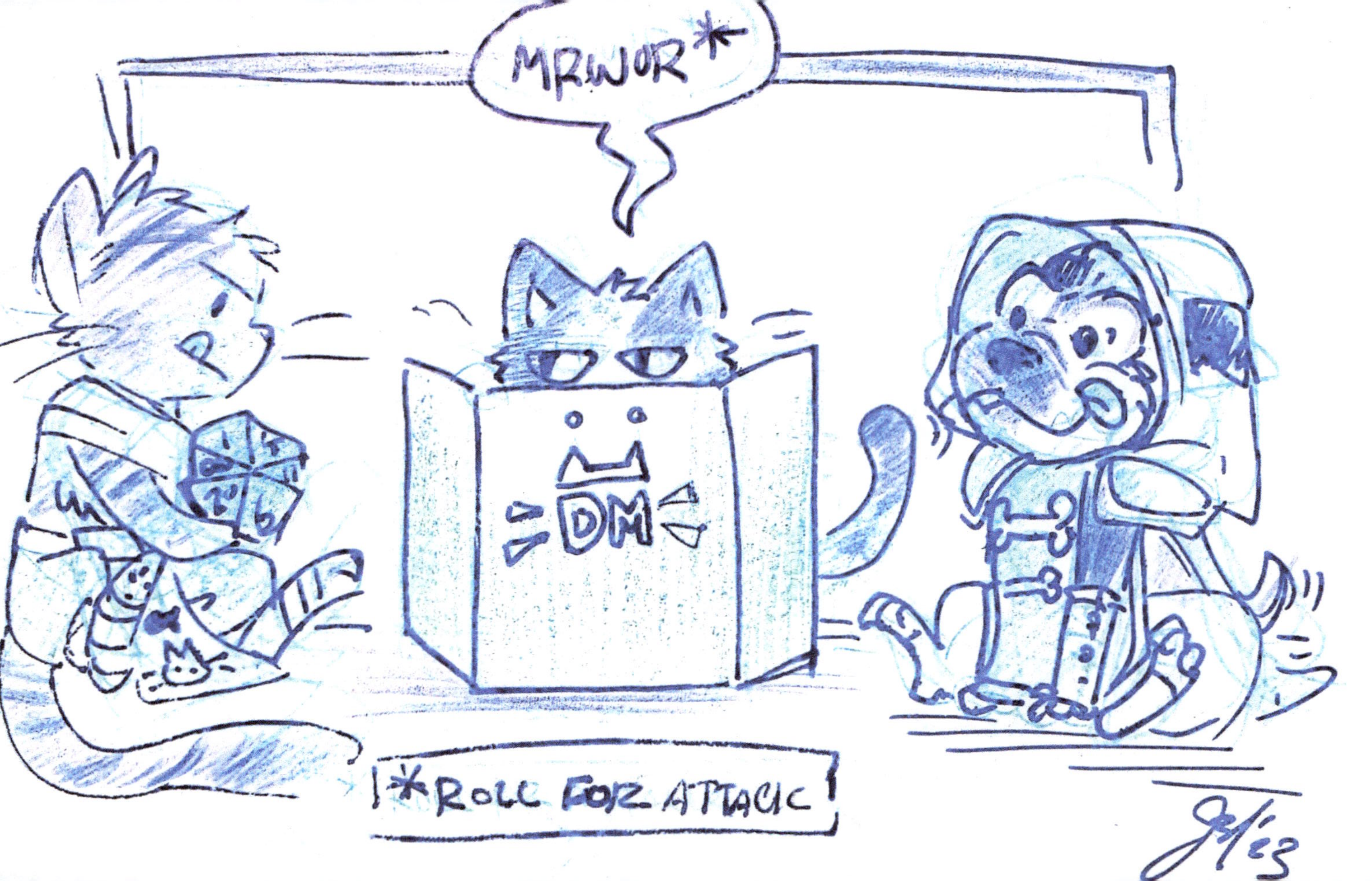

MRWOR *
DM
* ROLL FOR ATTACK

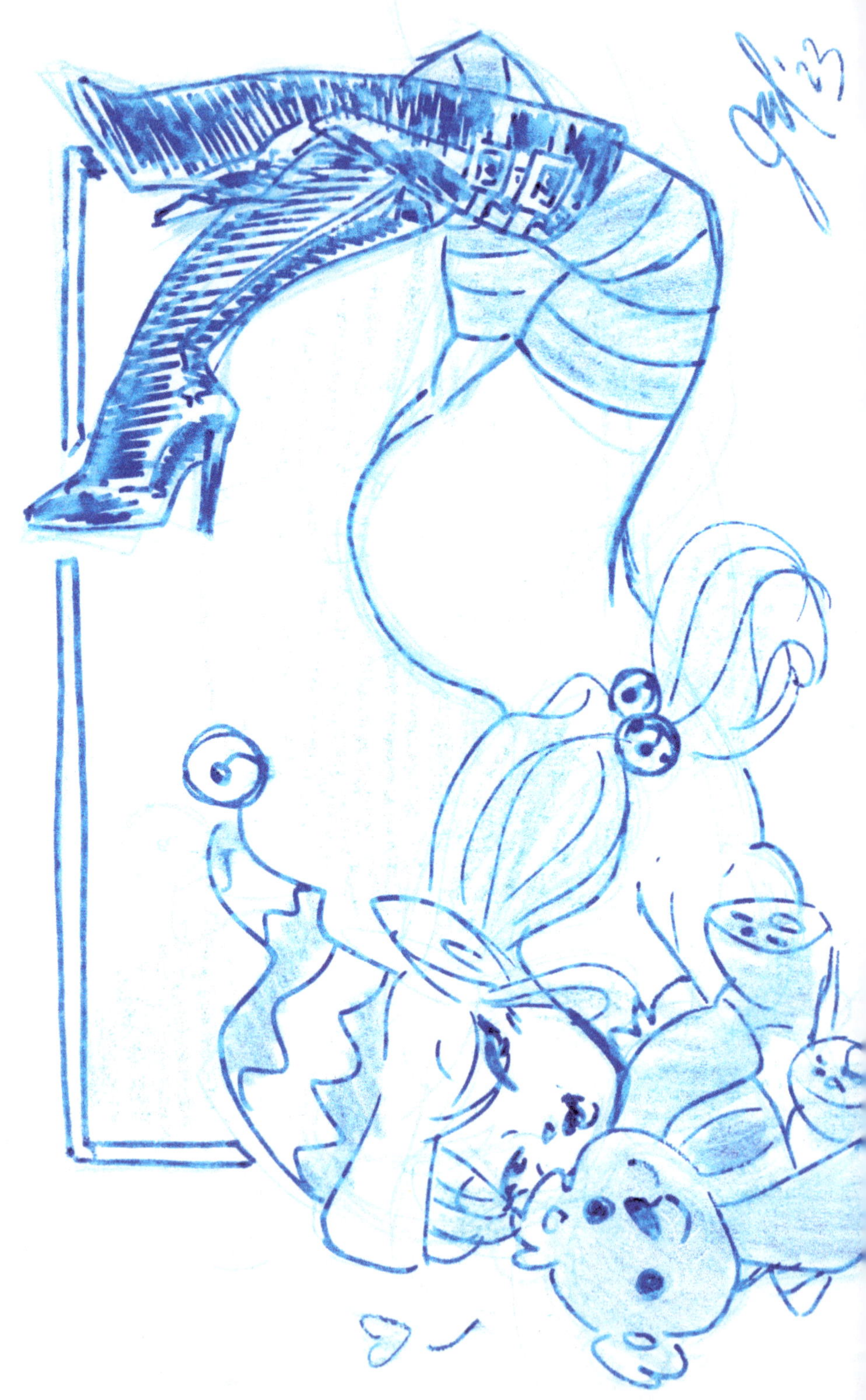

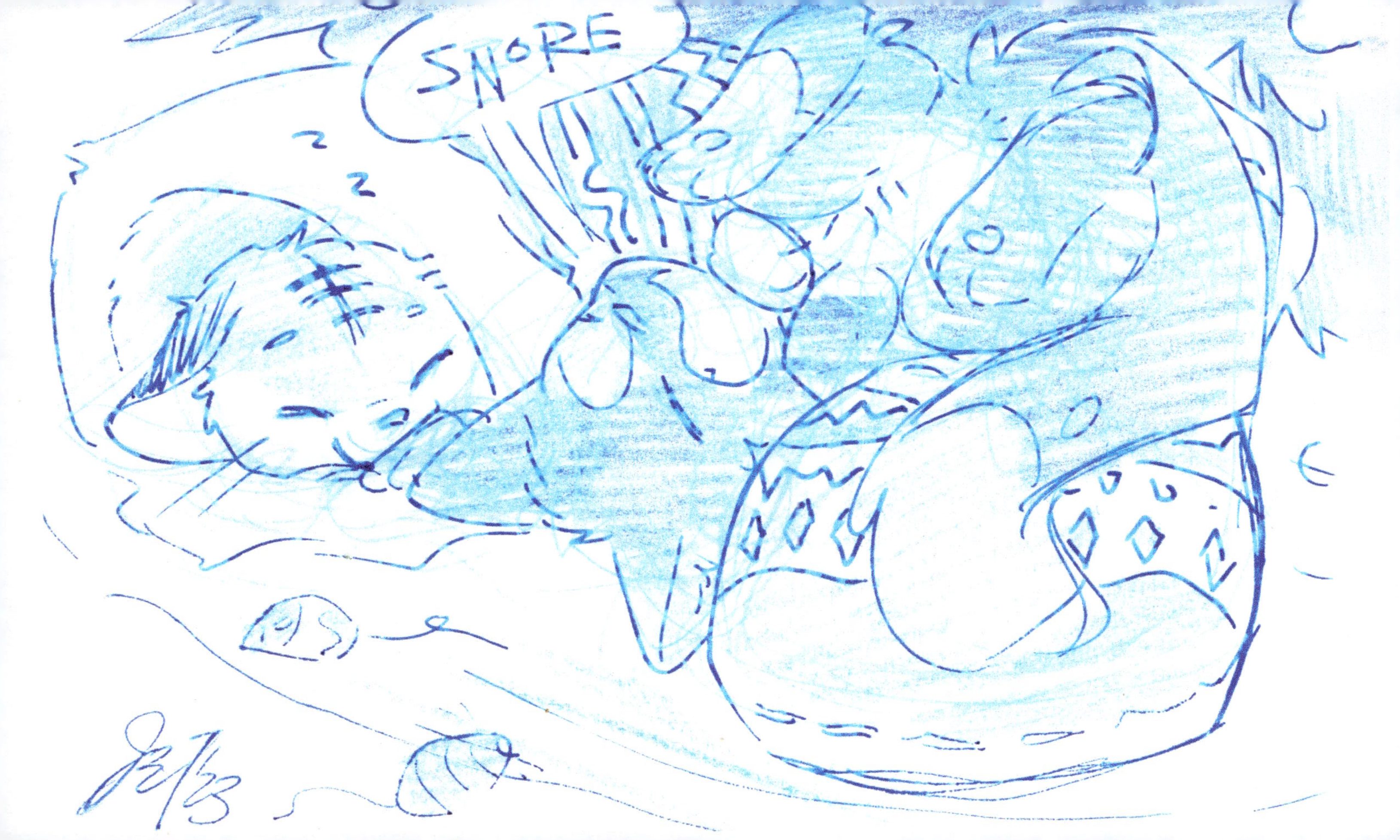

SNORE

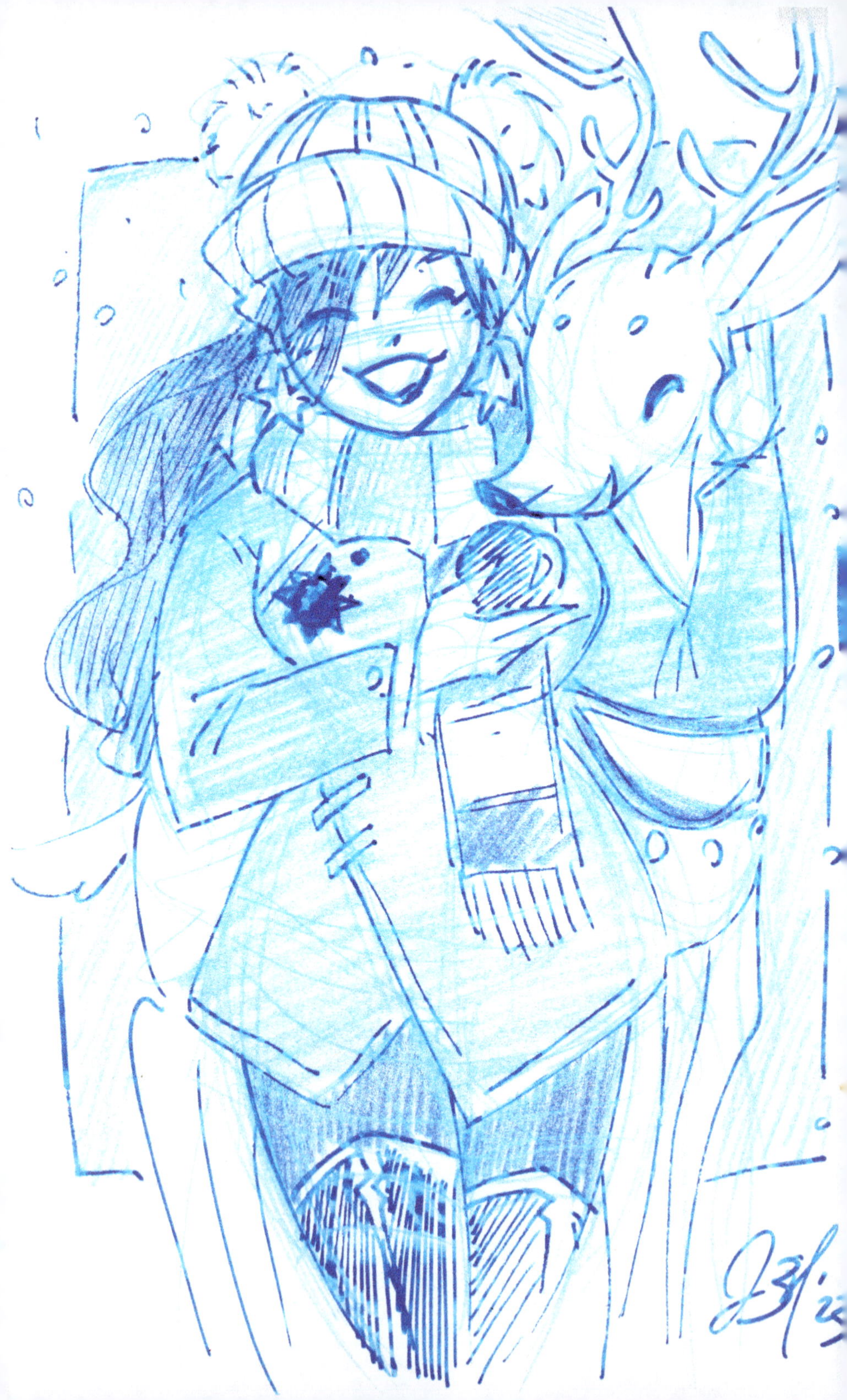

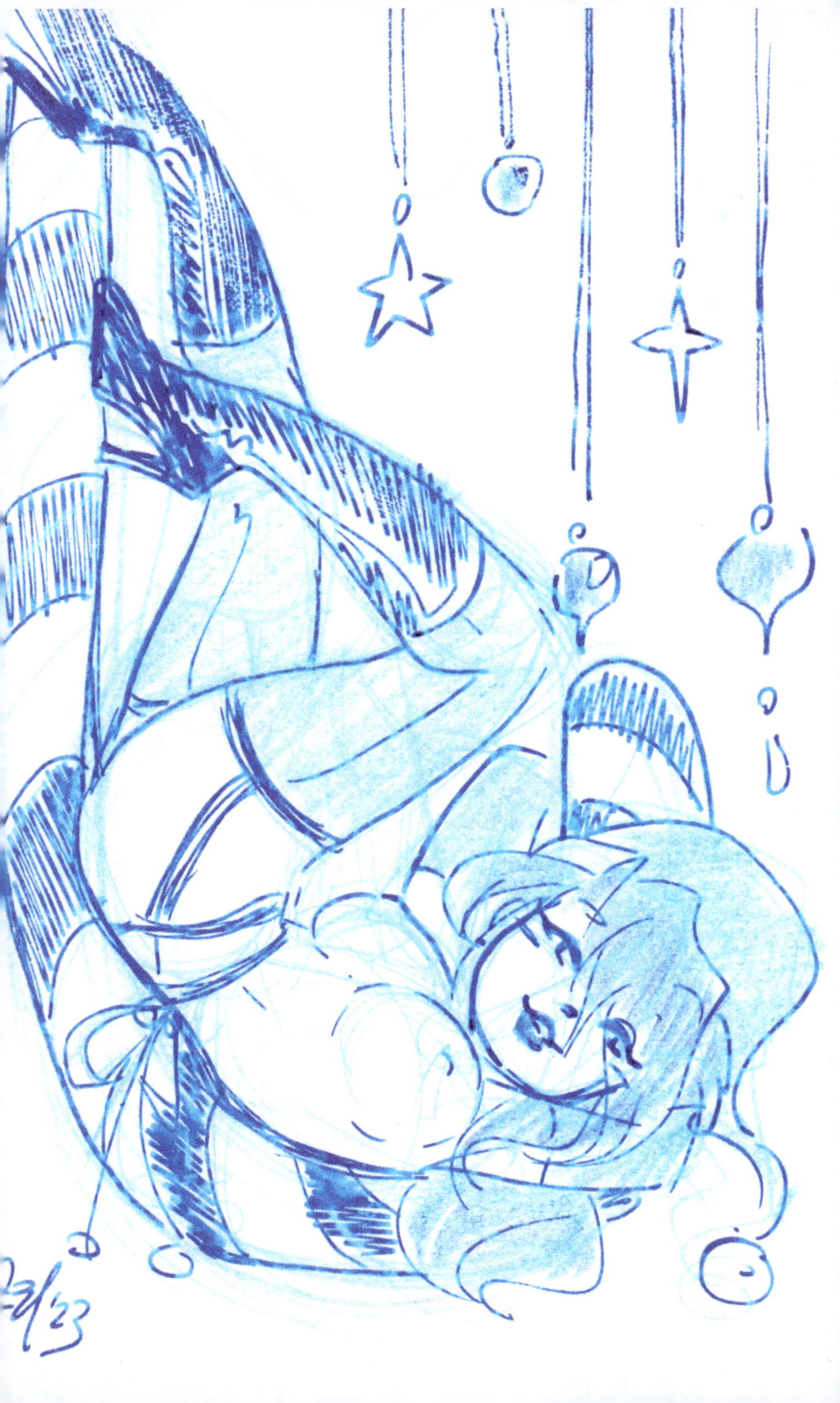

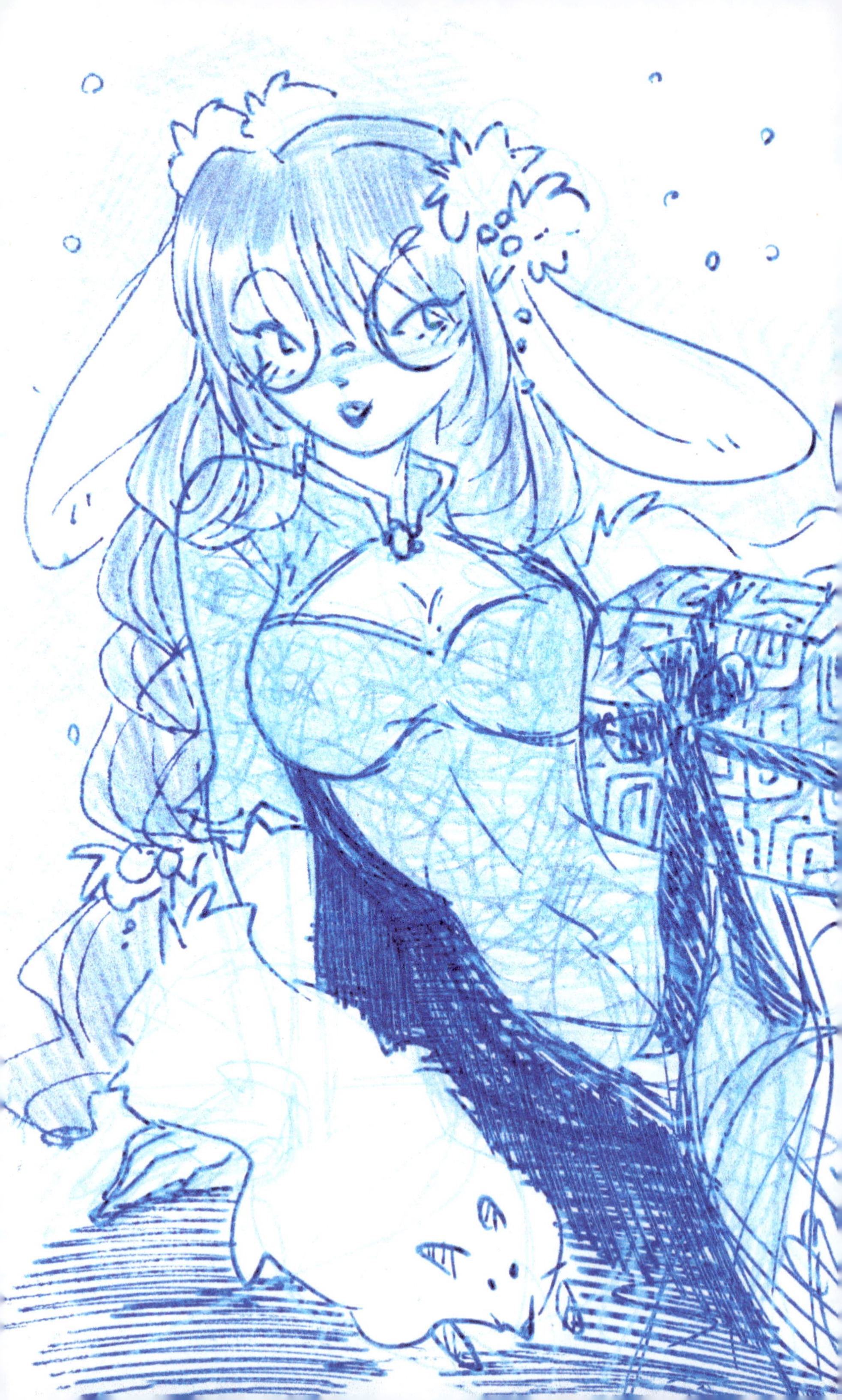

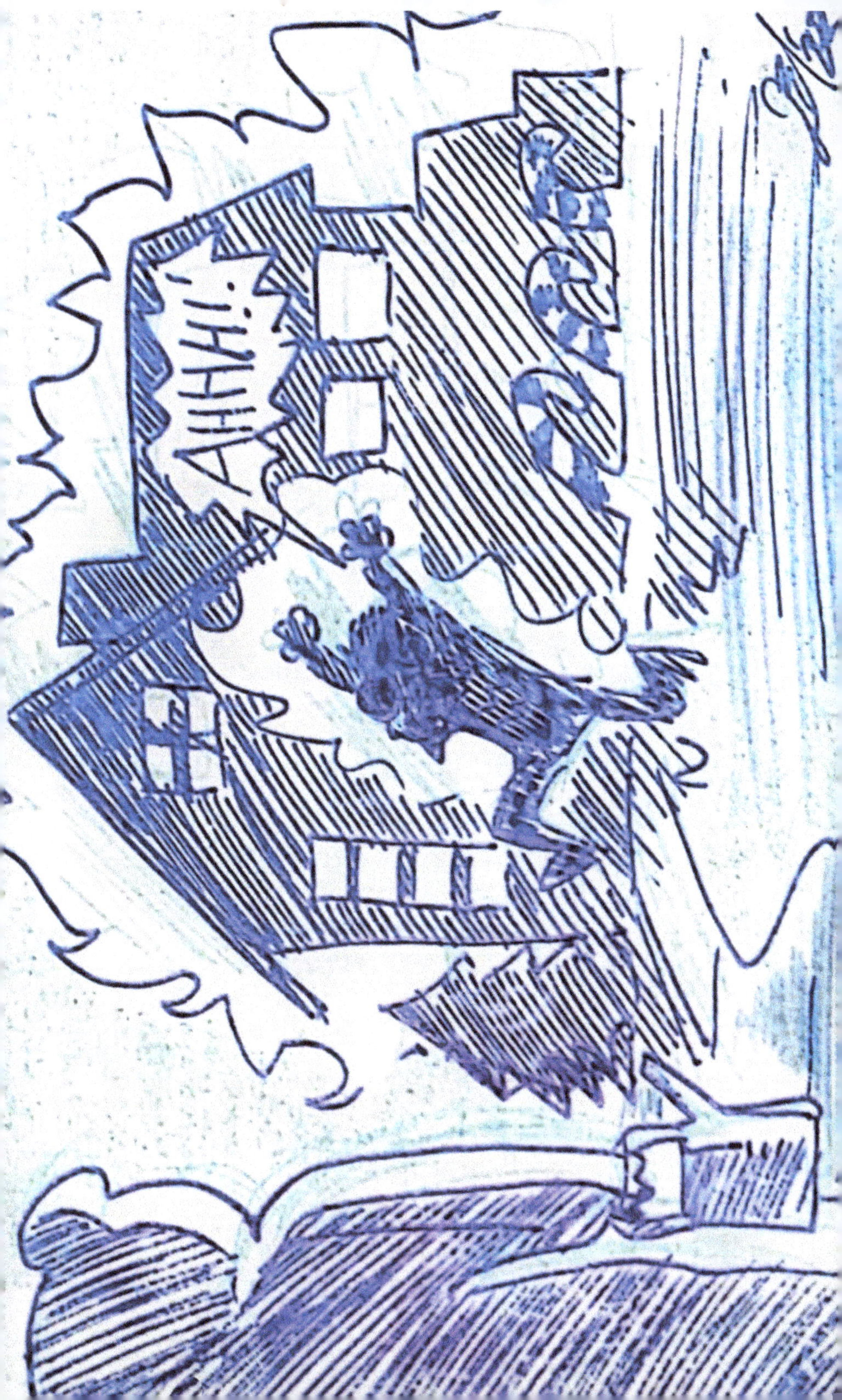

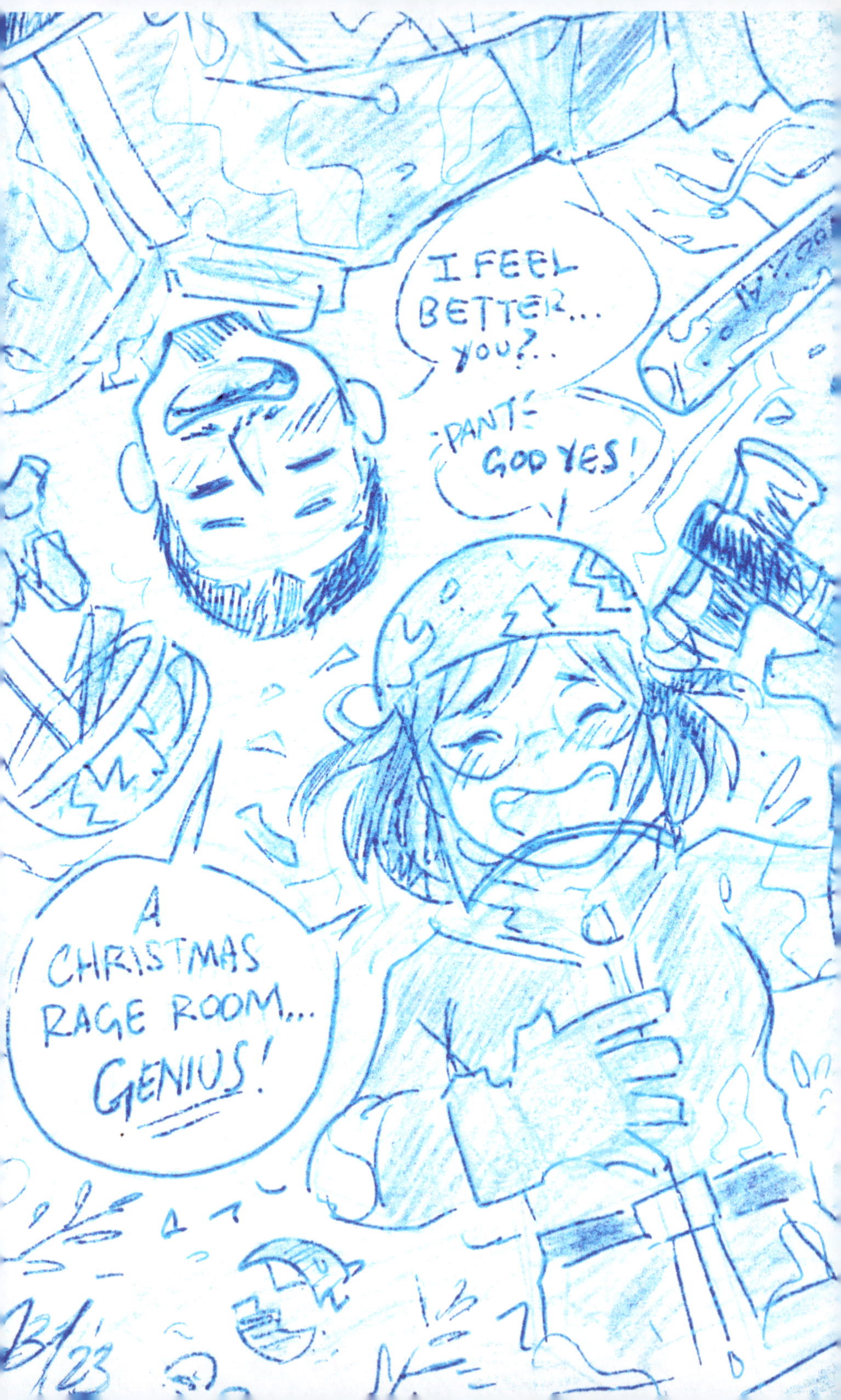

I FEEL BETTER... YOU?...
PANT GOD YES!
A CHRISTMAS RAGE ROOM... GENIUS!

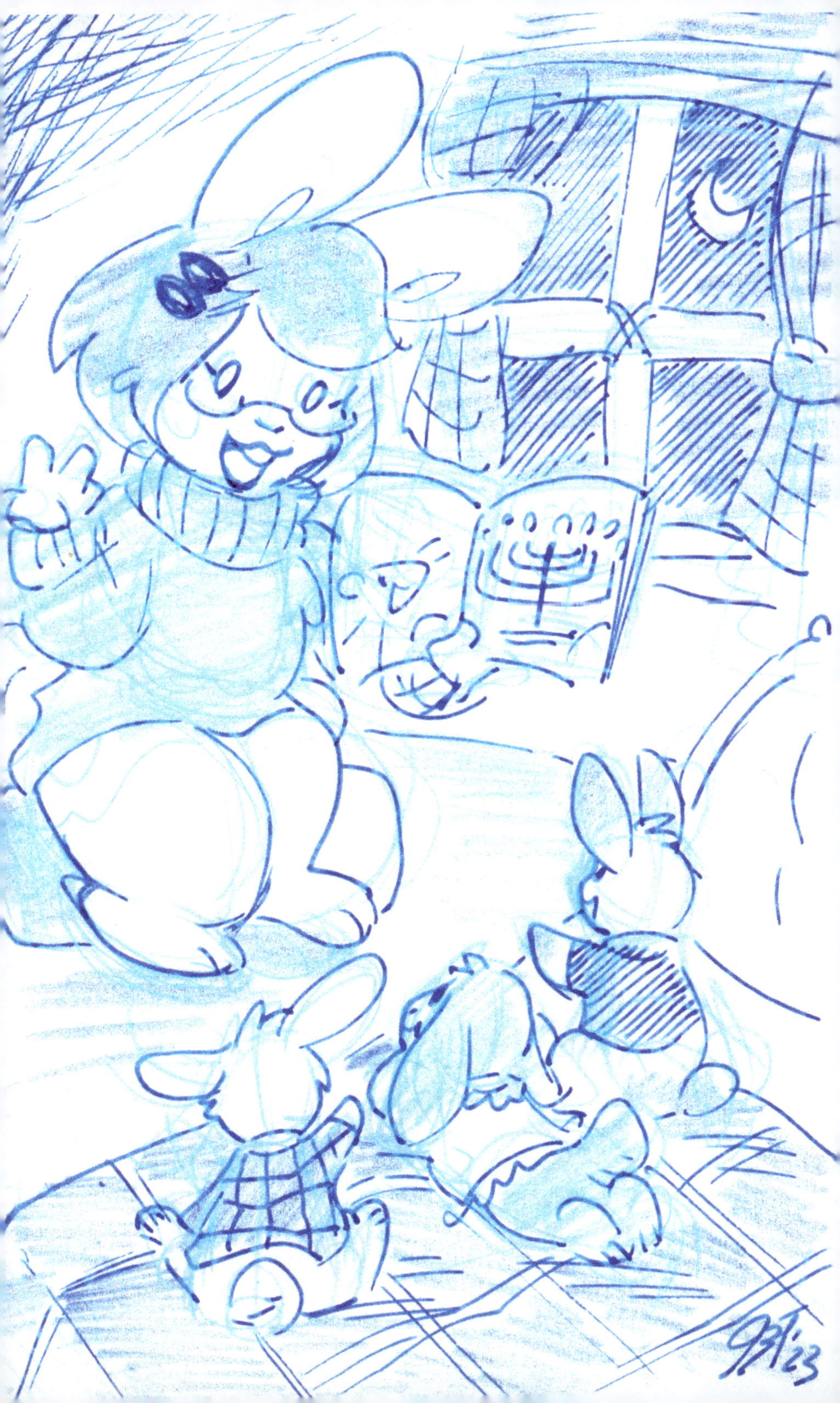

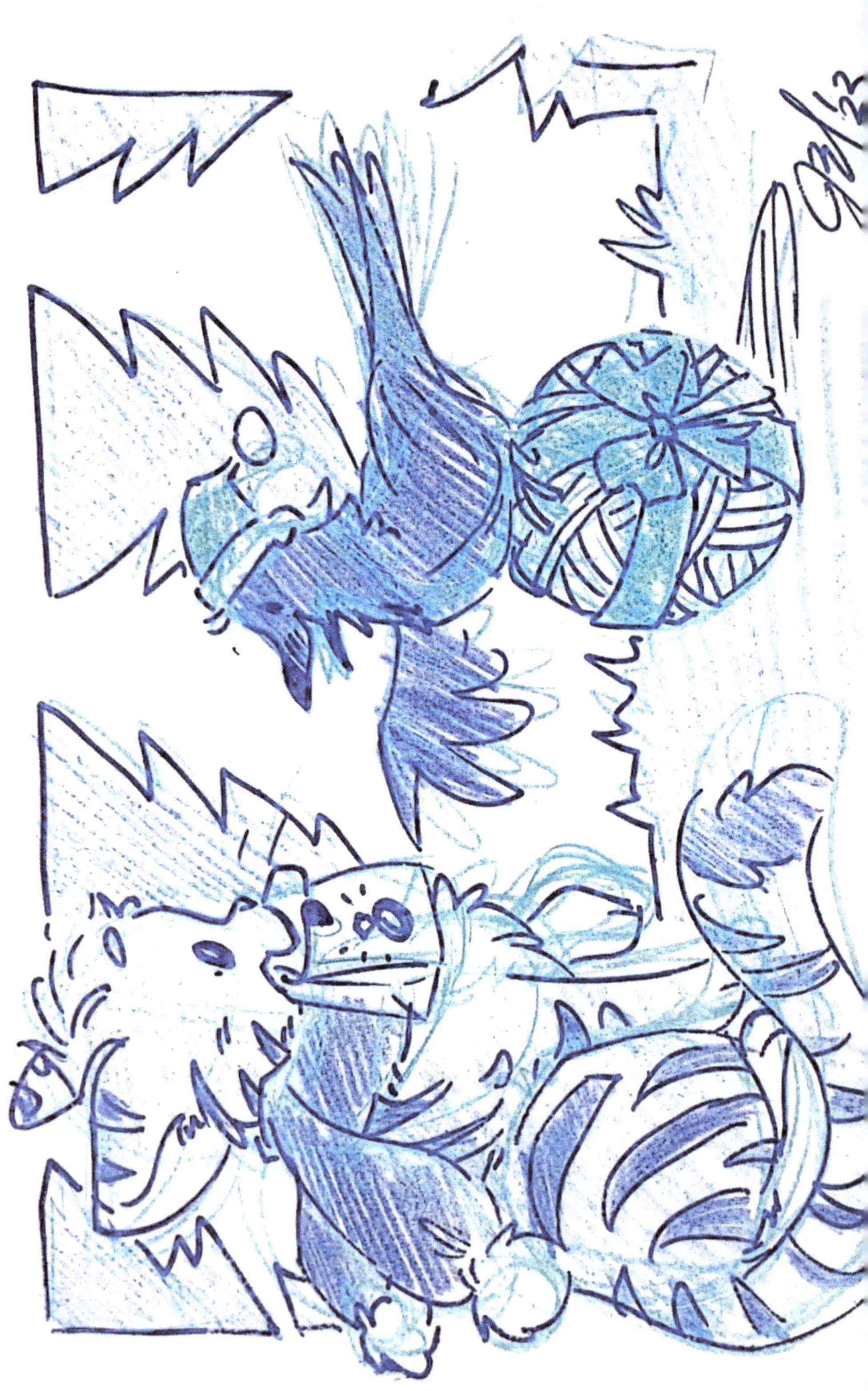

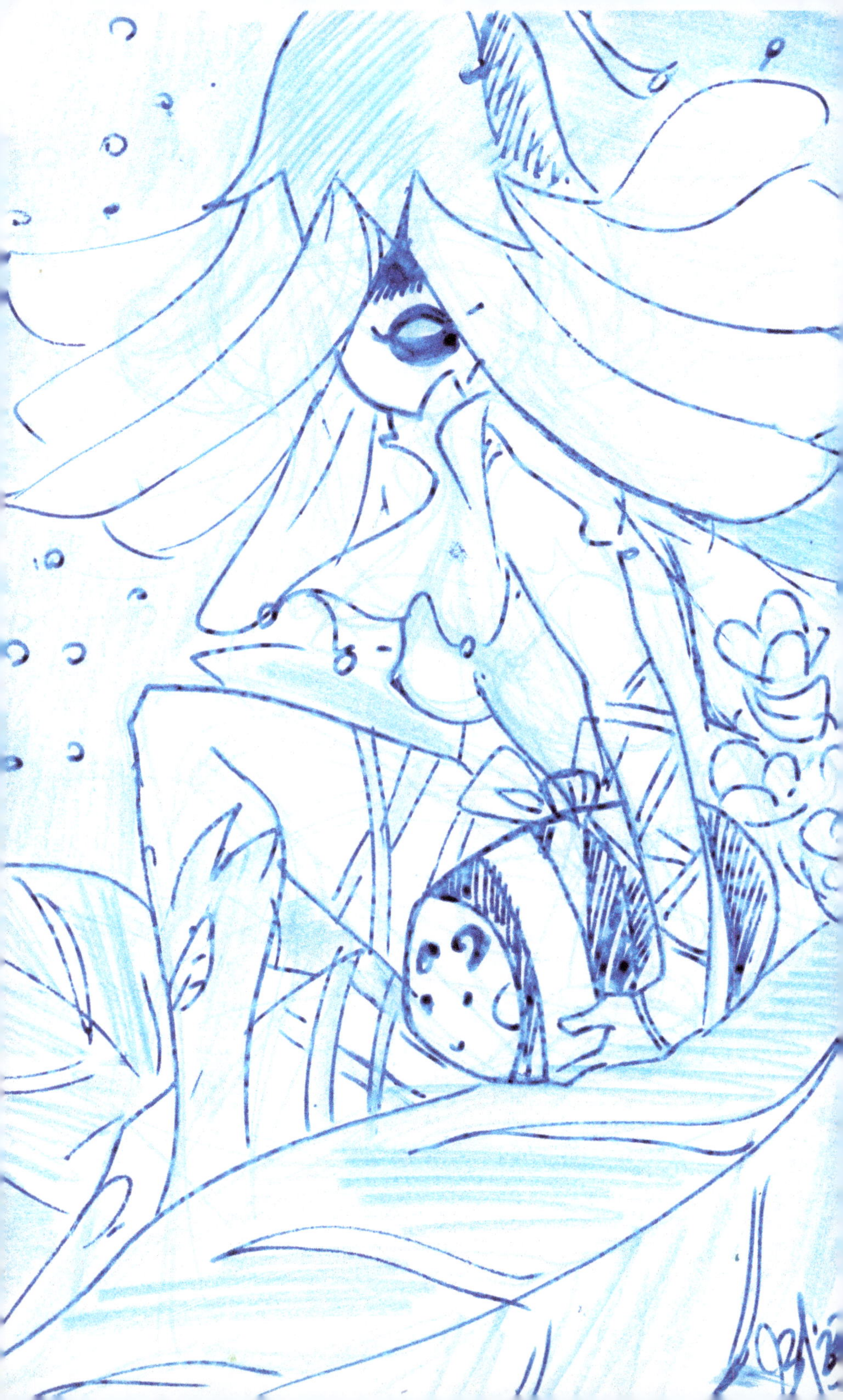

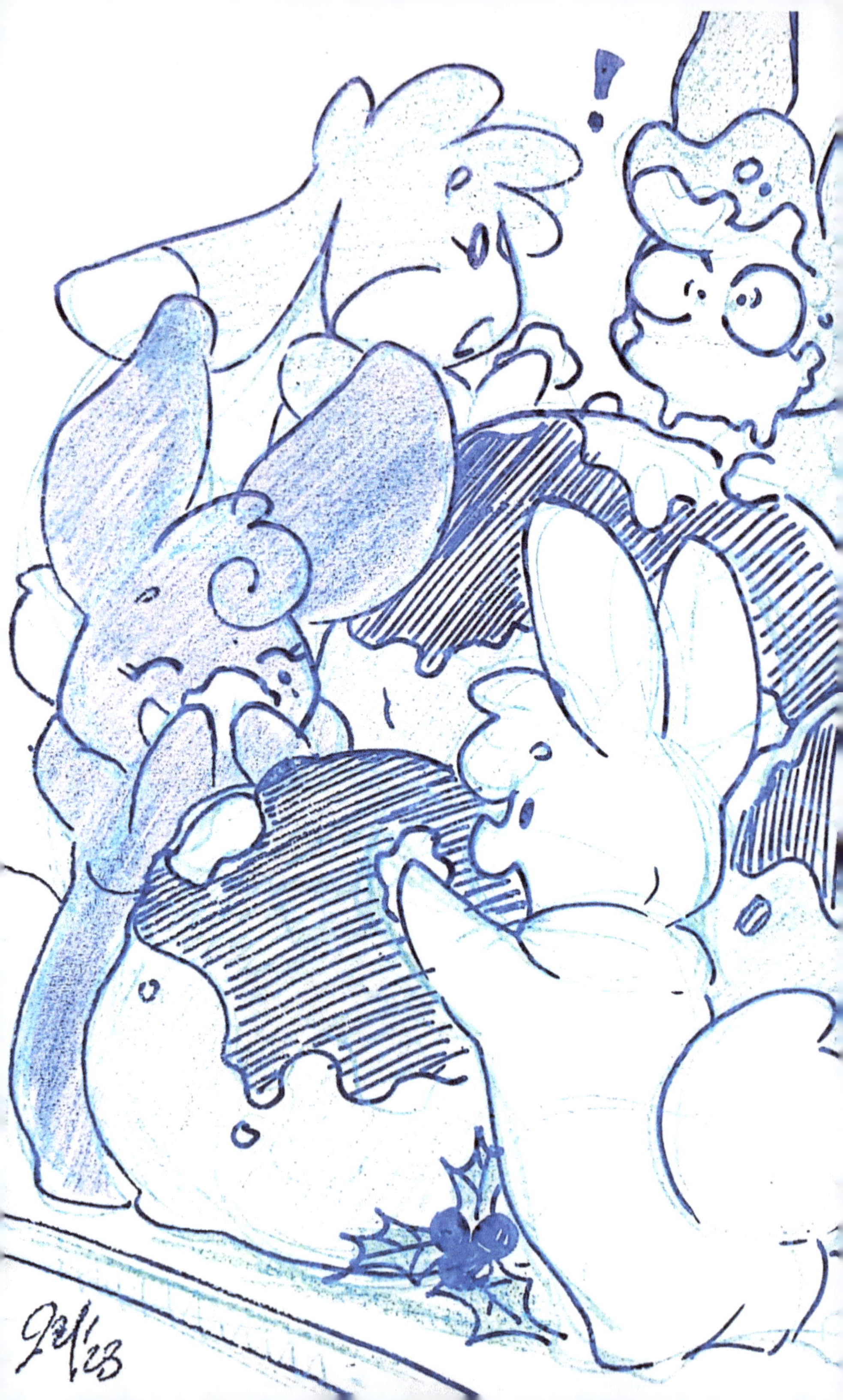

THAT'S IT...
JUST A BIT TO
RIGHT...AHN...
KEEP YOUR
STROKES
STEADY....
AM...I...
CLEAR?...
KNEAD
KNEAD
YES MA'AM...
I MEAN MY
QUEEN!
GOOD
BOY.

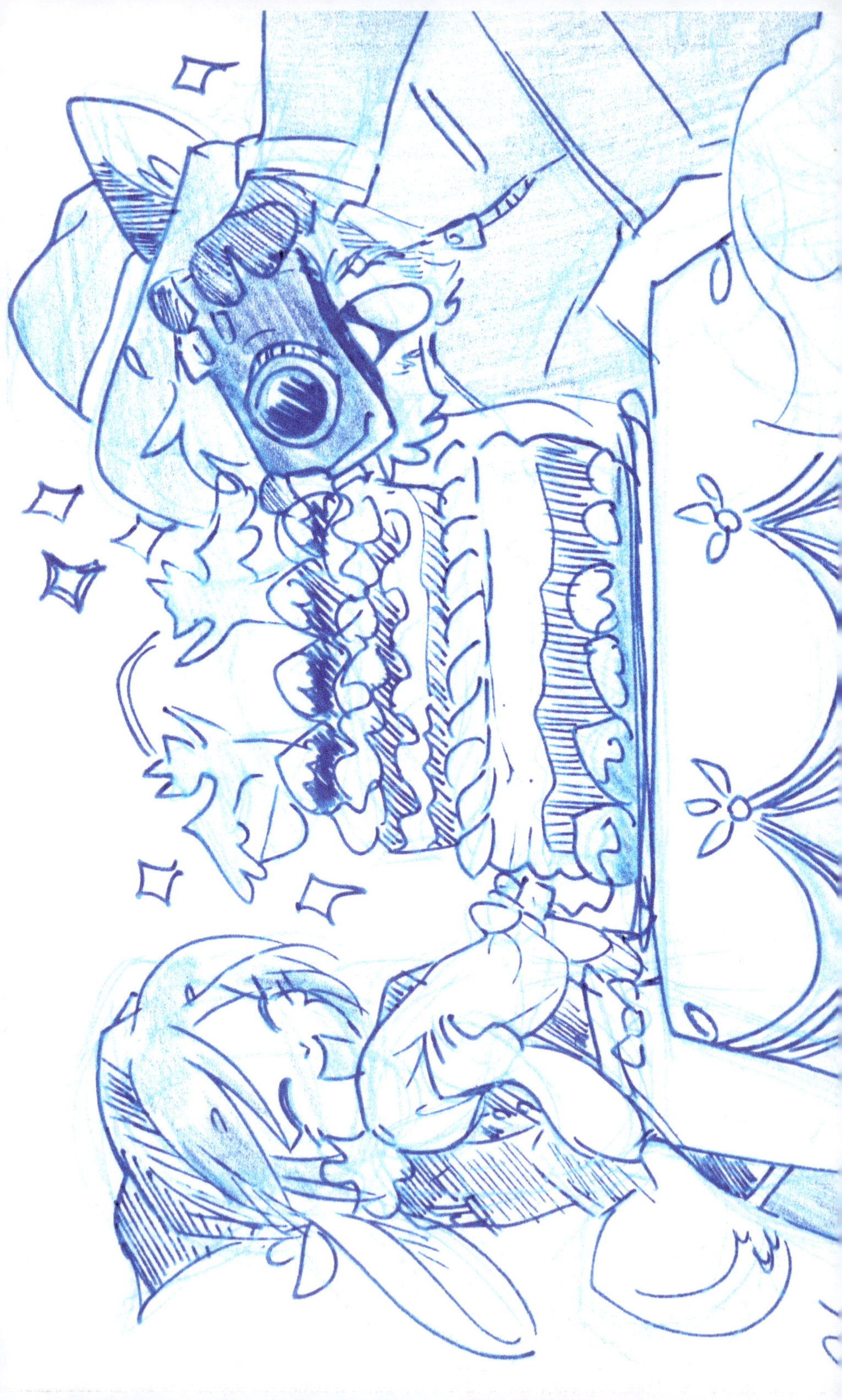

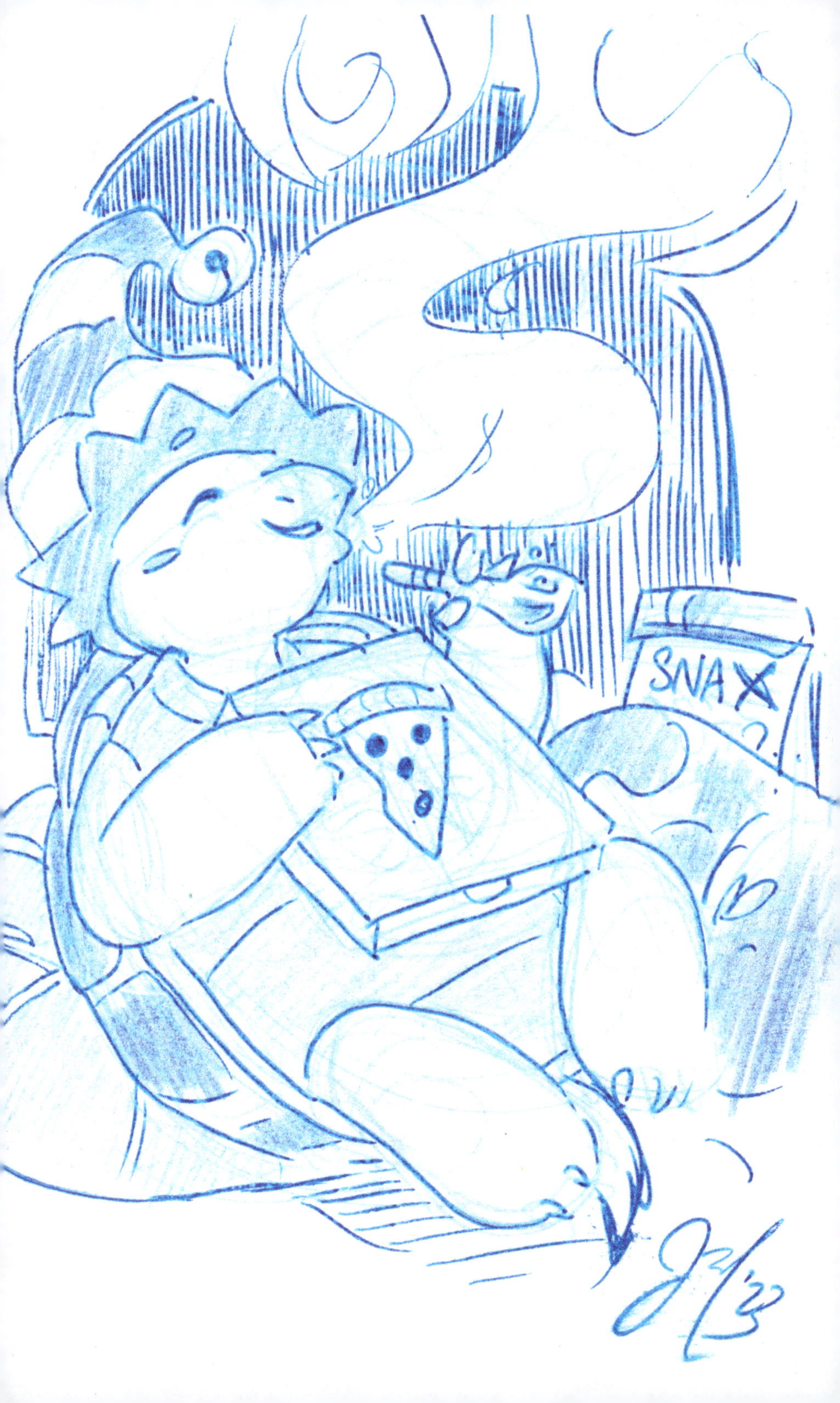

SNAX

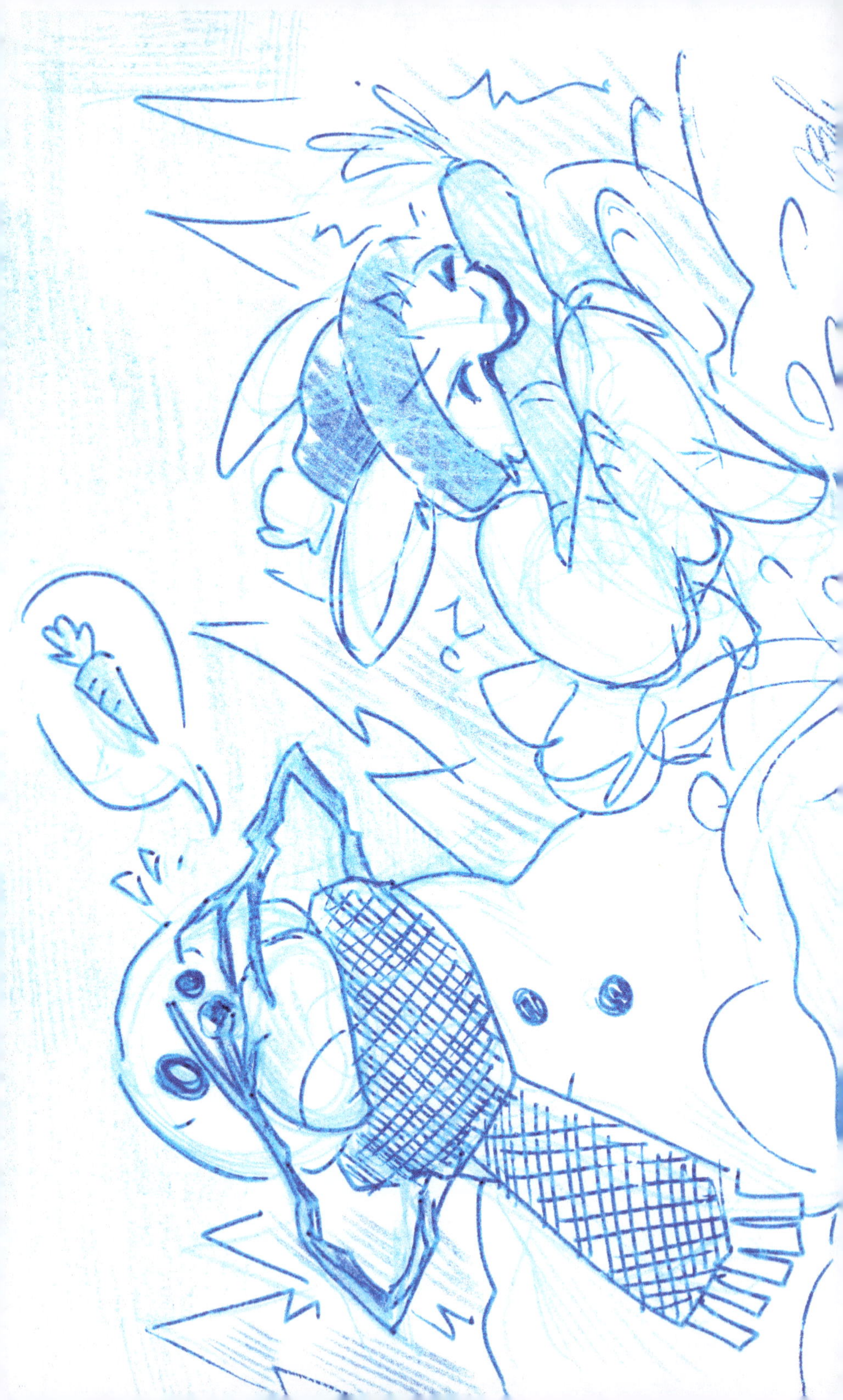

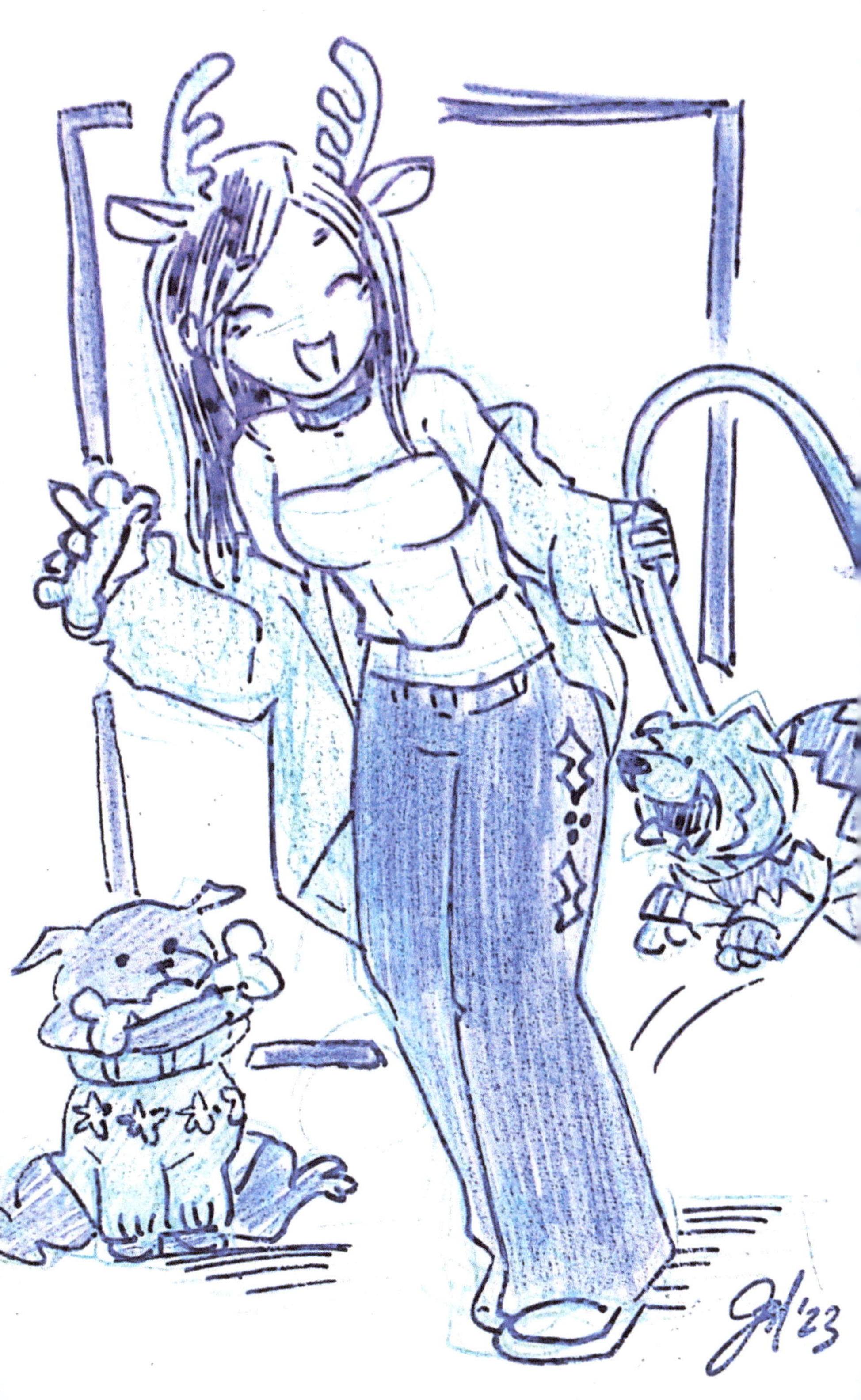

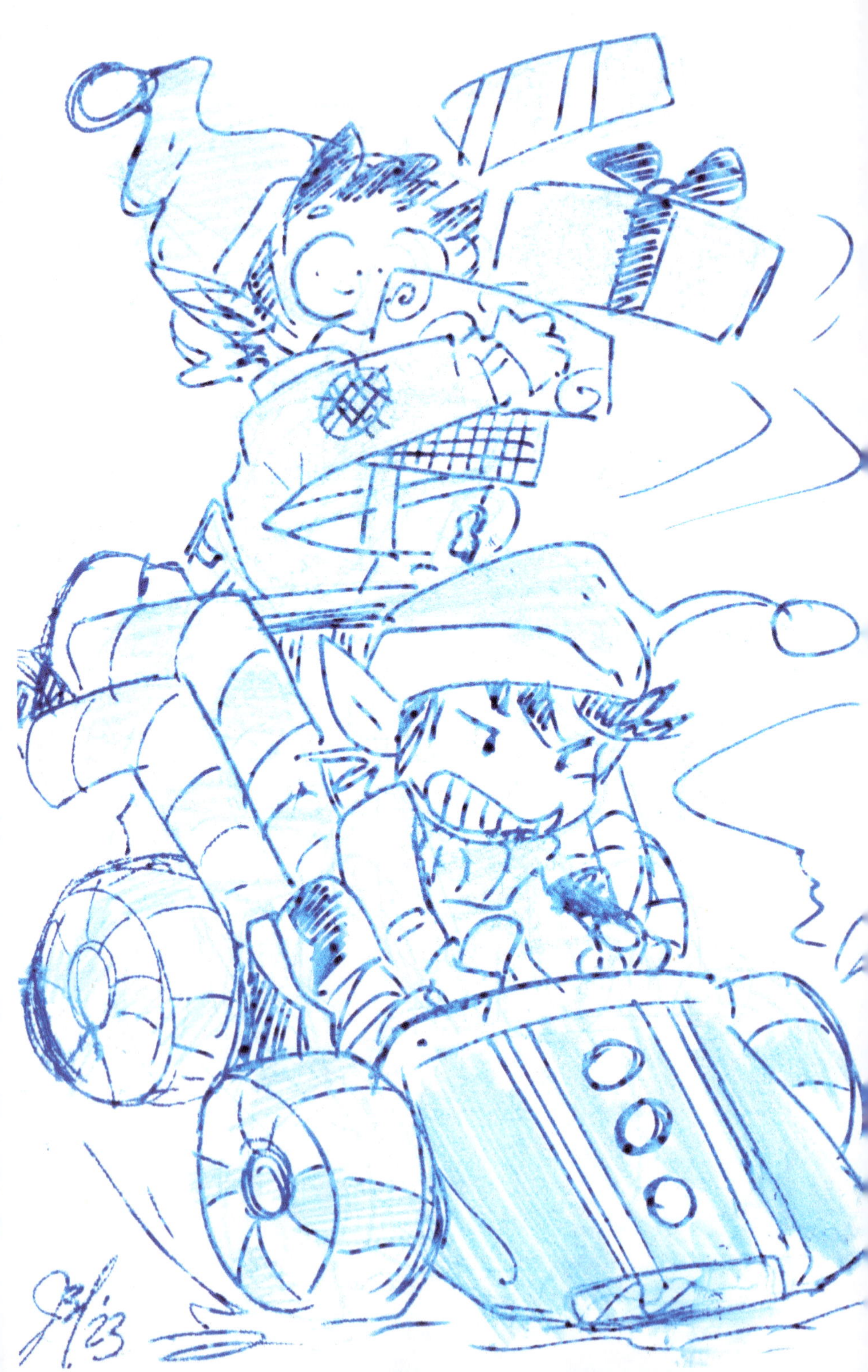

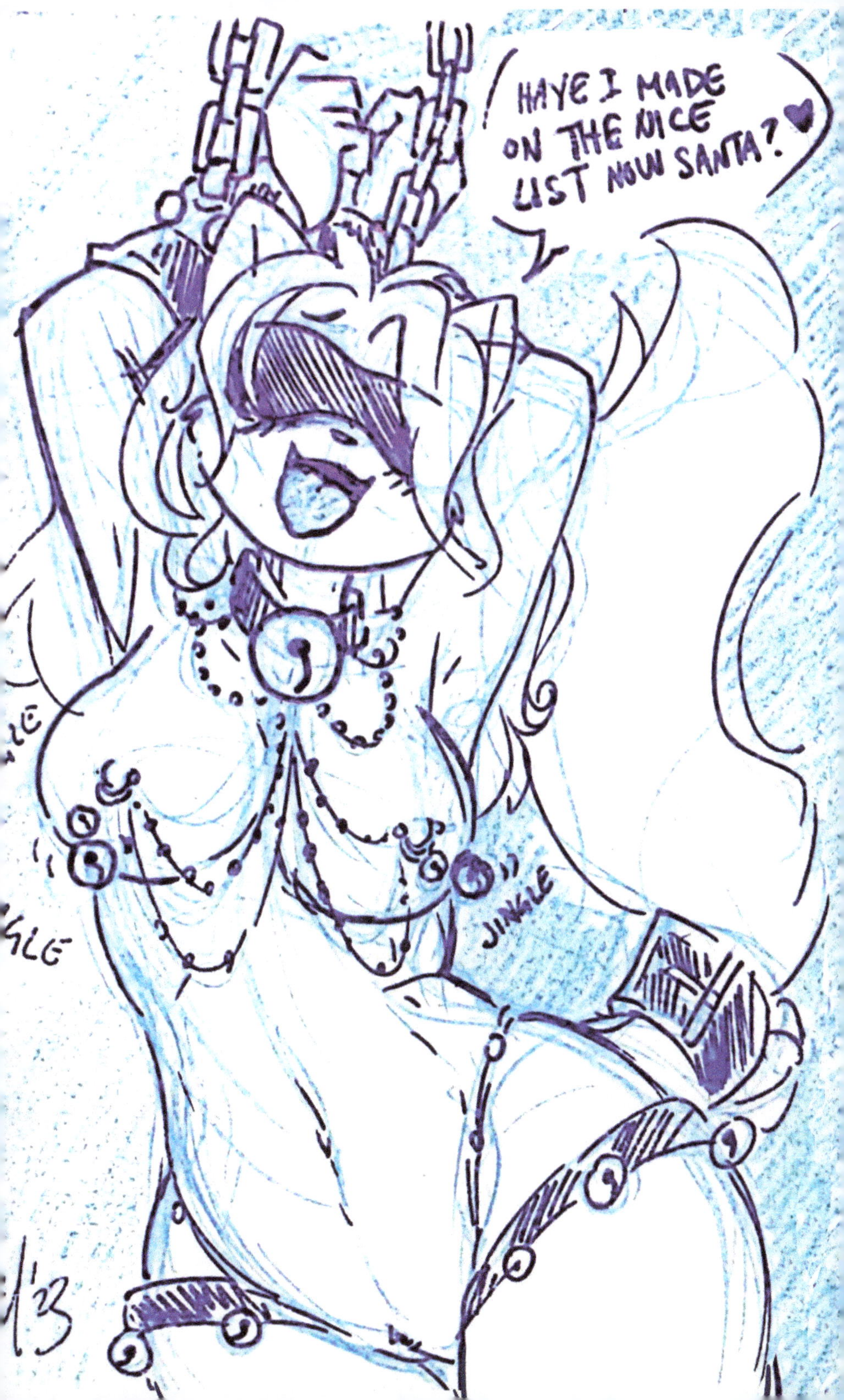

HAVE I MADE ON THE NICE LIST NOW SANTA?
JINGLE
JINGLE
'23

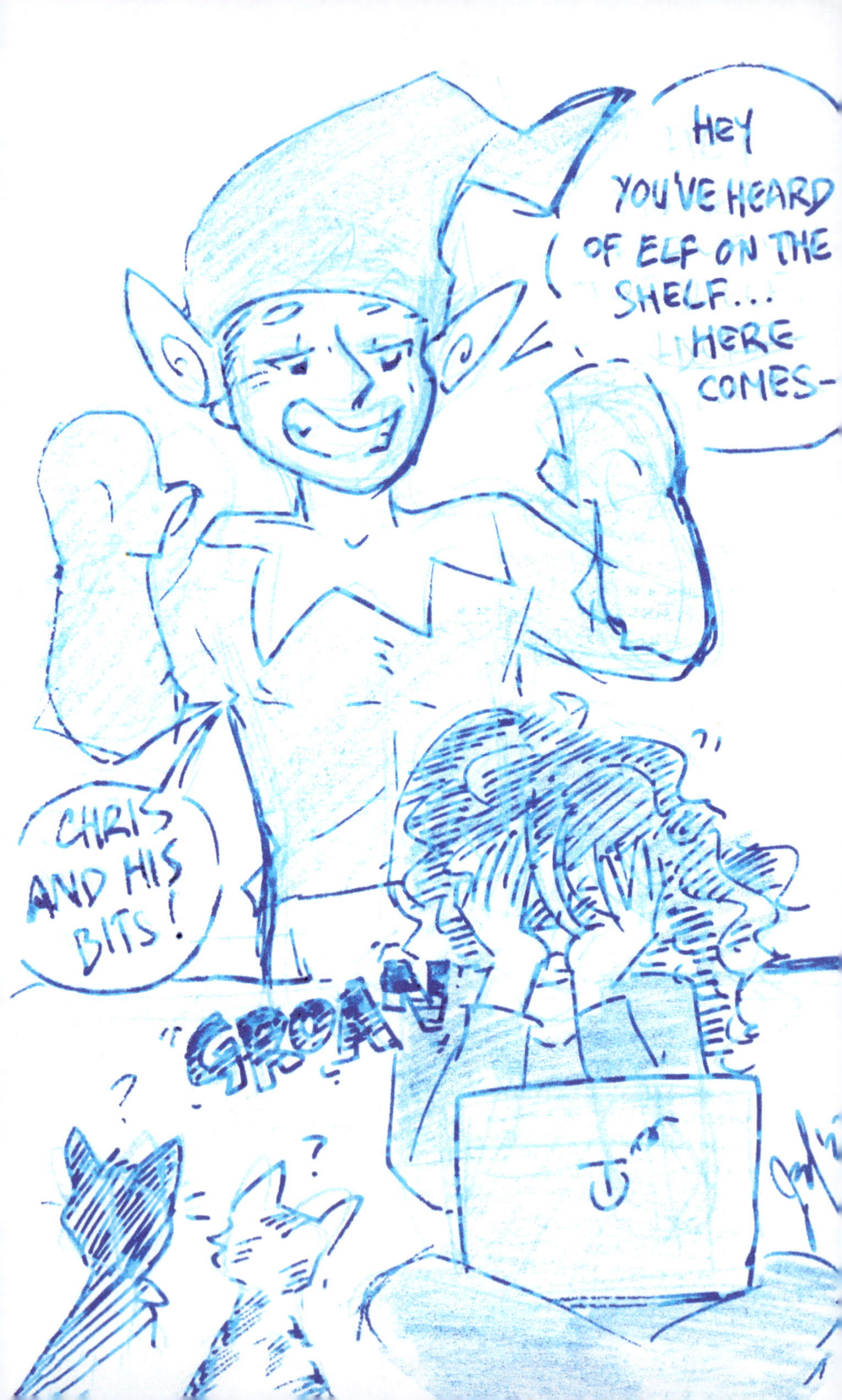

HEY YOU'VE HEARD OF ELF ON THE SHELF... HERE COMES-
CHRIS AND HIS BITS!
GROAN

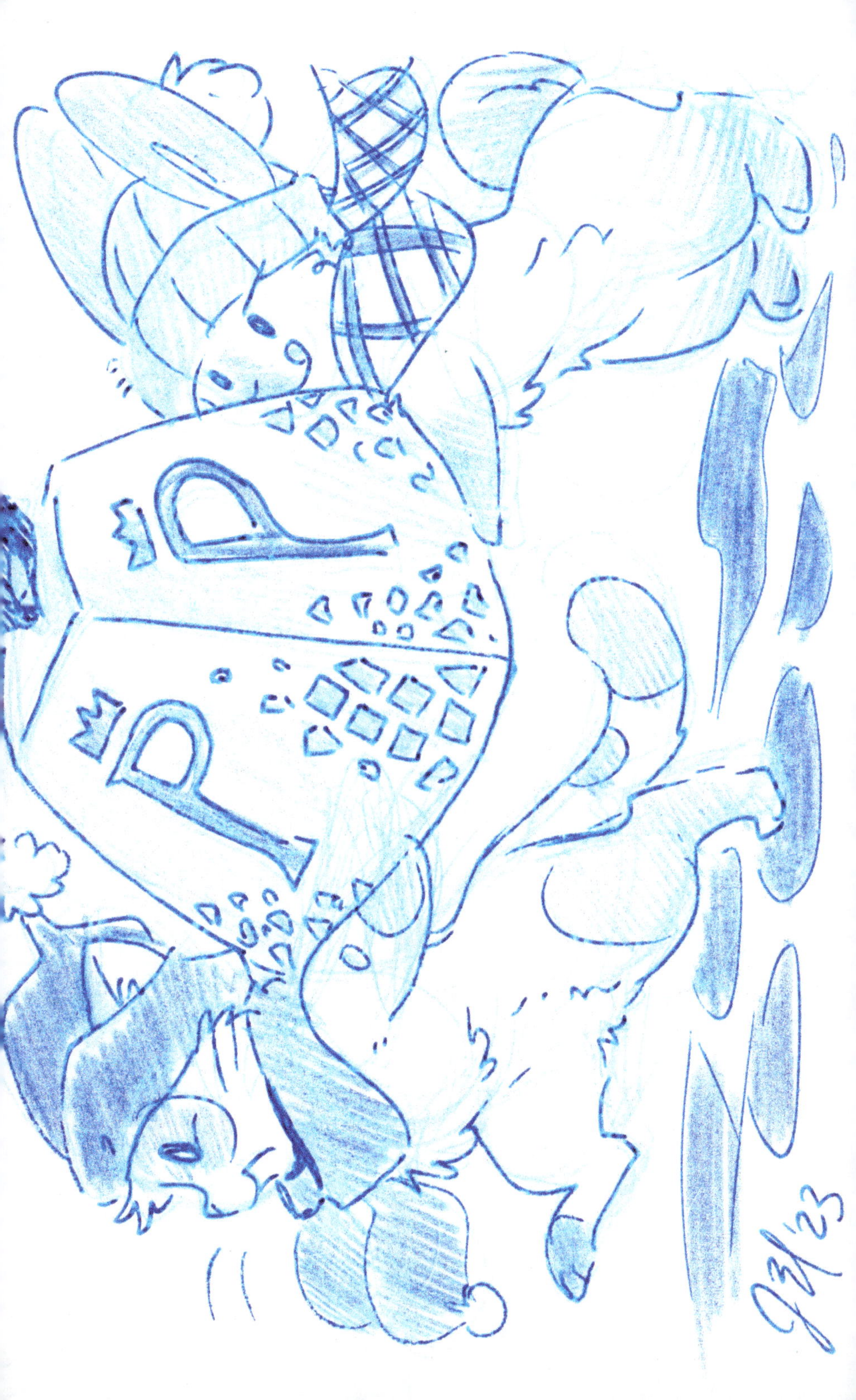

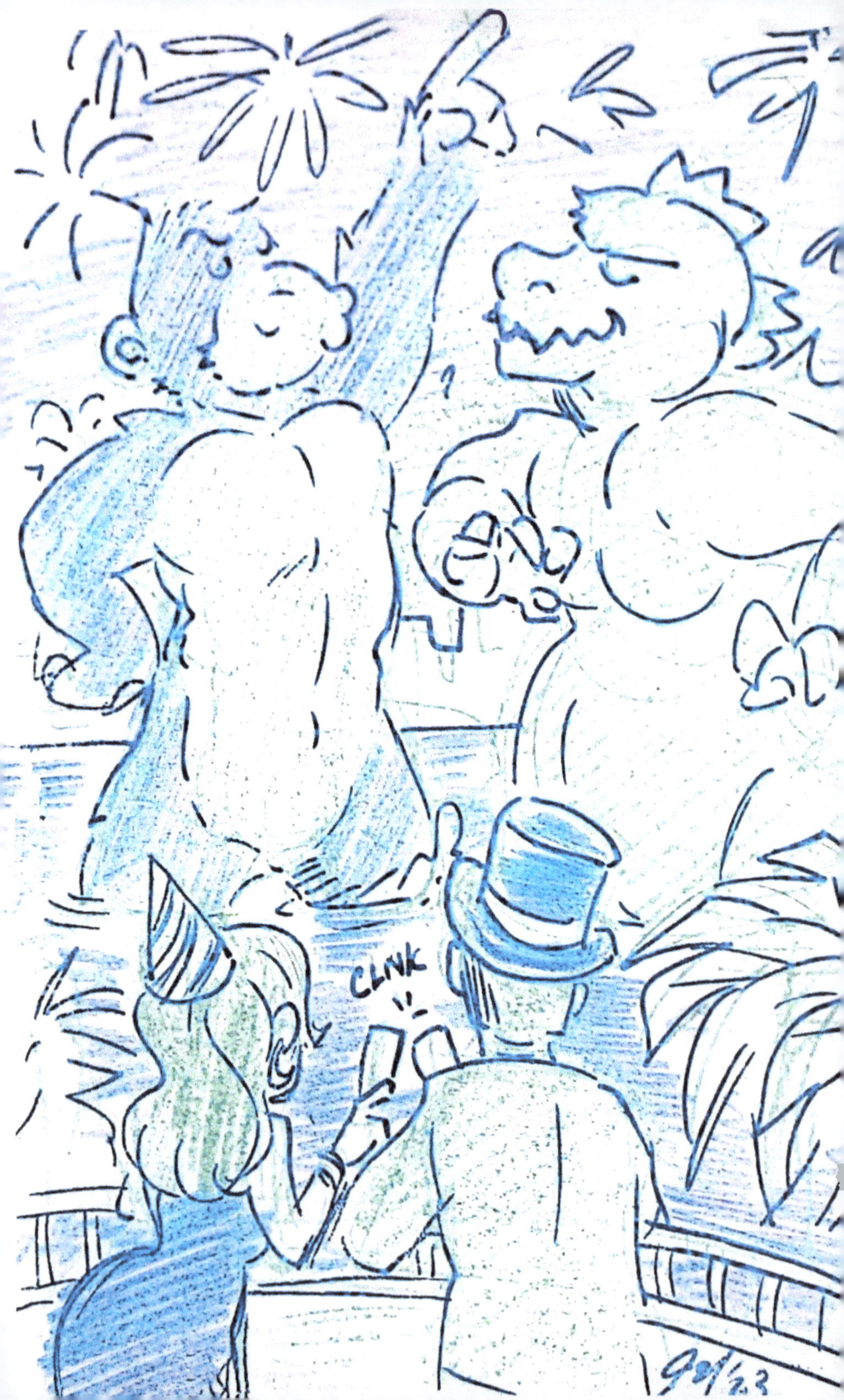

CLINK

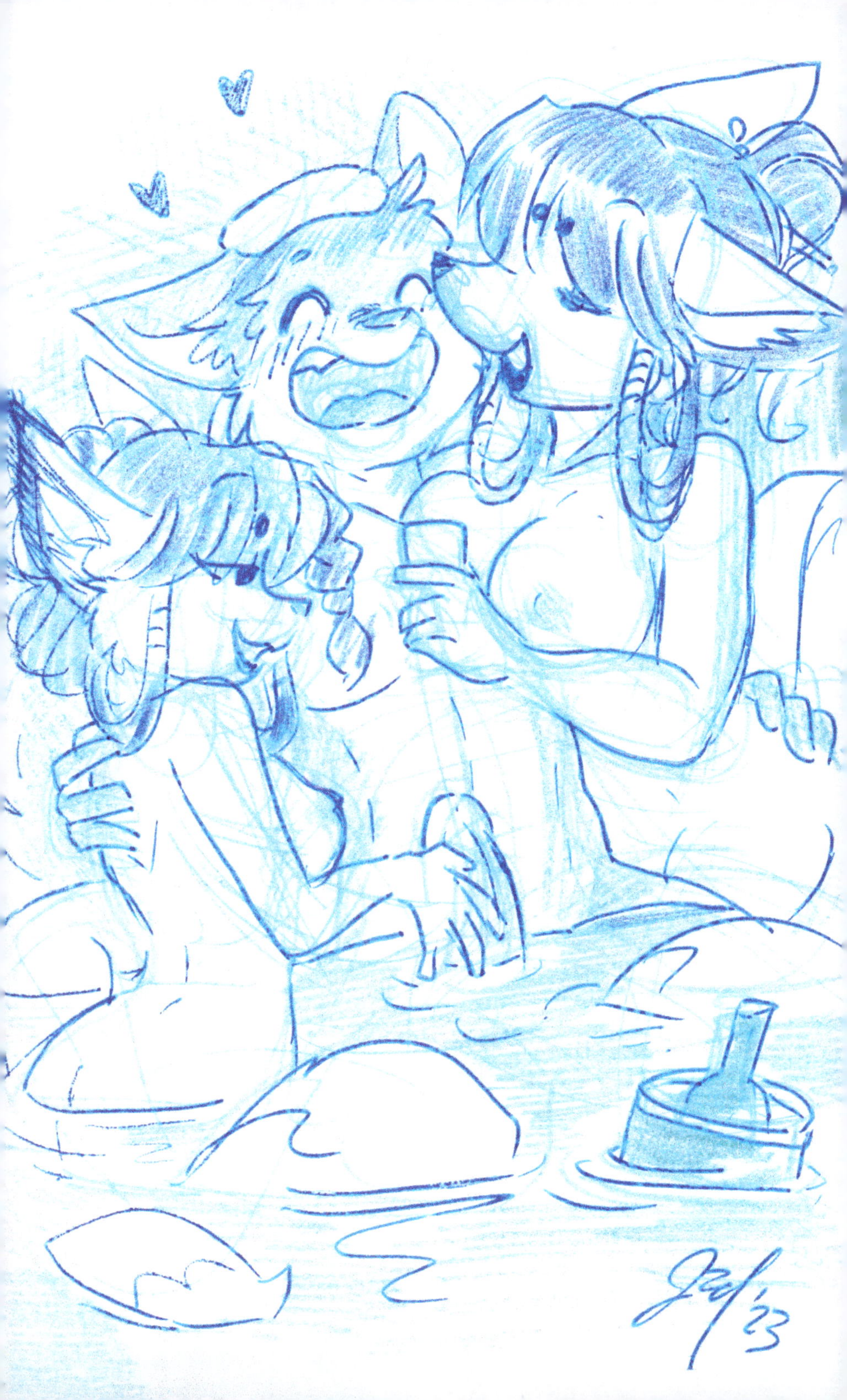

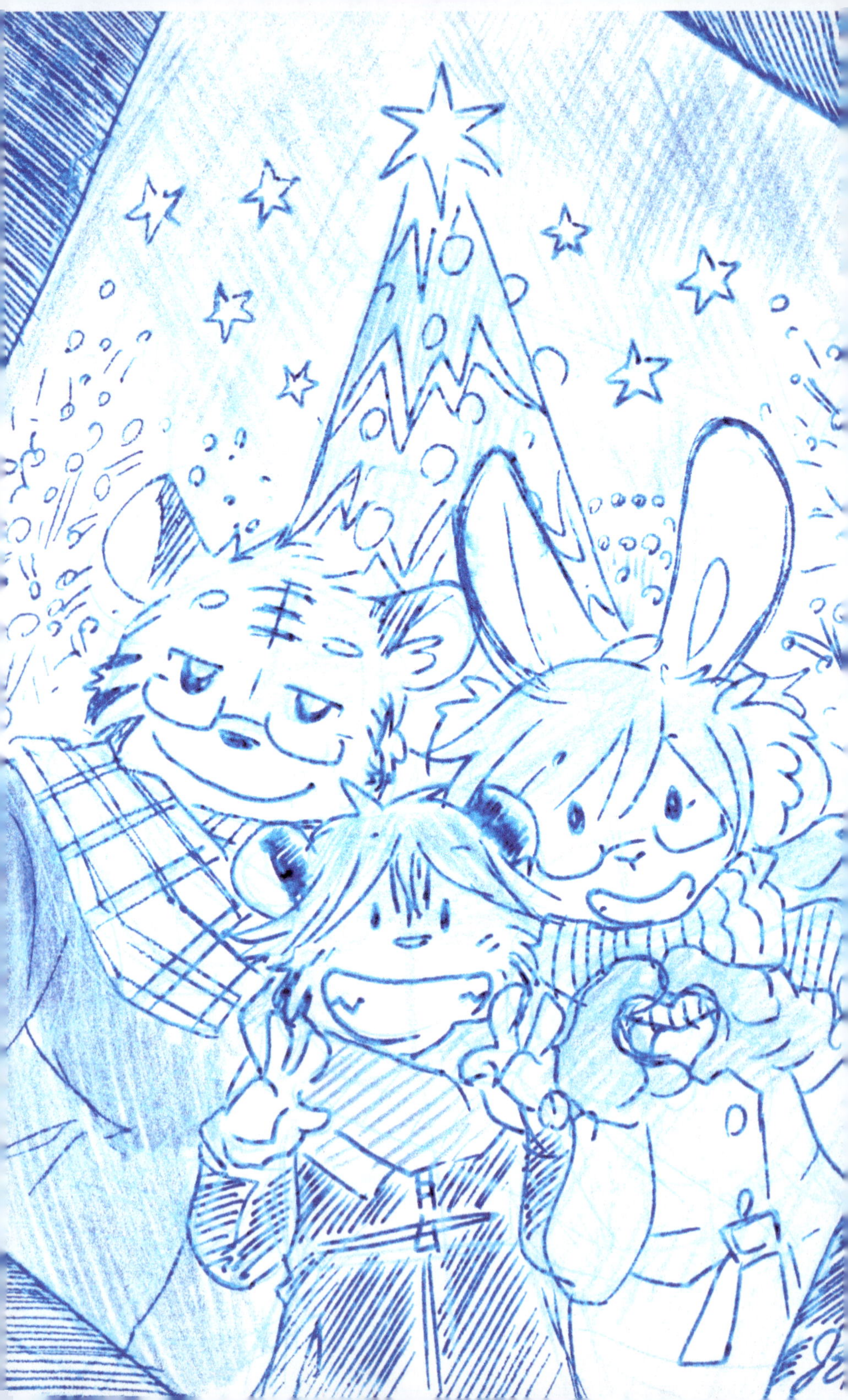

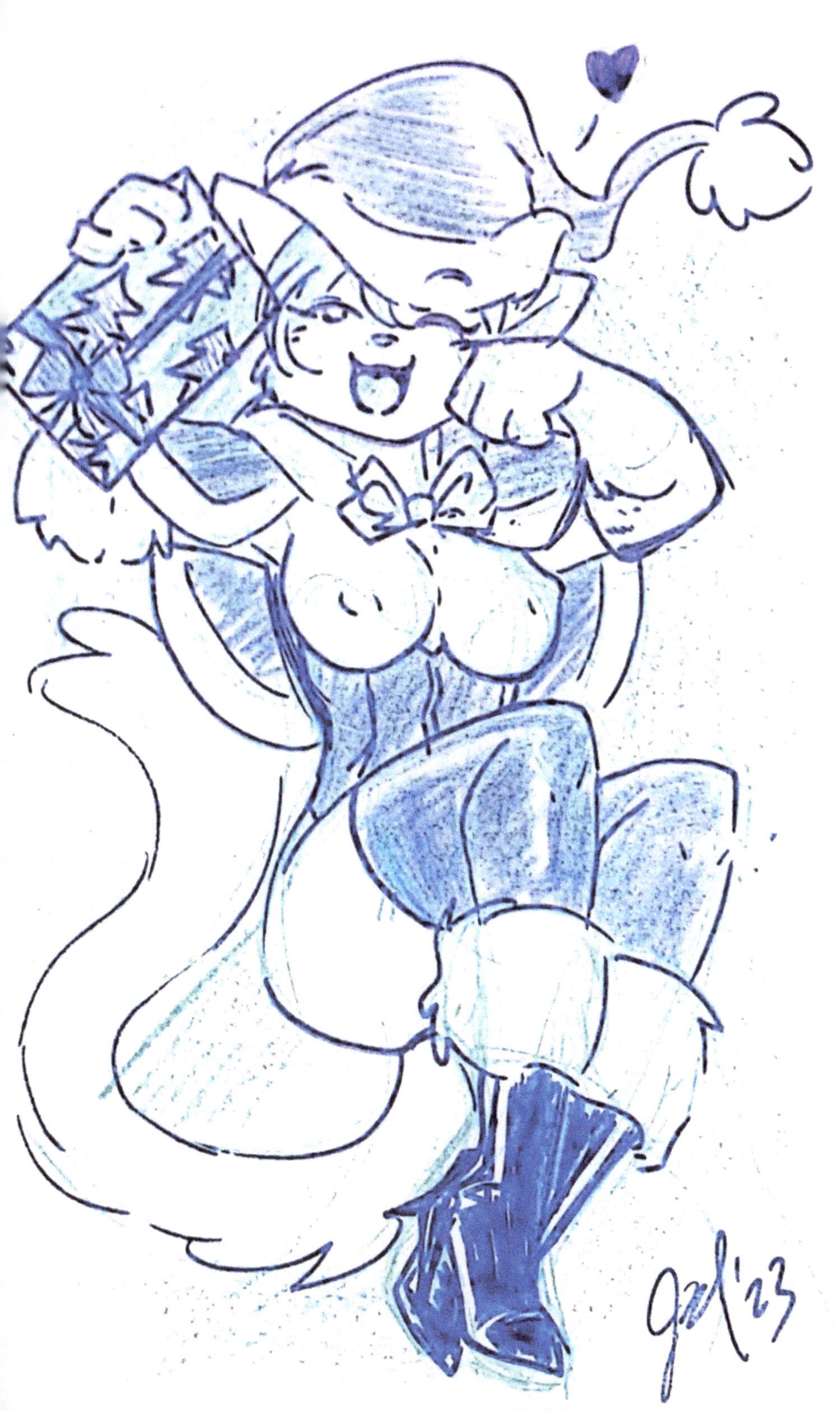

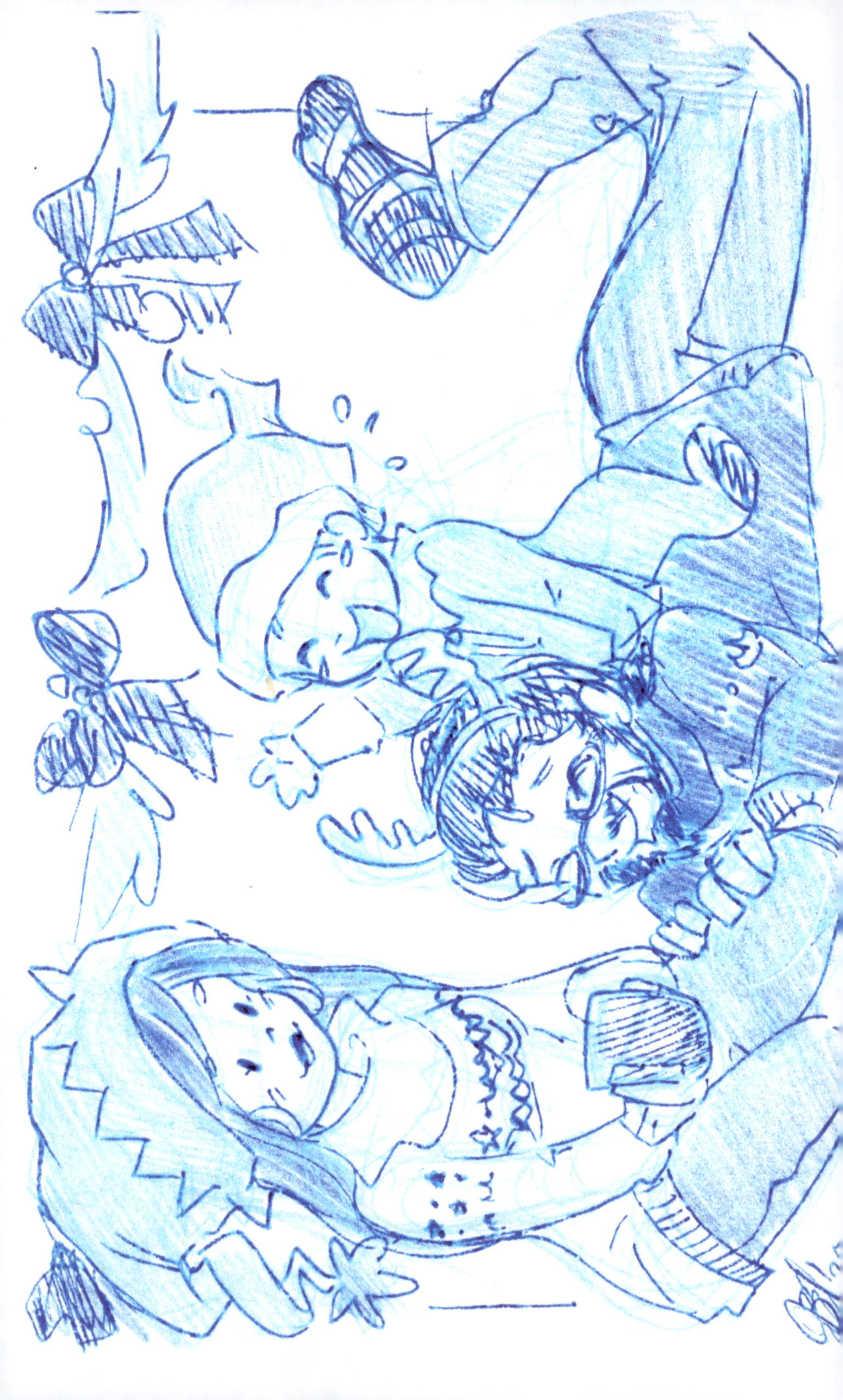

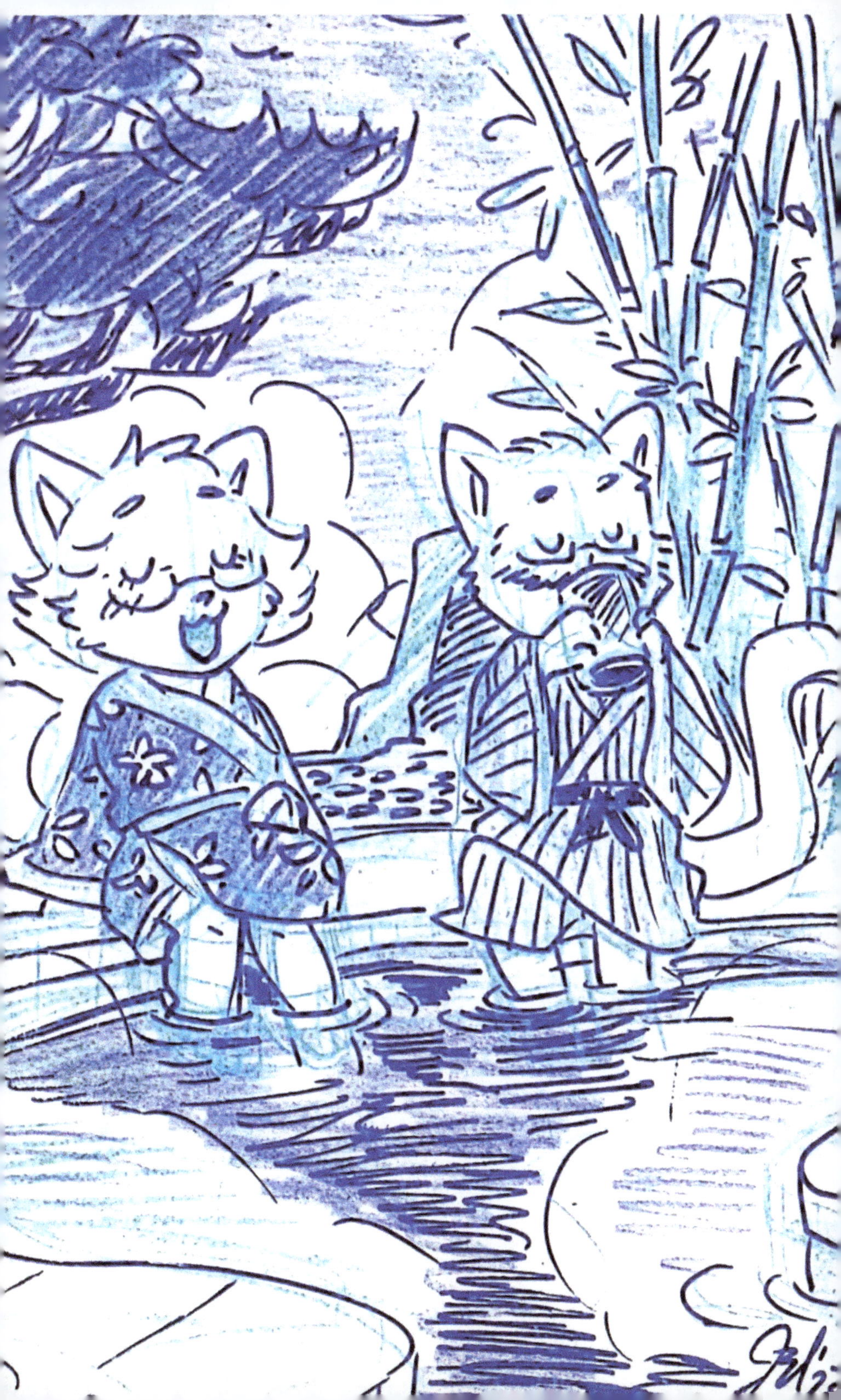

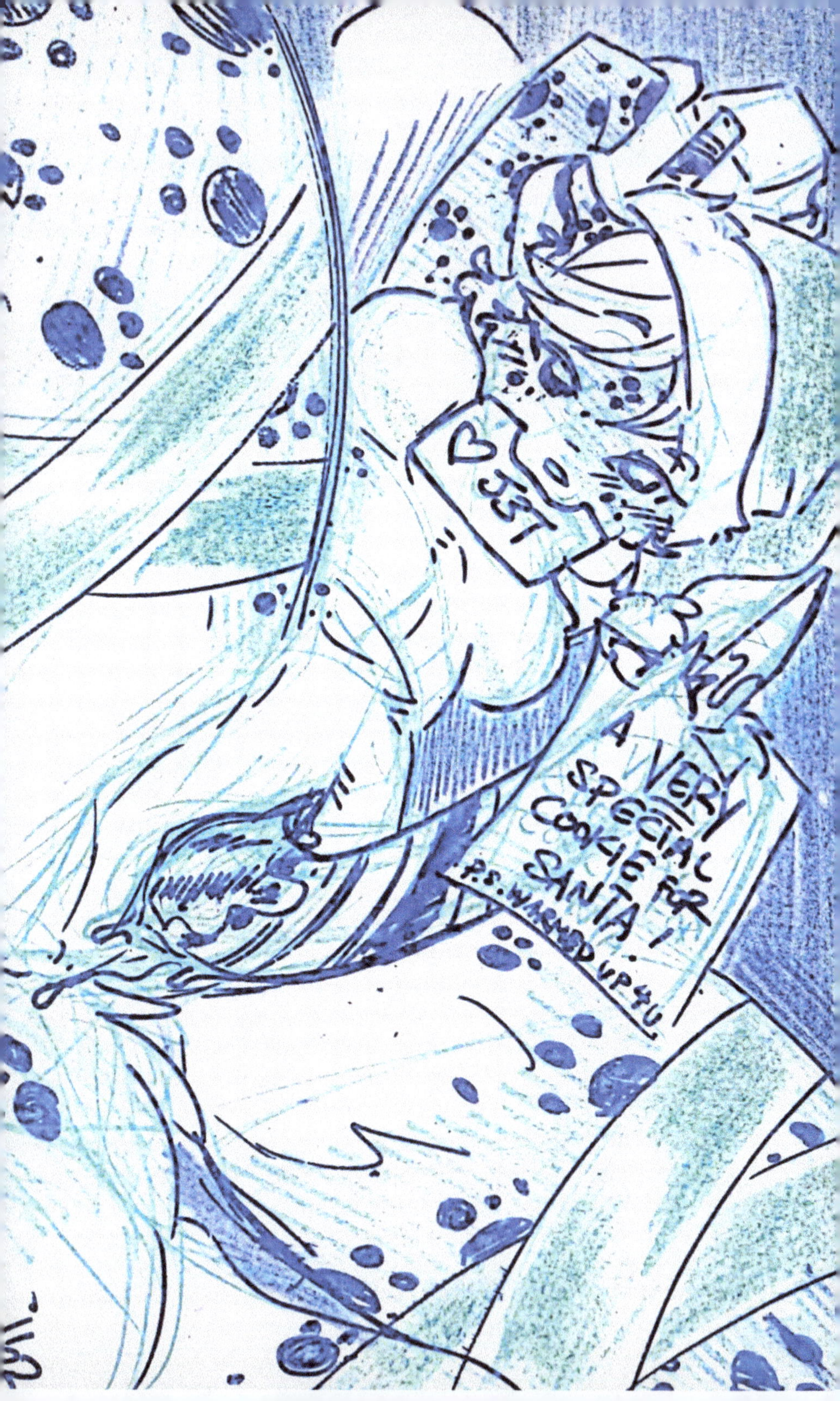
♡ 35¢
A VERY
SPECIAL
COOKIE FOR
SANTA !
P.S. WARMD UP 4U

Naughty?
Or Nice?